KNITTING IT OLD SCHOOL

43 Vintage-Inspired Patterns

By Stitchy McYarnpants and Caro Sheridan

WILEY

Wiley Publishing, Inc.

Published by Wiley Publishing, Inc., Hoboken, New Jersey
Published simultaneously in Canada

For general information on our other products and services or to obtain technical support please contact our Customer Care Department within the U.S. at (877) 762-2974, outside the U.S. at (317) 572-3993 or fax (317) 572-4002.

Wiley also publishes its books in a variety of electronic formats. Some content that appears in print may not be available in electronic books. For more information about Wiley products, please visit our web site at www.wiley.com.

Library of Congress Cataloging-in-Publication data is available from the publisher upon request.
ISBN: 978-0-470-52466-4 (pbk)
ISBN: 978-0-470-63874-3 (ebk)

Printed in United States of America

10 9 8 7 6 5 4 3 2 1

Book production by Wiley Publishing, Inc. Composition Services

Credits

Senior Editor
Roxane Cerda

Senior Project Editor
Donna Wright

Technical Editor
Kristi Porter

Copy Editor
Marylouise Wiack

Editorial Manager
Christina Stambaugh

Publisher
Cindy Kitchel

Vice President and Executive Publisher
Kathy Nebenhaus

Interior Design
Lissa Auciello-Brogan

Cover Design
Susan Olinsky

Acknowledgments

We'd like to thank Linda Roghaar for her guidance, Roxane Cerda and Donna Wright at Wiley for their patience and humor during the bookmaking process, Denise Siegel and Tommi Zabrecky for bringing our visions of retro style to fruition, and all of our designers who made this project possible. Without them, we'd still be talking to ourselves about this great idea for a book we have. We would also like to thank our husbands, Jon and Boon, for their support, techie wisdom, mixed drinks and delicious lunches as we slaved over hot laptops.

This book is dedicated to our mums, who passed on their creative genes and a love of vintage fashion (we'll overlook the fact that it wasn't actually vintage yet when they were wearing it). They rocked the beehive wigs and sharp pantsuits like nobody's business. And to our dads, who recognized and nurtured our independent spirits. Thank you for understanding that well behaved women seldom make history. We solemnly swear to continue in our endeavor to resist behaving well.

Photo Credits

Photography: Denise Siegel, Caro Sheridan, Adrian Bazilla

Stylist: Tommi Zabrecky

Makeup: Lori Depp

Models: Scott Aschenbrenner, Kay Davis, Caroline Gleich, Chante Griffin, Camille Moitoret, Jerry Turner, Ruta Vaisnys, Mai Vo, Rob Zabrecky, Tommi Zabrecky, Christian Zollenkopf

Car Owners: Tom Lamb, Bob Navarro, Elana Scherr

Table of Contents

About the Authors

Debbie Brisson a.k.a. Stitchy McYarnpants was born to be a knitter. Her parents met at Pandora, a sweater mill set on the Merrimack River in Manchester, NH, known for its vast number of textile mills. To this day, her parents still regale the days of working the cut-and-sew machines and how much nicer the full-fashion sweaters were because they were made with more care than the cut-and-sew line.

So you see, she can't help it. She is powerless against knitting. Add to that her love for all things vintage, the kitschier the better, and you've got a good look at what makes Debbie tick. If it's goofy, mostly useless, and steeped in the irony of popular culture's most embarrassing moments, she'll take two. As the creator and curator of the *Museum of Kitschy Stitches*, an online (www.yarnpants.com) and in print gallery of notorious knits, she is no stranger to vintage fashion.

When she isn't knitting, sewing or trying to resist the siren's call of eBay, she can be found slaving away in the software mines of Massachusetts. She shares a home in Chelsea, MA with her husband, Jon, and four cats, Chloe, Dot, Chi Chi and Mike. They swore they were going to stop at two, but cats, as it turns out, are like potato chips. Once you start with them, it's hard to stop.

Caro Sheridan was born on the West Coast of Canada and spent her formative years in creative environs surrounded by fabric and yarn. While her mother taught knitting, embroidery, and couture tailoring from home, Caro played Barbies under the table, seemingly oblivious. Fabric cutting tables have osmotic properties though and the wee girl learned how to set in sleeves and turn hems before she was seven years old.

When the spare room of your house is filled with fabric and notions, it gets in your blood. Caro had the best-dressed dolls west of the Canadian Shield courtesy of her Mum's formal training. Knitted coats, handsewn vinyl boots, matching pant suits for Barbie, dolly and cutey Caro, it's no wonder that designing comes so easily.

Although she tried her hand at professional dancing and snowboarding for several years, she has since returned to her roots and is putting her knitting and sewing skills to better use. Caro's craft blog, Splityarn.com, features sewing and knitting tutorials that have been featured on WhipUp.net, the Craft Magazine Blog, Instructables.com and many other prominent sites. She also designs, sews and sells her creations online through Splityarn.com.

She currently lives in Boston, Massachusetts with her husband Boon and three feline rapscallion companions (Teek and Mother, the darlings of Flickr, and Indy, Teek's, their more sedate older sister).

Introduction

Welcome to our book; we're so glad you could make it! Consider this a mixed tape made of yarn—from us to you. It's chock-full of our favorite things: vintage style, retro color combinations, adorable models, and fake eyelashes. And that's before we even get to the knitting and crocheting. We've even got sewing in here!

When we first set out to create this book, we knew we wanted to provide readers and crafters with an experience that goes beyond the simple act of making a sweater. We asked ourselves a lot of questions, the hardest being, "Why should our book be on every knitter's shelf?" After much thought, the answer was that we didn't want it sitting on the shelf at all. Our goal was to create a book that stays on your coffee table long after you've woven in the ends on your new crocheted hot pants. Our hope is that you won't want to put it away because there's always something else you want to make, or just because you love to flip through it and admire the campy styles. It's the book we've been searching for; who knew we'd ending up making it ourselves?

We've touched on fashion trends from the 40s to the 70s (we're not quite ready to embrace the 80s yet; the wounds are still too fresh, the legwarmers too warm), and included 43 pieces that range from classic to kitschy. There are matchy-matchy sweater sets for him and her, versatile garments that will move stealthily throughout your wardrobe, and modern interpretations of ultra-mod visions of the future from the past. No, seriously . . . you'll see.

One of the more unusual things about this pattern book is the use of finer-gauge yarns for pieces that are larger than socks. We're knittin' it old school, folks. It's the yarn of choice in many vintage patterns and just one look tells you why—amazing drape, flattering fit, and a sturdy, long-wearing garment. If making beautiful clothes was good enough for our mothers and grandmothers, it's good enough for us!

chapter 1

Beach Blanket Bonfire

When it comes to fun in the sun, modern beachwear is barely there. Summer clothes don't leave much to the imagination, and some might say that there's a plan afoot to warm the globe in an attempt to make clothes even skimpier. But there was a time when looking hotter than the summer sun involved a little more fabric and lot more imagination. Did you know that imagination takes off ten pounds? It's true! Just ask Frankie, Annette, Gidget, and all those crazy beach bums with names like Riff, Moondoggie, and Eric Von Zipper. Honestly, we're not sure if Gidget even had a bellybutton, but she sure looked cute in her boy shorts and tankinis.

Summer fashions and knitting might not be obvious companions, but not all yarn is wooly and warm. Lightweight cottons, linens, silks, and even corn and bamboo are perfect for cool, comfortable clothes; and they drape perfectly for a sexy silhouette. What better way to show off your handiwork than letting it shine? In this chapter, we've combined bright colors, airy yarns, and just the right amount of quirky style that seems to come easy when the weather is right.

Wiley Wahine

by Robyn Chachula

Whether you wear it as a cover-up after a swim or pair it with a flowing skirt and sandals, Wiley Wahine is a versatile crocheted piece that will take you from a day at the beach to a late-night bonfire. We wanted to evoke the popular peasant-style tops of the 70s with an open, airy feel. The flattering neckline takes a graceful dip, and brightly colored detailing adds just the right amount of island splash. Slits at the sides and roomy sleeves add to the easy fit, and naturally we wanted to use a yarn that would convey a summertime feeling. And what's more summery than corn? Yarn made of corn is certainly unusual, but the bright colors and smooth texture make this the perfect thing for the next clambake. Just go easy with the butter.

Sizes

S (M, L, 1X, 2X)

Finished Measurements

Chest: 36 (39½, 43, 48¾, 52½)"

Materials

Cornucopia by Kollage Yarns CYCA #4 (100% Corn) 100 yd./ 34g hank

MC: #6001 Antique Lace; 17 (18, 22, 24, 27) hanks

CC1: #6023 Sapphire; 1 hank for all sizes

CC2: #6030 Coral Fusion; 1 hank for all sizes

CC3: #6032 Gold; 1 hank for all sizes

CC4: #6010 Island Sea; 1 hank for all sizes

U.S. H-8 (5mm) crochet hook *or size needed to match gauge*

Spray bottle

Blocking pins

Yarn needle

Stitch markers

Gauge

17 dc × 10 rows = 4" over patt

Special Stitches and Terms

sc3tog: (Insert hook into next st, yo, draw up loop) 3 times. Yo, draw through rem loops on hook.

dc5tog: (Yo, insert hook into next st, yo, draw up loop, yo, draw through 2 loops on hook) 5 times. Yo, draw through rem loops on hook.

A note on stitch counts: Ch 3 at beg of row is counted as dc.

DC Stitch Pattern

Ch 21.

Row 1: 2 dc in 5th ch from hook, skip 1 ch, *2 dc in next ch, skip 1 ch, rep from * to last ch, dc in last ch, turn (18 dc).

Row 2: Ch 3, 2 dc between next 2 dc pairs and each across, dc in top of t-ch, turn.

Rep Row 2.

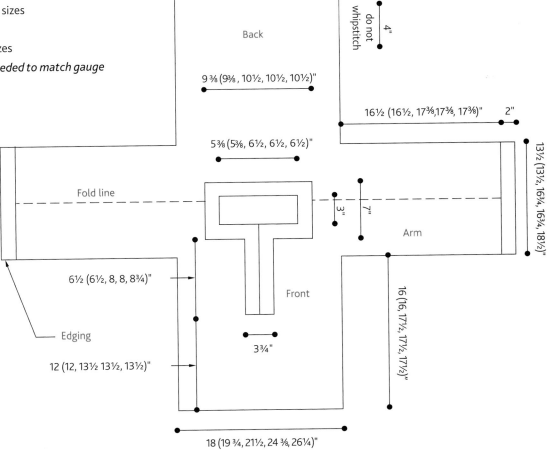

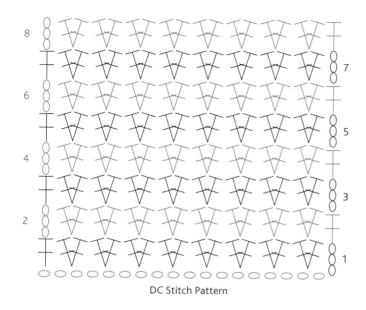

DC Stitch Pattern

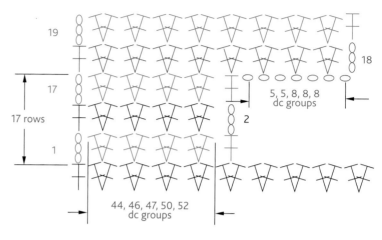

5, 5, 8, 8, 8
dc groups

44, 46, 47, 50, 52
dc groups

Left Sleeve and Neck Opening

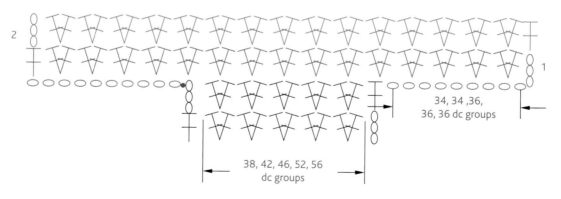

34, 34 ,36,
36, 36 dc groups

38, 42, 46, 52, 56
dc groups

Sleeves

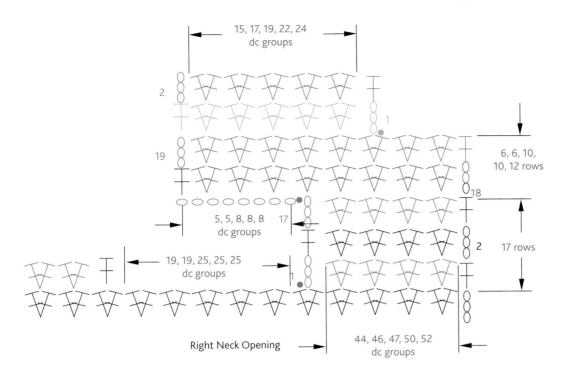

15, 17, 19, 22, 24
dc groups

2

19

6, 6, 10,
10, 12 rows

18

5, 5, 8, 8, 8
dc groups

17

17 rows

2

19, 19, 25, 25, 25
dc groups

1

Right Neck Opening

44, 46, 47, 50, 52
dc groups

chain

slip stitch

single crochet

sc3tog

double crochet

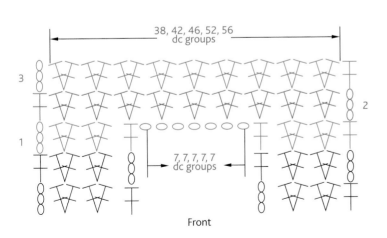

38, 42, 46, 52, 56
dc groups

3

1

2

7, 7, 7, 7, 7
dc groups

Front

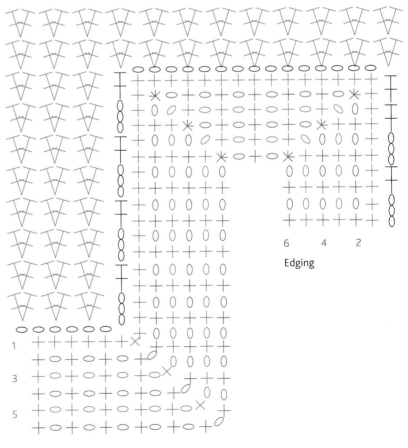

6   4   2

Edging

1

3

5

Directions

Back

Ch 81, 89, 97, 109, 117 with MC.

Row 1 (RS): As Row 1 of DC Stitch Pattern (78, 86, 94, 106, 114 dc).

Row 2: Work Row 2 of DC Stitch Pattern 39 (39, 43, 43, 43) times.

Sleeves

Ch 72 (72, 76, 76, 76), drop yarn. Attach new strand of MC to opposite end of this row with sl st. Ch 70 (70, 74, 74, 74), fasten off [chains form the foundation for the sleeves]. Pick up dropped yarn, 2 dc in 5th ch from hook, sk 1 ch, *2 dc in next ch, sk 1 ch, rep from * across to last ch, sk last ch, 2 dc in first dc, 2 dc between next 2 dc pairs and each across, 2 dc in top of t-ch, sk ch. Rep from * to last ch, dc in last ch, turn. (218, 226, 242, 254, 262 dc).

Work Row 2 of patt 10 (10, 14, 14, 16) times.

Left Sleeve and Neck Opening

Row 1 (WS): Ch 3, 2 dc between next 2 dc pairs and each across for 44 (46, 47, 50, 52) 2 dc pairs total, dc between next 2 dc pairs, turn. (90, 94, 96, 102, 106 dc).

Rows 2–17: As Row 2 of patt.

Row 18: Ch 14 (14, 20, 20, 20), 2 dc in 5th ch from hook (t-ch count as dc), sk 1 ch, *2 dc in next ch, sk 1 ch, rep from * to last ch, sk last ch, 2 dc in first dc, 2 dc between next 2 dc pairs and each across, dc in top of t-ch, turn. (102, 106, 114, 120, 124 dc).

Work Row 2 of patt 5 (5, 9, 9, 11) times.

Left Front Neck Opening

Row 1 (RS): Ch 3, work in patt for 15 (17, 19, 22, 24) pairs total, dc between next 2 dc pairs, turn. (32, 36, 40, 46, 50 dc)

Work Row 2 of patt 9 times, turn, drop yarn.

Right Sleeve and Neck Opening

Row 1 (WS): Sk 18 (18, 24, 24, 24) 2 dc pairs, attach MC between next 2 dc pairs with sl st. Ch 3, 2 dc between next 2 dc pairs and each across, dc in top of t-ch, turn. (90, 94, 96, 102, 106 dc).

Rows 2–17: As Row 2 of patt.

Row 18: Drop yarn and attach new ball of MC to opposite end of row with sl st. Ch 12 (12, 18, 18, 18), fasten off. Pick up dropped yarn. Ch 3, 2 dc between next 2 dc pairs and each across, 2 dc in top of t-ch, sk 1 ch, *2 dc in next ch, sk 1 ch, rep from * to last ch, dc in last ch, turn. (102, 106, 114, 120, 124 dc).

Work Row 2 of patt 5 (5, 9, 9, 11) times, fasten off, weave in ends.

Right Front Neck Opening

Row 1 (RS): Sk 34 (34, 36, 36, 36) 2 dc pairs, join MC with sl st between next 2 dc pairs. Ch 3, 2 dc between next 2 dc pairs and each across, dc in top of t-ch, turn. (32, 36, 40, 46, 50 dc).

Work Row 2 of DC Stitch Pattern 8 times, fasten off, weave in ends.

Front

Row 1 (WS): Pick up dropped yarn from left front neck opening. Ch 3, 2 dc between next 2 dc pairs and each across, dc in top of t-ch, ch 13, dc in dc on right side, 2 dc between next 2 dc pairs and each across, dc in top of t-ch, turn. (64, 72, 80, 92, 100 dc).

Row 2: Ch 3, 2 dc between next 2 dc pairs and each across, 2 dc in dc, sk 1 ch, *2 dc in next ch, sk 1 ch, rep from * across to last ch, sk last ch, 2 dc in dc, 2 dc between next 2 dc pairs and each across, dc in top of t-ch, turn. (78, 86, 94, 106, 114 dc).

Rep Row 2 of DC Stitch Pattern for 29 (29, 33, 33, 33) times, fasten off.

Finishing

Pin body to schematic size, spray with water, and leave to dry. When dry, fold body in half with right sides together. With yarn needle and leftover yarn, seam sleeves and body with whipstitch to 4" from bottom. Fasten in ends neatly on wrong side.

Bottom Edging

With RS of back facing, attach MC yarn with sl st at bottom edge. Ch 1, sc around bottom edge. Join with sl st to first sc. Fasten off. Weave in ends.

Sleeve Edging

Attach MC to RS of sleeve with sl st at seam.

Rnd 1: Ch 1, sc around sleeve edge in multiple of 2, join with sl st to 1st sc, turn.

Rnd 2: Ch 1, *sc in next sc, ch 1, sk next sc, rep from * around, join as before, turn.

Rnd 3: Ch 1, *sc in next sc, ch 1, sk next ch-1 sp, rep from * around. Join. Turn.

Rep Rnd 3 three times, fasten off MC.

Rnd 7: Attach CC1, ch 3 (counts as dc), dc in each sc and ch-1 sp around, join with sl st to top of t-ch, ***do not turn,*** fasten off CC1.

Rnd 8: Attach CC2, ch 1, sc in each dc around, join as before. Fasten off, weave in ends.

Collar Edging

With RS of back facing, attach MC at right side of neck with sl st.

Rnd 1: Ch 1. Sc evenly around neckline with 3 sc in each outside corner, for a total sc edging in a multiple of 2. Join with sl st to 1st sc. Turn. Place a marker (**M**) in center st of all inside and outside corners.

Rnd 2: Ch 1, *sc in next sc, ch 1, sk next sc **. Rep from * to 1 sc before **M** at inside corner, sc3tog over next 3 sc, ch 1, sk next sc, rep from * to 1 sc before **M** at inside corner, sc3tog over next 3 sc, ch 1, sk next sc, rep from * to **M** at outside corner, [sc, ch 1, sc] in next sc, ch 1, sk next sc, rep from ** around. Join with sl st to first sc, turn. Move markers to sc3tog on inside corners and ch-1 sp on outside corners.

Rnd 3: Ch 1, *sc in next sc, ch 1, sk next ch-1 sp, ** rep from * to **M** at inside corner, sk [ch-1 sp, sc3tog, ch-1 sp], sc in next sc, ch 1, sk next ch-1 sp, rep from * to **M** at inside corner, sk [ch-1 sp, sc3tog, ch-1 sp], sc in next sc, ch 1, sk next ch-1 sp, rep from * to **M** at

outside corner, [ch 1, sc, ch 1] in **M** ch-1 sp, rep from ** around, sl st to first sc, turn. Move markers to sc on outside corners and ch-1 sp on inside corners.

Rnd 4: Ch 1, *sc in next sc, ch 1, sk next ch-1 sp, ** rep from * to 1 sc before **M** at inside corner, sc3tog over next [sc, ch-1 sp, sc], ch 1, sk next ch-1 sp, rep from * to 1 sc before **M** at inside corner, sc3tog over next [sc, ch-1 sp, sc], ch 1, sk next ch-1 sp, rep from * to **M** at outside corner, [sc, ch 1, sc] in next sc, ch 1, rep from ** around, sl st to first sc, turn. Move markers to sc3tog on inside corners and ch-1 sp on outside corners.

Rep Rnds 3–4 once, fasten off MC.

Rnd 7: Attach CC1 at center front of neck edge in center, sc with sl st and RS facing. Sk [ch-1 sp, sc3tog], **dc in each sc and ch-1 sp across to **M** at outside corner, 3 dc in outside corner ch-1 sp, *dc in each sc and ch-1 sp across to 1 sc before **M** at inside corner, dc5tog over next [sc, ch-1 sp, sc3tog, ch-1 sp, sc], rep from * twice more, rep from ** to beg, sl st same sc, ***do not turn,*** fasten off CC1. Move markers to dc5tog on inside corners and center dc on outside corners.

Rnd 8: Attach CC2 with sl st, **sc in each dc across to **M** at outside corner, 3 sc in next dc, *sc in each sc across to 1 dc before **M** at inside corner, sc3tog over next 3 dc, rep from * twice more, rep from ** to beg, sl st to same sc, fasten off, weave in ends.

Embroidery

Using the photo on page 4 as a guide, sl st embroider lines on sleeve and collar.

Hala Kahiki Beach Tote

by Regina Rioux

If you're hitting the beach, take along our sturdy Hala Kahiki bag (that's Hawaiian for pineapple, doncha know). This faux fruit is roomy enough to fit everything you need for a day of watching surfers go by. The ingenious scalloped stitch pattern captures the bumpy texture and spiny leaves of a pineapple so cleverly. A drawstring just below the leaves cinches the bag in perfect pineapple form, and a strap allows you to throw it over your shoulder as you make your way across the sandy landscape. It's crocheted with plastic raffia, so you don't have to worry about getting it wet, it's easy to clean, and sand shakes right off.

Finished Measurements

When flat, 16" wide × 17" height (from inner points of leaves)

Materials

Wraffia Ribbon (100% Synthetic) ¼" × 100 yd.

MC1: Kraft—4 spools

MC2: Terracotta—4 spools

CC1: Daffodil—1 spool

CC2: Forest Green—1 spool

U.S. I-9 (5.5mm) crochet hook *or size needed to match gauge*

Tapestry needle

Gauge

16 sts × 6 rows = 4" in dc

Directions
Body of the Bag

Rnd 1: With CC1, ch 4, 15 dc in 4th ch from hook, sl st in 3rd ch of beg ch 3 to join (16 sts). Beg ch sts count as 1 dc. This remains true throughout the pattern.

Rnd 2: Ch 3, 1 dc in same st as beg ch, 2 dc in every st, sl st in t-ch to join (32 sts).

Rnd 3: Ch 3, 2 dc in next st, [1 dc, 2 dc in next st] 15 times, sl st in t-ch to join (48 sts).

Rnd 4: Ch 3, 1 dc, 2 dc in next st, [2 dc, 2 dc in next st] 15 times, sl st in t-ch to join (64 sts).

Rnd 5: Ch 3, 2 dc, 2 dc in next st, [3 dc, 2 dc in next st] 15 times, sl st in t-ch to join (80 sts).

Rnd 6: Ch 3, 3 dc, 2 dc in next st, [4 dc, 2 dc in next st] 15 times, sl st in t-ch to join (96 sts). Break off CC1 and attach MC1.

Rnd 7: With MC1, ch 3, working in back loops only, dc in next 95 sts, sl st in t-ch to join (96 sts). Drop MC1, but do not break off.

Rnd 8: Attach MC2, ch 3, working in back loops only, 4 dc, 2 dc in next st, [5 dc, 2 dc in next st] 15 times, sl st in t-ch to join (112 sts). Drop MC2.

Rnd 9: With MC1, ch 4, working in back loops only, tr in next 111 sts, sl st in t-ch to join (112 sts). Drop MC1 and begin working with MC2.

Rep Rnd 9, alternating between MC1 and MC2, 12 more times. After the last rnd has been completed, break off both MC1 and MC2 and attach CC2.

Crown

Rnd 10: With CC2, ch 3, work 1 dc in next 111 sts, sl st in t-ch to join (112 sts).

Rnd 11: Ch 3, 1 dc, ch 1 and sk 1, [2 dc, ch 1 and sk 1] 36 times, 1 dc, sl st in t-ch to join.

Ch 4, tr in next 111 sts, sl st in t-ch to join (112 sts).

Points

Row 1: Ch 3, work 1 dc in next 7 sts, turn.

Row 2: Ch 3, work 1 dc in next 2 sts, dc2tog twice, 1 dc, 1 dc in t-ch, turn.

Row 3: Ch 3, 1 dc, dc2tog 3 times (includes last 2 dc and the t-ch), turn.

Row 4: Ch 3, dc2tog, dc3tog (includes next 2 dc and the t-ch), turn.

Row 5: Ch 3, dc3tog (includes first 2 dc and the t-ch), fasten off; do not turn.

Attach CC2 in st immediately to the left of finished point and ch 3, beginning in the next st beside the st with the beg ch, work 7 dc across, turn. Continue with Rows 2–5 of point pattern. Repeat until 14 points have been completed.

Scallops

Scallops are worked in the rem front loops of Rnds 7–20 in the same color as the rnd itself.

Rnd 1: Begin at the bottom of the bag at Rnd 7—the top of the bag (points) should be closest to you, while the bottom of the bag faces outward—and attach at back seam with MC1 (same color as Rnd 7). Ch 1, 1 sc in same st as ch 1, *sk 2, 5 dc in next st, sk 2, 1 sc, rep from * until rnd is complete, sl st to beg sc to join and fasten off (16 scallops made—sk 1 instead of 2 on either side of last scallop as spacing becomes tight).

Rnd 2: With MC2, work as Rnd 1 (19 scallops).

Rnd 3: With MC1, ch 1, 1 sc in same st as ch 1, *sk 2, 5 tr in next st, sk 2, 1 sc in next st, rep from * until rnd is complete, sl st to beg sc to join and fasten off (19 scallops made—sk 1 instead of 2 on either side of last scallop as spacing becomes tight).

Alternating colors as determined by the color of the rnd you are working, rep scallop Rnd 3 until all scallop rnds have been completed.

Drawstring

With CC1, ch 141, beg in 2nd ch from hook, 140 sc, fasten off. Weave in rem ends and then weave drawstring through Rnd 12 of crown.

Strap

With CC1, ch 71.

Row 1: Beg in 2nd ch from hook, sc in next 70 sts, turn.

Row 2: Ch 1, sc in next 70 sts, turn.

Row 3: Ch 1, sc in next 70 sts. Do not turn. Work 4 sc along short side of strap, work 70 sc along bottom of foundation chain, do not fasten off.

Pin strap to bottom of bag at back "seam." Secure strap to bottom of bag by making 4 sc through strap and front loops of rnd 6 of bag body. Continue with a sc in each front loop of Rnd 6 of bag body. Sl st to beg sc in rnd to join. Fasten off.

Sew top of strap to last of rnd of MC1 below crown with a whip-stitch and your tapestry needle. Make sure that strap is not twisted and lays straight vertically along back of bag.

Finishing

Weave in rem ends.

Clara

by Claire Moore

No summer wardrobe is complete without your favorite tank top. Clara is an unusual summer number that brings to mind the sweetly modest swimwear of the 1920s. Clever short-row shaping combined with sturdy elastic bands give the top portion excellent support for your delicate décolletage. The unexpected diamond stitch pattern is the bee's knees, whether you're having fun in the sun or waiting for the weekend at the office. Pair it with shorts or wear over a long sleeve shirt for an entirely different look.

Sizes

S (M, L, 1X, 2X)

Finished Measurements

Chest: 28 (33, 36½, 39, 44½)"

Hip circumference: 30 (34, 38, 42, 46)"

Materials

2nd Time Cotton from Knit One Crochet Too (180 yd./100g per skein)

MC: #485 Ochre; 3 (3, 3, 4, 4) skeins

CC: #922 Coal; 3 (3, 3, 4, 4) skeins

U.S. 6 (4mm) circular needles, 24" or 36" length, *or size needed to match gauge*

U.S. 4 (3.5mm) circular needles, 24" or 36" length

Openable stitch markers or safety pins

Darning needle

Elastic, 1" wide for bands

Gauge

20 sts × 28 rows = 4" in St st on larger needles

Special Stitches and Terms

Double Knitting: Holding both colors together, knit first stitch in pair using one color, then bring both colors forward and purl second stitch with second color. Bring both colors to back of work. One pair of double knitting stitches will be made.

Pattern Notes

Knit from the bottom up in the round. Double knitting is employed for portions requiring elastic, and for straps.

Directions

Body

Optional faced hem: With smaller needles and MC, CO 168 (192, 210, 228, 252) sts. Pm to indicate start of round, and join in the round, being careful not to twist. Knit 6 rows, then switch to CC. Knit until piece measures 1" from CO edge. Purl 1 row to create turning ridge. Switch to larger needles and knit 2 rows in CC.

Non-faced hem (pictured): CO 168 (192, 210, 228, 252) sts in CC. Join for knitting in the round, pm to mark start of round, and knit 1 round in CC.

All continue: Begin Diamond Pattern working from chart with Row 1. Work even in diamond pattern until piece measures approximately 12½ (12¾, 13, 13¼, 13½)" from CO edge, ending with Row 4 of pattern.

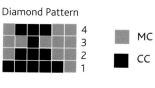

Diamond Pattern

MC

CC

Using CC, knit 1 decrease round as follows, decreasing 42 (38, 40, 38, 42) sts evenly spaced:

- **Size S:** *K2, k2tog, rep from * around.
- **Size M:** K1, *k3, k2tog, rep from * to last st, k1.
- **Size L:** *K3, k2tog, k3, k2tog, k3, k2tog, k4, k2tog, rep from * around.
- **Sizes 1X** and **2X:** *K4, k2tog, rep from * around 126 (154, 170, 190, 210) sts rem. Do not break yarn or bind off. You will now use double knitting to knit the first elastic band casing.

Band

Set up for Double Knitting: In first stitch, knit with CC but do not slip from left needle. Bring both colors forward and purl with MC into same stitch. Now let stitch drop from left needle. One Double Knitting pair completed. Repeat for all stitches.

Double knit for 7 rounds.

Next rnd: Using CC, knit first st from first pair of sts (the CC st) and slip the second st from the pair (the MC st) onto a holder. Rep for first 10 sts. This creates an opening in the band that elastic can be threaded through. Ssk all rem stitch pairs in CC. 126 (154, 170, 190, 210) sts rem.

Bodice

Begin Increasing for Bust

Rnd 1: In MC, k31 (38, 42, 47, 52), pm, k63 (77, 85, 95, 105), pm, k32 (39, 43, 48, 53). New markers indicate the left and right side seams of the garment; the round begins in the center back of the tank.

Rnd 2: *Knit to 2 sts before side marker, M1, k2, sm, k2, M1, rep from * once, knit to end of round. 130 (158, 174, 194, 214) sts.

Rep Rnds 1 and 2 twice more: 138 (166, 182, 202, 222) sts.

Rnds 7–9: Knit.

Short-Row Shaping for Front Bodice

Rnd 10: K5 sts, place contrasting marker, knit to 6 sts before end of round, place contrasting marker, knit to end of round. New markers will guide you through short-row shaping.

Rnd 11: Knit to second contrasting marker, remove marker, wrap next st, and turn.

Rnd 12: P6, replace marker, purl to first contrasting marker, remove marker, wrap next st, and turn.

Rnd 13: K6, replace marker, knit to second contrasting marker, remove marker, wrap, and turn.

Repeat the last 2 rnds 2 (3, 3, 4, 4) times, then rep Rnd 12 once.

Next rnd: Knit around, knitting wrapped sts together with their wraps through the back loop.

Band and Straps
Top Band

Next rnd: Set up for Double Knitting: In first stitch, knit with CC but do not slip from left needle. Bring both colors forward and purl with MC into same stitch. Now let stitch drop from left needle. One Double Knitting pair completed. Repeat for all stitches.

Double knit for 7 rounds.

Bind off all but last 10 pairs of sts in CC, leaving an elastic pocket opening as in the under-bust band and a long tail of yarn to finish binding off when elastic is in place.

Try on the garment, wearing the bra you want to wear with the finished garment. Have a buddy mark the places where the bra straps emerge from the bodice. Use these markers to position your garment straps.

Straps

Straps are double knit on smaller needles for structure. Measure distance over your shoulder from marker to marker to determine length of strap.

Using smaller needles, CO 5 pairs of sts using backward loop method: *make 1 loop in MC, make 1 loop in CC, repeat from * 4 more times. Double knit until strap is long enough to travel from marker to marker, bind off, and sew into place. Repeat for other side.

Finishing

With optional faced hem: Sew hem into place.

With standard hem: Knit a three-stitch I-cord border around bottom hem. To make the I-cord, pick up sts along the bottom of the camisole. CO on 3 sts in CC on the left needle, *K2, sl 1, k1, psso*. Put sts back on left needle and holding yarn firmly behind the work, repeat from * until all the bottom sts are incorporated into the border.

Wet-block the piece to finished measurements.

Sunshine Day

by Maryse Roudier

Sunshine Day is a reproduction
of an actual 1970s sweater that
combined eye-popping colors
and detailed components that
sang to us. It hit a few off-
notes, so we reworked it and
now it's a superstar! Flirty cap
sleeves and a lace-up front
have vintage flair to spare. The
flowered waistband ties in the
back so you can adjust the fit
to your liking. (You can create a
matching headband by cro-
cheting a second waistband.)
The yarn used is available in a
huge array of colors, so you
can create looks that range
from psychedelic to soothing.
Depending on your height, this
will either be a tunic-length
top or a daring micro-mini
dress—either way, you'll be the
brightest girl in the bunch.

Sizes

S (M, L, 1X)

Finished Measurements

Chest: 34 (37, 40, 43)"

Materials

Berroco Pure Pima (100% cotton; 115 yd./50g per skein)

Yarn A: #2237 Olive; 2 (3, 3, 3) skeins

Yarn B: #2252 Navy; 4 (5, 6, 6) skeins

Yarn C: #2206 Gold; 2 (2, 3, 3) skeins

Yarn D: #2201 Cream; 2 (2, 3, 3) skeins

Yarn E: #2233 Orange; 2 (2, 3, 3) skeins

U.S. G-6 (4mm) crochet hook *or size needed to match gauge*

Openable stitch markers or safety pins

Yarn needle

Gauge

17 sts × 9 rows = 4" in dc

1 mini granny square = 2" square

Pattern Notes

This tunic is constructed top down from a yoke. The top front and back are crocheted separately with the top front sewn into the granny square band. The whole piece is then seamed together at the sides from the underarms down.

When changing colors, hold the old yarn behind the work while you work the first few stitches with the new color, then cut the old yarn. This technique will mean fewer ends to weave in while finishing.

Directions

Mini Granny Square Band

For the foundation ring: Using size G-6 hook, and Yarn D, form a loose slipknot on the hook.

Rnd 1: Ch 3 (counts as 1 dc), 2 dc into slipknot ring, ch 3, *3 dc in slipknot ring, ch 3; rep from * 2 more times, join with a sl st into 3rd chain of ch 3. Sl st into next 2 dc until the next 3 ch space. Tighten slipknot end by pulling free end of yarn.

Rnd 2: Join Yarn A to the 3 ch space, holding Rnd 1 yarn in back. Ch 3 (counts as 1 dc), [2 dc, ch 3, 3 dc] into same space, *ch 1, [3 dc, ch 3, 3 dc] into next ch 3 space; rep from * 2 more times, ch 1, join with sl st into 3rd ch of ch 3. Sl st into next 2 dc to the next 3 ch space. Break both yarns.

Sizes S and M: Make 7 squares: 3 in D and A, 2 in C and A, 2 in E and A.

Sizes L and 1X: Make 8 squares: 2 in D and A, 2 in C and A, 2 in E and A, 2 in B and A.

Join the squares together by holding the right sides together and whipstitching in Yarn A through the back loops to form a band.

For sizes M and 1X, single crochet 2 rows on each short edge side of the bands.

With RS facing, join Yarn A to one corner in a ch 3 sp. Ch 1 (first 1 sc), 1 sc into corner ch 3 space, *sc into each stitch to next corner, 4 sc into ch 3 space, rep from * twice more, sc in each st to next corner, end with 2 sc into corner. Sl st into ch 1.

The band will have 58 (62, 70, 74) sc sts on the top and bottom and 9 sts on each short side.

Set band aside for later.

Yoke

With Yarn A, and G-6 hook, ch 71.

Row 1 (RS): Dc in 4th chain from hook, dc into each chain across to end; turn. 68 sts.

Row 2 (WS): Ch 3 (counts as first dc), (dc in next dc, 2 dc in next dc, dc in next dc) 22 times, dc in next dc; turn. 90 sts.

Row 3: Join Yarn B and ch 3, dc into each dc across to end; turn. 90 sts.

Row 4: Ch 3, (1 dc in next dc, 2 dc in next dc, dc in next 2 dc) 22 times, dc in last dc; turn. 112 sts.

Row 5: Join Yarn C and ch 3, dc into each dc across to end; turn. 112 sts.

Row 6: Ch 3, (dc in next 2 dc, 2 dc in next dc, dc in next 2 dc) 22 times, dc in last dc; turn. 134 sts.

Row 7: Join Yarn D and rep Row 3. 134 sts.

Row 8: Ch 3, (dc in next 2 dc, 2 dc in next dc, dc in next 3 dc) 22 times, dc in last dc; turn. 156 sts.

Row 9: Join Yarn E and rep Row 3. 156 sts.

Row 10: Ch 3, (dc in next 3 dc, 2 dc in next dc, dc in next 3 dc) 22 times, dc in last dc; turn. 178 sts.

Row 11: Join Yarn A and rep Row 3. 178 sts.

Row 12: Ch 3, (dc in next 3 dc, 2 dc in next dc, dc in next 4 dc) 22 times, dc in last dc; turn. 200 sts.

For Sizes S and M Only:

Place markers as follows:

Left armhole: Place marker after stitch 28.

Left side back: Place marker after stitch 71.

Right side back: Place marker after stitch 129.

Right armhole: Place marker after stitch 172.

For Sizes L and 1X Only:

Row 13: Continuing with Yarn A, rep Row 3. 200 sts.

Row 14: Ch 3, (dc in next 4 dc, 2 dc in next dc, dc in next 4 dc) 22 times, dc in last dc; turn. 222 sts.

Place markers as follows:

Left armhole: Place marker on stitch 34.

Left side back: Place marker on stitch 77.

Right side back: Place marker on stitch 145.

Right armhole: Place marker on stitch 188.

Left Front

Row 1 (RS): Join Yarn B, and ch 3, dc in next 28 (28, 34, 34) dc; turn. 29 (29, 35, 35) sts.

Row 2: Ch 3, dc in each dc; turn.

Row 3: Join Yarn C and ch 3, dc in next 26 (26, 32, 32) dc, 2 dc in next 2 dc; turn. 31 (31, 37, 37) sts.

Row 4: Ch 3, 2 dc in next 2 dc, dc in next 28 (28, 34, 34) dc; turn 33 (33, 39, 39) sts.

Row 5: Ch 3, dc in next 30 (30, 36, 36) dc, 2 dc in next 2 dc; turn. 35 (35, 41, 41) sts.

Row 6: Ch 3, 2 dc in next 2 dc, dc in next 32 (32, 38, 38) dc; turn. 37 (37, 43, 43) sts.

For Sizes S and L Only:

Row 7: Ch 3, dc in each dc; turn.

Row 8: Rep Row 7.

Row 9: Join Yarn D and rep Row 7.

Row 10: Rep Row 7.

For Sizes M and 1X Only:

Row 7: Ch 3, dc in next (34, 40) dc, 2 dc in next 2 dc; turn. (39, 45) sts.

Row 8: Ch 3, dc in each dc; turn.

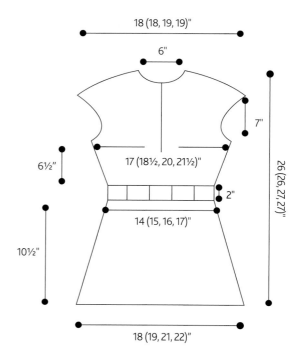

Row 9: Join Yarn D and rep Row 8.

Row 10: Rep Row 8.

For All Sizes

Place marker at 22nd (22nd, 28th, 28th) st from armhole edge.

Row 11: Ch 3, dc in each dc until 1 st before marker, decrease 1 st, dc to end of row; turn. 36 (38, 42, 44) sts.

Rows 12–14: Rep Row 11 three times. 33 (35, 39, 41) sts.

Break yarn.

Right Front

Join Yarn B at right armhole marker at stitch 172 (172, 188, 188).

Row 1 (RS): Ch 3, dc in next 28 (28, 34, 34) dc; turn. 29 (29, 35, 35) sts.

Row 2: Ch 3, dc in each dc; turn.

Row 3: Join Yarn C and ch 3, 2 dc in next 2 dc, dc in next 26 (26, 32, 32) dc; turn. 31 (31, 37, 37) sts.

Row 4: Ch 3, dc in next 28 (28, 34, 34) dc, 2 dc in next 2 dc; turn. 33 (33, 39, 39) sts.

Row 5: Ch 3, 2 dc in next 2 dc, dc in next 30 (30, 36, 36) dc; turn. 35 (35, 41, 41) sts.

Row 6: Ch 3, dc in next 32 (32, 38, 38) dc, 2 dc in next 2 dc; turn. 37 (37, 43, 43) sts.

For Sizes S and L Only:

Row 7: Ch 3, dc in each dc; turn.

Row 8: Rep Row 7.

Row 9: Join Yarn D and rep Row 7.

Row 10: Rep Row 7.

For Sizes M and 1X Only:

Row 7: Ch 3, 2 dc in next 2 dc, dc in next (34, 40) dc; turn. (39, 45) sts.

Row 8: Ch 3, dc in each dc; turn.

Row 9: Join Yarn D and rep Row 8.

Row 10: Rep Row 8.

For All Sizes:

Place marker at 22nd (22nd, 28th, 28th) st from armhole edge.

Row 11: Ch 3, dc until 1 st before marker, decrease 1 st, dc until end of row; turn. 36 (38, 42, 44) sts.

Rows 12–14: Rep Row 11 three more times. 33 (35, 39, 41) sts.

Join the Front

Row 15: Join Yarn E and ch 3, dc until 1 st before marker, decrease 1 st, dc to end. **Do not turn.** Ch 2 and continue to left front. Dc across left front to marker. Decrease 1 st at marker. Continue in dc to edge of left front. Turn. 66 (70,78, 82) sts.

Row 16: Ch 3, dc in each dc, skipping 2 chains that join the two fronts together, turn. 64 (68, 76, 80) sts.

Row 17: Ch 3, skip 1 st, dc until 1 st before end of row; turn. 62 (66, 74, 78) sts.

Row 18: Rep Row 17. 60 (64, 72, 76) sts.

Row 19: Rep Row 17. 58 (62, 70, 74) sts.

Row 20: Ch 3, dc across row to end; turn. 58 (62, 70, 74) sts.

With right sides facing, whipstitch granny square band to the bottom of front crocheted edge using Yarn A.

Join Yarn B to bottom edge of granny square band.

Next row: Ch 3, dc in each sc of granny square band to end; turn. 58 (62, 70, 74) sts.

Next row: Ch 3, 2 dc in next dc, dc to last st, 2 dc in last dc; turn. 60 (64, 72, 76) sts.

Repeat this every 3rd row 8 times more. 76 (80, 88, 92) sts. Break yarn.

Back

Join Yarn B at the left-side back marker at stitch 71 (71, 77, 77).

Row 1 (RS): Ch 3, dc in next 59 (59, 69, 69) dc; turn. 60 (60, 70, 70) sts.

Row 2: Ch 3, dc in each dc; turn.

Row 3: Join Yarn C and ch 3, 1 dc in base of ch 3, 2 dc in next dc, dc until the last 2 dc; 2 dc in last 2 dc; turn. 64 (64, 74, 74) sts.

Row 4: Ch 3, 2 dc in next 2 dc; dc until the last 2 dc; 2 dc in last 2 dc; turn. 68 (68, 78, 78) sts.

Row 5: Ch 3, 2 dc in next 2 dc; dc until the last 2 dc; 2 dc in last 2 dc; turn. 72 (72, 82, 82) sts.

Row 6: Ch 3, 2 dc in next 2 dc; dc until the last 2 dc; 2 dc in last 2 dc; turn. 76 (76, 86, 86) sts.

For Size S and L Only:

Row 7: Ch 3, dc in each dc; turn.

Row 8: Rep Row 7.

For Sizes M and 1X Only:

Row 7: Ch 3, 2 dc in next 2 dc; dc until the last 2 dc; 2 dc in last 2 dc; turn. (80, 90) sts.

Row 8: Ch 3, dc in each dc; turn.

For All Sizes:

Row 9: Join Yarn D and ch 3, dc in each dc; turn.

Row 10: Rep Row 9.

Row 11: Ch 3, sk 1 st, dc until 1 st before end of row; turn. 74 (78, 84, 88) sts.

Row 12–14: Rep Row 11, decreasing 2 sts every row. 68 (72, 78, 82) sts.

Row 15: Join Yarn E and rep Row 11. 66 (70, 76, 80) sts.

Row 16–19: Rep Row 11, decreasing 2 sts every row. 58 (62, 68, 72) sts.

Row 20: Ch 3, dc to end; turn.

Row 21: Join Yarn A and ch 3, dc to end; turn.

Row 22–25: Rep Row 20.

Row 26: Join Yarn B and ch 3, dc to end; turn.

Row 27: Ch 3, 2 dc in next dc, dc to last st, 2 dc in last dc; turn. 60 (64, 70, 74) sts.

Repeat this row every 3rd row 8 (8, 9, 9) times. Break yarn.

Finishing

With right sides facing, sew front and back together, leaving armholes open.

Join Yarn C to bottom of garment at seam. Ch 1, sc in each st around, sl st to join to first ch 1. Break yarn and weave in ends.

Armhole

Join Yarn B to yoke and ch 1, sc 6, hdc 7, dc 15, hdc 7, sc 7; turn.

Next row: Repeat previous row. Break yarn.

Join Yarn C at the seam, ch 1 and sc around the perimeter of the armhole. Sl st to join to first ch 1. Break yarn and weave in end.

Repeat for second armhole.

Neckline

Join Yarn E at left front neck edge, ch 1, sc 50 along left front edge, distributing the stitches evenly; 1 sc in each chain stitch at bottom of neck edge, then sc 51 along right front edge. Break yarn.

Join Yarn E again at left front neck edge, ch 1, 1 sc, ch 2 while skipping 2 st from row before. Repeat (2 sc, ch 2, sk 2) pattern 11 times; 1 sc in each stitch around the bottom of the placket; (ch 2, sk 2, 2 sc) 12 times. Ch 2 in corner space, then 1 sc into each dc around neck edge to right front neck edge. Sl st into ch 1. Break yarn.

Weave in ends.

Using Yarn E, make a chain long enough to lace through ch 2 spaces.

Back ties (optional): At side edge of granny square band, join Yarn A, pick up and ch 1, then 10 sc across width of square; turn. 11 sts.

Row 1: Ch 1, 9 sc; turn. 10 sts.

Row 2: Ch 1, 8 sc; turn. 9 sts.

Continue decreasing 1 each row until there are 6 sts.

Next row: Ch 1, 5 sc.

Repeat this row for 24" or until ties are long enough to tie in back. Break yarn, weave in end.

Repeat on other side of granny square band.

Cheeky Hot Pants

by Marnie MacLean

Show off your cheeky side with a pair of irresistible hot pants in sizzling colors. Crocheted hot pants are a staple of kitschy couture, so we just had to include them in this homage to vintage style. Let's face it, they're silly but you kind of want a pair, don't you? The possibilities are endless with these shortest of shorts. Change up the colors and stripes, add a granny square pocket to hold your fat comb and root beer-flavored lip gloss, or use some funky buttons for added flair. You can even wear them under a skirt for a secret that will give you a Mona Lisa smile wherever you go. You can't go wrong with crocheted hot pants, even if they're for your eyes only.

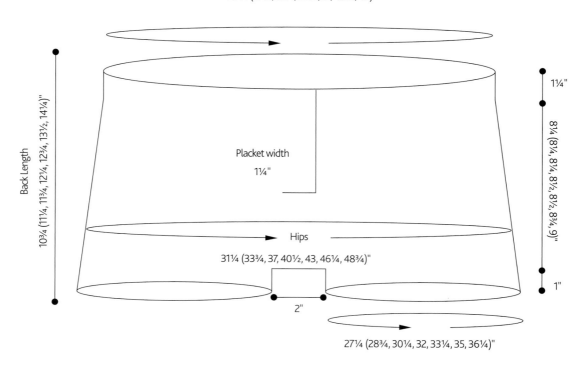

25¼ (27¾, 31¼, 33¾, 37, 40½, 43)"

Placket width
1¼"

Back Length
10¾ (11¼, 11¾, 12¼, 12¾, 13½, 14¼)"

1¼"

8¼ (8¼, 8¼, 8½, 8½, 8¾, 9)"

Hips
31¼ (33¾, 37, 40½, 43, 46¼, 48¾)"

1"

2"

27¼ (28¾, 30¼, 32, 33¼, 35, 36¼)"

Sizes

To fit hip circumference of 32 (35, 38, 41, 44, 47, 50)"

Finished Measurements

Note: The following measurements are of the actual garment, not the size it fits including any ease.

Hips: 31¼ (33¾, 37, 40½, 43, 46¼, 48¾)"

Materials

Tahki Cotton Classic (100% mercerized cotton; 108 yd./50g per skein)

MC: #3401 Light Bright Orange; 4 (4, 4, 4, 5, 5, 5) skeins

CC1: #3942 Light Purple; 1 skein for all sizes

CC2: #3947 Bright Purple; 1 (1, 1, 1, 1, 2, 2) skeins

CC3: #3540 Light Orange; 1 skein for all sizes

U.S. G-6 (4mm) crochet hook *or size needed to match gauge*

6 openable stitch markers or safety pins

Darning needle

7 buttons, ½" diameter

Gauge

19 sts × 20 rows = 4" in sc

Special Stitches and Terms

Short-row stair step: When working over the stair step formed by a short row, work the lower stitch next to the short row together with a loop pulled through the side of the short row stair step, as if to decrease.

Pattern Notes

Every butt is unique and crochet isn't as elastic as knit, so with this project, it's important to try on as you go. To adjust hip width, add or subtract increase rounds from the waist down (shaping at side seams). To adjust for a rounder or flatter tush, adjust the number of short rows after the crotch shaping. Extending that section will also change the leg circumferences.

Directions

Begin Waist

With MC, ch 126 (138, 154, 166, 182, 198, 210). Ch 1 more and turn.

Row 1: Skip first ch, sc in each subsequent ch. 126 (138, 154, 166, 182, 198, 210) sc. Ch 1, turn.

Row 2 (Buttonhole Row): Sc in next 3 sc, ch 2, skip 1 sc, sc in all rem sc. Ch 1, turn.

Rows 3–5: Sc in each sc, ch 1, turn.

Row 6: Rep Row 2.

Increase to Hips

You will begin the stripe pattern on Row 9 (9, 9, 10, 11, 12, 13), *at the same time,* you will increase to shape the hips, and continue creating buttonholes every 4th row.

Stripe Pattern

Work stripes as follows as you shape the hips:

4 rows in CC1

2 rows in CC3

6 rows in CC2

2 rows in CC3

4 rows in CC1

Increases are complete. Cut yarn and begin next section with MC.

Place locking st markers or safety pins 31 (34, 38, 41, 45, 49, 52) sts in from each end to separate fronts from back. Each front has 6 sts for the button band/placket. Back is 64 (70, 78, 84, 92, 100, 106) sts.

Row 7 (Increase Row): *Sc to st before marker. Work 2 sc in st before marker. Work sc in st with marker, moving marker to the new st, work 2 sc in next sc. Rep from *, sc to end, ch 1, turn. 4 sts increased.

Repeat the Increase Row every 3 (3, 3, 3, 3, 3, 4) rows 4 (4, 4, 3, 2, 1, 6) times, then every 4 (4, 4, 4, 4, 4, 0) rows 2 (2, 2, 3, 4, 5, 0) times.

For rows between increases, work as for Row 3 above. Remember to move the side seam markers up as you go. After 27 (27, 27, 28, 29, 30, 31) rows, there are a total of 148 (160, 176, 192, 204, 220, 232) sts.

Join to Work in the Round

Cut yarn and hold garment so that buttonhole band is on right side (as worn) and is in front of the button band, overlapping by 6 sts. Attach MC at right side seam marker. Keep the side seam markers and add two markers at the center front (one in each of the two middle sts of the button placket) and two markers at the center back directly opposite the front markers.

Crotch Shaping Part 1

Increase rounds are worked as follows:

Next rnd (Increase Round 1): Work to first center marker, *sc twice into marked st, placing marker into second st made, sc twice into next st, placing marker into first st made (so markers are side by side), work to back center marker and rep from *, sc to end of round. 4 sts added, 2 each to center front and center back.

Repeat Increase Rnd 1 every 4th rnd 3 times.

Crotch Shaping Part 2

Work 2 rnds even.

Next rnd (Increase Round 2): *Work to first center marker, sc twice in next sc, placing marker in first st made, sc 2 times in following marked st, placing marker in second st made. Rep from * once, work to end of row. (Increased sts are added between markers.)

Repeat Increase Round 2 every 3 rounds twice more, then every other round twice. 54 (54, 54, 55, 56, 57, 58) rnds have been completed; there are 178 (190, 206, 222, 234, 250, 262) sts.

Short Rows

This section is what gives you enough extra length in back to fit whatever shape you may be. Adjust the number of short rows as needed, keeping in mind that you'll add 2 more inches after, to close the rem gap.

Sc in each sc until you get to the side marker before the back section of the garment.

Increase as for *Crotch Shaping* every other row, keeping markers 10 sts apart while you work this section.

Rows 1–2: Sc in patt to 10 sts before side marker, ch 1, turn.

Rows 3–10: Sc in patt to 5 sts before side marker, ch 1, turn.

Finish Crotch

Stop crotch increases.

Work to second center st marker in back section. (There should be 10 sts between center markers.) Work 8 rows in sc across just these 10 sts. Cut yarn leaving a long tail to seam. Sew the center 10 back sts to the center 10 front sts to close crotch.

Legs

Work identically on both legs.

Rnd 1: Join yarn to center inside of leg. Work 3 sts along crotch, sc in every sc around leg, then 3 more sc along crotch to finish the round.

Rnds 2–4: Sc in every sc.

Work one row each of CC1, CC3, and CC2.

Finishing

Work 2 rows of CC1 across entire waist band. *Hint:* If you need to, you can ease in the waist a little, at this point, to better fit you. Just evenly space decreases around the waist. Work 1 row of CC3 across entire waistband

With CC2, sc up front edge of placket, across the entire waistband and down the back placket.

Cut all ends.

Weave in all ends. Sew on buttons.

Ahoy, Sailor

by Diana Loren

Get set to sail the seven seas with Ahoy, Sailor, a fine-gauge sweater with striped sleeves, a slimming shape, and an adorable nautical collar. This cool cotton sweater has great waist shaping and a shortened middy to give a nod to sailors of yore without looking costume-y. Striping inside the cuffs and bottom hem are small details that will have a big impact. Creamy white and deep, dark blue are a classic combination that will fit any wardrobe.

Sizes

XS (S, M, L, 1X)

Finished Measurements

Chest: 30 (34, 38, 42, 46)"

Materials

Rowan Cotton Glace (100% cotton; 126 yd./50g per skein)

MC: #730 Oyster; 7 (7, 8, 8, 9) skeins

CC: #746 Nightshade; 3 (3, 4, 4, 5) skeins

U.S. 4 (3.5mm) needles *or size needed to match gauge*

Removable stitch marker

Tapestry needle

Gauge

23 sts × 37 rows = 4" in St st

Pattern Notes

This is a close-fitting sweater. Choose a size closest to your own bust circumference.

Directions

Front

Using CC, CO 86 (94, 110, 120, 132) sts.

Working in St st, beginning with a knit row, *work 2 rows with CC, then 2 rows with MC, rep from * once; knit 2 rows with CC; the second knit row creates a turning ridge.

Continue in St st in CC for 10 rows, then switch to MC until piece measures 4 (4½, 5, 5¾, 6¾)" from the turning ridge.

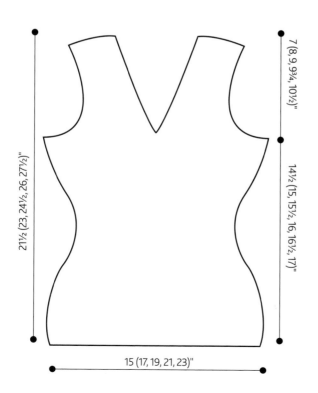

21½ (23, 24½, 26, 27½)"

7 (8, 9, 9¾, 10½)"

14½ (15, 15½, 16, 16½, 17)"

15 (17, 19, 21, 23)"

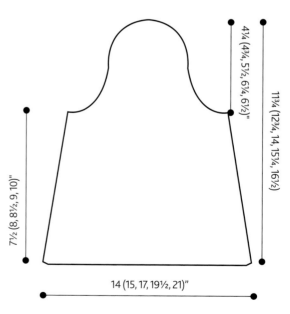

4¼ (4¾, 5½, 6¼, 6½)"

11¾ (12¾, 14, 15¼, 16½)"

7½ (8, 8½, 9, 10)"

14 (15, 17, 19½, 21)"

Waist Shaping

Next row (Decrease Row): K1, ssk, knit to the last 3 sts, k2tog, k1.

Work in St st for the next 3 rows.

Repeat these 4 rows 6 more times. 72 (80, 96, 106, 118) sts.

Work even in St st until piece measures 9½ (10, 10½, 11¼, 12¼)" from turning ridge.

Increase Row: K1, M1, knit to last st, M1, k1.

Work in St st for the next 5 rows.

Repeat these 6 rows 6 more times. 86 (94, 110, 120, 132) sts rem.

Work even until piece measures 14½ (15, 15½, 16¼, 17¼)" from turning row, ending with a WS row.

Armhole and Neck Shaping

Read through this section entirely before knitting, as you will be shaping the neck and armholes at the same time.

Place marker at 43 (47, 55, 60, 66) sts for the center of the V-neck. You will work both sides of neck shaping at the same time by attaching a new ball of yarn after the marker.

Next row: Bind off 3 (4, 4, 5, 5) sts, knit to 3 sts before marker, k2tog, k1, attach a second ball of yarn, and with it k1, ssk, knit to end of row.

Next row: Bind off 3 (4, 4, 5, 5) sts, purl to neck edge, switch yarns and purl to end of row.

Bind off 0 (2, 2, 3, 3) sts at the beginning of next 2 rows (at the armholes only).

Next row: K1, ssk, knit to 3 sts before neck edge, k2tog, k1, switch yarns and k1, ssk, knit to last 3 sts, k2tog, k1.

Work 1 row even.

Next row: K1, ssk, knit to neck edge, switch yarns, knit to last 3 sts, k2tog, k1.

Work 1 row even.

Repeat these 4 rows 7 (6, 7, 7, 8) times more. Armhole shaping is complete.

Next row: Knit to 3 sts before neck edge, k2tog, k1, switch yarns and k1, ssk, knit to end of row.

Work 3 rows even.

Repeat these 4 rows 2 (5, 7, 7, 9) more times. 20 (20, 27, 29, 33) sts rem on each side at the end of shaping.

Work even until armhole measures 7 (8, 9, 9¾, 10¼)".

Shape Shoulders

Beginning on the outside shoulder edge of each side (RS rows for left side, WS rows for right side):

Bind off 5 (5, 7, 7, 9) sts, work to end of row. Work 1 row even.

*Bind off 5 (5, 7, 7, 8) sts, work to end of row. Work 1 row even. Rep from * once more, then bind off rem sts.

Back

Work the back the same as the front to the beginning of armhole shaping. The back measures 14½ (15, 15½, 16¼, 17¼)" from turning row, ending with a WS row.

Armhole Shaping

Bind off 3 (4, 4, 5, 5) sts at the beginning of next 2 rows.

Bind off 0 (2, 2, 3, 3) sts at the beginning of next 2 rows.

Next row (RS): K1, ssk, knit to last 3 sts, k2tog, k1.

Work 1 row even.

Repeat these 2 rows 8 (7, 8, 8, 9) times more. 62 (66, 80, 86, 96) sts rem. Work even until armhole measures 7 (8, 9, 9¾, 10¼)".

Shape Shoulders

Bind off 5 (5, 7, 7, 9) sts at the beginning of the next 2 rows.

Bind off 5 (5, 7, 7, 8) sts at the beginning of the next 6 rows.

Bind off center 22 (26, 28, 30, 30) sts.

Sleeves (Make 2)

Using CC, CO 80 (86, 98, 112, 120) sts.

Working in St st, beginning with a knit row, *work 2 rows with CC, then 2 rows with MC, rep from * once; knit 2 rows with CC; the 2nd knit row creates a turning ridge.

Continuing in St st, work CC for 10 rows, then begin a stripe pattern, alternating 2 rows of MC and 2 rows of CC.

Maintaining stripe pattern, when sleeve measures 2" from turning ridge ending with a WS row, decrease 1 st each side as follows:

Next row: K1, ssk, knit to last 3 sts, k2tog, k1.

Work 3 rows even.

Repeat these 4 rows 4 (3, 3, 6, 7) more times. 70 (78, 90, 98, 104) sts rem.

Continue working even in stripe pattern until sleeve measures 7½ (8, 8½, 9, 10)" from turning row, ending with a WS row.

Sleeve Cap Shaping

Bind off 4 (5, 5, 6, 6) sts at the beginning of the next 2 rows.

Bind off 3 sts at the beginning of the next 2 rows.

Bind off 2 sts at the beginning of the next 2 rows.

Next row: K1, ssk, knit to last 2 sts, k2tog, k1.

Work 3 rows even.

Repeat these 4 rows 10 (10, 12, 13, 13) more times. 30 (36, 44, 48, 54) sts rem.

Bind off 3 sts at the beg of next 8 rows. Bind off rem 16 (18, 22, 26, 30) sts.

Finishing

Block lightly to measurements. Sew shoulder seams. Set in sleeves. Sew side and sleeve seams.

Collar

Using CC, CO 54 (58, 62, 66, 70) sts. Knit 4 rows.

Continue the rest of the collar in St st, maintaining first and last 3 sts in garter st. Begin alternating 2-row stripes of MC and CC. Work until collar measures 2 (2, 2, 2½, 2½)" ending with a WS row.

Divide for Neck

Work first 16 (16, 17, 18, 20) sts, bind off center 22 (26, 28, 30, 30) sts, and work rem 16 (16, 17, 18, 20) sts. You will work both sides of the neck at the same time, maintaining striping throughout. Continue working the 3 outside sts on each side of the collar in garter st.

Work 1" more of St st stripes on each side of the collar, ending with a WS row.

Begin decreasing on the next row as follows:

Decrease Row (RS): On the right side of collar: K3, ssk, knit to end; on the left side of collar: knit to last 5 sts, k2tog, k3.

Repeat the Decrease Row every 8 rows 7 (7, 8, 9, 11) more times. 8 sts rem.

Work even until both sides of neck measure 7 (8, 9, 9¾, 10¼)".

Bind off all sts.

Using mattress stitch, attach collar to sweater, making sure to sew the RS of collar to WS of neck. At the bottom of the V-neck, sew the two bound-off edges of the collar together.

Bottle Buddies

by Tamie Snow

Throughout history, fashions have come and gone and come back again. Everything from shoulder pads and capri pants to ponchos and flared jeans. Hemlines go up and down, men's ties get wider and skinnier. But there's one thing that never goes out of style: a well-dressed bottle of hooch.

Even the cheapest bottom-shelf whiskey takes on an air of sophistication when you pay some extra attention to its presentation. And what better way to jazz up that cabinet of half-empty bottles of booze, er, your collection of exotic liqueurs, than with a finely *sewcheted* (sewn and crocheted) Bottle Buddy?

It could be the fact that we've already imbided a number of bottles in preparation of this exciting tutorial, but we feel there's nothing that some pom-poms, bits of colorful felt, and a couple of well-placed googly eyes can't do. If you agree, then you're going to love turning your bottle-strewn apartment into a veritable zoo of colorful characters who would never judge you for your shortcomings or expect you to have a better job by now, especially after spending all that time and money on your education (although it seems like you spent more time socializing than studying and no one is really sure what you're supposed to do with that degree in Mythology, anyway). Nope, these little guys and their delicious liquid innards will always be there for you.

We're giving you the bare essentials to make a naked, faceless Buddy. With a little creativity, it will turn out to be whatever you like, be it animal, vegetable, or mythically handsome and caring creature. The poodle in our example was made using pom-poms, googly eyes, a button nose, and bits of felt for the ears.

What You'll Need

- 8½" × 11" piece of fabric
- Thread
- Sewing machine
- Less than one skein of Red Heart yarn
- U.S. size 7 (4.5mm) crochet hook
- Embroidery needle
- Poly-fill stuffing material
- All manner of crafty offal including, but not limited to, pom-poms, googly eyes, felt, pipe cleaners, feathers, buttons, ribbon, rick-rack, rhinestones, glue, and tufts of cat hair from behind the door.

Gauge: 18 sts × 24 rows = 4" in sc.

Finished Measurements: Approximately 10". Size can vary widely by tension. Use a tight tension for optimal effect.

What to Do

Sew Bottle Sleeve

1. Cut out your fabric piece using an 8½" × 11" piece of paper as your pattern.
2. Fold the long edges of the fabric down ½" and press. With a ¼" seam allowance, topstitch along the length of those newly pressed edges.
3. With right sides together using a ½" seam allowance, sew the short sides of the fabric together to complete your sleeve.

Crochet Head and Neck

This project is crocheted in rounds. You will need to mark your stitches to keep your place. To help keep track, place a stitch marker at the beginning of the first round, then slip the marker when you come to it on each round. Use a pencil and notepad or a row counter to keep track of the rounds you have worked.

Head

Rnd 1: Ch 2, 6 sc in 1st chain, place marker. Continue in the round.

Rnd 2: 2 sc in each sc around, move marker (mm)—12 sts.

Rnd 3: *2 sc in first sc, 1 sc in next sc, rep from * around, mm—18 sts.

Rnd 4: *2 sc in first sc, 1 sc in next 2 sc, rep from * around, mm—24 sts.

Rnd 5: *2 sc in first sc, 1 sc in next 3 sc, rep from * around, mm—30 sts.

Rnd 6: *2 sc in first sc, 1 sc in next 4 sc, rep from * around, mm—36 sts.

Rnds 7–16: Sc in each sc around, mm.

Rnd 17: *Sc2tog, 1 sc in next 4 sc, rep from * around, mm—30 sts.

Rnd 18: *Sc2tog, 1 sc in next 3 sc, rep from * around, mm—24 sts.

Rnd 19: *Sc2tog, 1 sc in next 2 sc, rep from * around, mm—18 sts.

Rnd 20: *Sc2tog, 1 sc in next 1 sc, rep from * around, mm—12 sts.

Fill your buddy's head with fluff.

Rnd 21: *Sc2tog, 1 sc in next sc, rep from * around—6 sts, finish off.

Leave a 6" tail, and use the tail to stitch up the hole.

Neck

Ch 15, sc in first chain to form ring.

Rnds 1–8: Sc in each stitch around—15 sts.

Finish off, leaving a 9" tail.

Stitch neck to head using whipstitch.

Weave in ends.

chapter 2

Snowbound

Whether you're schussing down the slopes or stringing together creative expletives as you shovel the six-car driveway that you raved about at your BBQ last summer, winter weather always makes an impression. Often it's an impression of your backside on a snowy hill. And through the years, people have strived to beat the cold by creating more and more advanced clothing. One can't help but imagine our ancestors wearing pelts of what was probably dinner from the night before. We've come a long way and now enjoy high-tech fabrics that wick, ventilate, and breathe. Almost seems like a step back from those non-living pelts, doesn't it?

There is a simple answer to nature's yearly cold shoulder that is beyond electric socks and blankets with sleeves—it's wool. Sheep swear by it! Woolen hand-knits and cold weather go together like marshmallows and hot cocoa, snow bunnies and ski bums, hot toddies and fuzzy memories. Remember, only microsheep wear real microfleece.

Staghorn Pullover

by Cheryl Burke

We put a cheeky twist on the classic reindeer motif with our Staghorn sweater. Big, strong bucks with regal antlers on the front of a yoked sweater have been a manly favorite for decades, but now we've captured the majesty of deer butts, too! Enhance his backside with these unusual "deer-ières" in gorgeous detail. Clever stranding charts on the sides of the sweater allow for easy sizing without disturbing the image. Rows of leaves, acorns, and squirrels add a quirky touch to the woodland theme. Contrasting piping, two-color corrugated ribbing, and sprawling trees along the edges add depth and detail that will make this a seasonal favorite.

Sizes

XS (S, M, L, XL, XXL, XXXL)

Finished Measurements

Chest: 34½ (37, 40, 42½, 45, 48, 53)"

Materials

Reynolds Whiskey (100% wool; 195 yd./50g per skein)

MC: #3608 Dark Blue; 5 (5, 6, 7, 7, 8, 9) skeins

CC1: #53 Blue; 3 (4, 4, 5, 5, 6, 6) skeins

CC2: #101 Safety Orange; 1 (1, 1, 1, 1, 1, 2) skeins

U.S. 5 (3.75mm) circular needle, 24" to 36" length, *or size needed to match gauge*

U.S. 5 (3.75mm) circular needle, 16" length, or double-pointed needles for sleeves

Stitch markers

Darning needle

DK weight waste yarn

Gauge

24 sts × 28 rows = 4" in St st and colorwork

Special Stitches and Terms

Corrugated rib: *K2 with CC1, p2 with MC, rep from *. Bring MC to the back after each set of purl sts.

Trapping the yarn held in the left hand: Insert right needle into the stitch. Bring the yarn in the left hand across the tip of the right needle in the back. Complete the stitch with the yarn in the right hand as usual.

Trapping the yarn held in the right hand: Insert right needle into the stitch. Wrap the yarn in the right hand as if to knit. Wrap the yarn in the left hand as if to knit. Unwrap the yarn in the right hand. Complete the stitch with the yarn in the left hand.

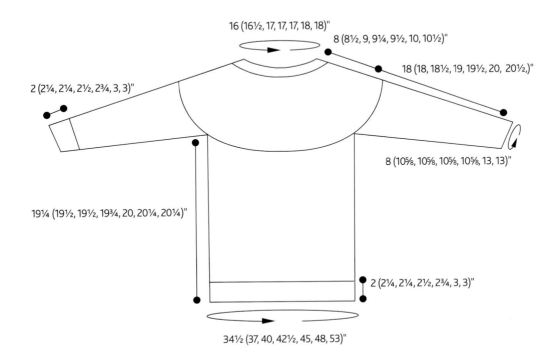

16 (16½, 17, 17, 17, 18, 18)"

8 (8½, 9, 9¼, 9½, 10, 10½)"

18 (18, 18½, 19, 19½, 20, 20½,)"

2 (2¼, 2¼, 2½, 2¾, 3, 3)"

8 (10⅝, 10⅝, 10⅝, 10⅝, 13, 13)"

19¼ (19½, 19½, 19¾, 20, 20¼, 20¼)"

2 (2¼, 2¼, 2½, 2¾, 3, 3)"

34½ (37, 40, 42½, 45, 48, 53)"

Chart A

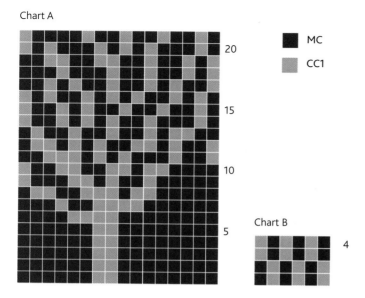

■ MC

■ CC1

Chart B

Work Row 1 of Chart B 1 (2, 3, 3, 4, 4, 5) times, pm, work Row 1 of Chart C as indicated for your size across 98 (100, 102, 110, 112, 120, 130) sts, pm. Work Row 1 of Chart B 1 (2, 3, 3, 4, 4, 5) times, pm. Work Row 1 of Chart D as indicated for your size across 98 (100, 102, 110, 112, 120, 130) sts.

Continue, working charts as set. Body will measure 19¼ (19½, 19½, 19¾, 20, 20¼, 20¼). Break yarn and set sts aside on spare needle or waste yarn.

Sleeves

With MC, CO 48 (64, 64, 64, 64, 80, 80) sts, pm, and join in round, being careful not to twist stitches.

Next rnd: Begin k2, p2 rib with MC.

Join CC1 and work corrugated rib for 2 (2¼, 2¼, 2½, 2¾, 3, 3)".

Work Row 1 of Chart A 3 (4, 4, 4, 4, 5, 5) times across round.

Work Rows 2–21 of Chart A as set. Drop MC and CC1; attach CC2.

Knit 1 round with CC2.

Purl 2 rounds with CC2. Break CC2.

Continue with MC only.

Next rnd (Increase Round): K1, M1L, work to 1 st before end of round, M1R, k1. 2 sts increased.

Continue sleeve shaping as follows: Repeat Increase Round every 6 (15, 7, 6, 5, 6, 5) rnds 12 (6, 10, 13, 15, 13, 15) more times until sleeve has 74 (76, 86, 92, 96, 106, 112) sts. Work even until sleeve measures 17 (18, 18½, 19, 19½, 20, 20½)" from cast-on edge, or desired length. Break yarn.

Place first 8 (9, 10, 10, 11, 12, 13) sts and last 9 (9, 10, 10, 11, 11, 13) sts on waste yarn or holder. 17 (18, 20, 20, 22, 23, 26) sts total on holder at underarm with beginning of round in center of held sts. Place rem 57 (58, 66, 72, 74, 83, 86) sts on separate length of waste yarn.

Rep for second sleeve.

Yoke

Rejoin MC to body stitches at beginning of round. Knit across front to 8 (9, 10, 10, 11, 12, 13) sts before side marker. Place the next 17 (18, 20, 20, 22, 23, 26) sts from the body on holder; attach first sleeve by holding underarm sts from both pieces parallel and

Pattern Notes

In a few areas on Charts A, C, and D, there are more than 7 stitches in a row of the same color. In order to avoid puckering, you may want to trap the longer floats of the unused color in the back. See the instructions for "Trapping the yarn" on the previous page.

Directions

Body

With MC, CO 208 (224, 240, 256, 272, 288, 320) sts. Pm and join in round, being careful not to twist stitches.

Next rnd: Mark position of side seams as follows: Work in k2, p2 rib with MC only across 104 (112, 120, 128, 136, 144, 160) sts, pm, continue in rib to end of round. Join CC1 and work in corrugated rib (see "Special Stitches and Terms") for 2 (2¼, 2¼, 2½, 2¾, 3, 3)".

Beginning with Row 1, work the 16-st repeat of Chart A 13 (14, 15, 16, 17, 18, 20) times across round.

Continue working Rows 2–21 of Chart A as set.

Drop MC and CC1, join CC2, and knit 1 round with CC2.

Purl 2 rounds in CC2. Break CC2.

knitting across the 57 (58, 66, 72, 74, 83, 86) sleeve sts with the same yarn, then continue across back to 8 (9, 10, 10, 11, 12, 13) sts before end of round marker. Place the next 17 (18, 20, 20, 22, 23, 26) sts from the body on a holder for underarm, removing end of round marker, knit across 28 (29, 33, 36, 37, 42, 43) sts of left sleeve, place end of round marker, knit across rem sleeve sts, keeping 17 (18, 20, 20, 22, 23, 26) of sleeve sts on holder in line with held body underarm sts. Knit until end of round. 288 (300, 332, 360, 376, 408, 440) sts total.

Next rnd: Evenly decrease 3 (0, 2, 0, 1, 3, 5) sts across round. 285 (300, 330, 360, 375, 405, 435) sts total.

Join CC2, and knit 1 round.

Purl 2 rounds with CC2. Break CC2.

Work Rows 1–56 of Chart E, joining yarns, changing colors, and decreasing as indicated. 114 (120, 132, 144, 150, 162, 174) sts rem at the end of Chart E. Break CC1 and continue in CC2 only.

For Sizes 34½" and 37" Only:

Decrease Round: [K4, k2tog 18] (20) times, knit to end of round. 96 (100) sts rem.

For Size 40" Only:

Decrease Round: [K2, k2tog, k3, k2tog] 14 times, knit to end of round. 104 sts rem.

For Size 42½" Only:

K6 rounds.

Decrease Round: [K4, k2tog] 24 times, knit to end of round.

K6 rounds.

Decrease Round: [K4, k2tog, k7, k2tog] 8 times, knit to end of round. 104 sts rem.

Chart C

100
95
90
85
80
75
70
65
60
55
50
45
40
35
30
25
20
15
10
5

End 53"
End 48"
End 45"
End 42½"
End 40"
End 37"
End 34½"

MC

CC1

Begin 34½"
Begin 37"
Begin 40"
Begin 42½"
Begin 45"
Begin 48"
Begin 53"

Chart D

MC

CC1

Begin 34½"
Begin 37"
Begin 40"
Begin 42½"
Begin 45"
Begin 48"
Begin 53"

Chart E

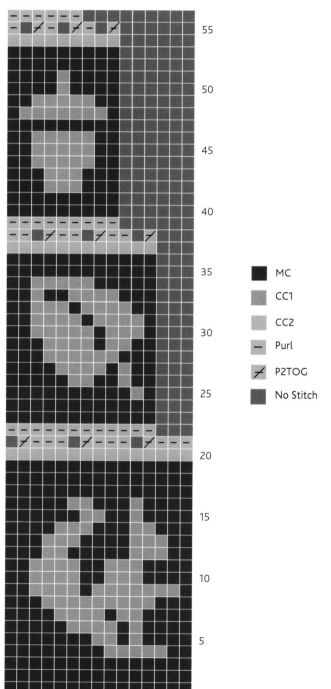

- MC
- CC1
- CC2
- — Purl
- ⁄ P2TOG
- No Stitch

For Size 45" Only:

Knit 8 rounds.

Decrease Round: [K3, k2tog] 30 times, knit to end of round.

Knit 8 rounds.

Decrease Round: [K5, k2tog, k6, k2tog] 8 times, knit to end of round. 104 sts rem.

For Size 48" Only:

Knit 8 rounds.

Decrease Round: [K4, k2tog] 27 times, knit to end of round.

Knit 8 rounds.

Decrease Round: [K3, k2tog] 27 times, knit to end of round. 108 sts rem.

For Size 53" Only:

Knit 10 rounds.

Decrease Round: [K2, k2tog] 43 times, knit to end of round.

Knit 10 rounds.

Decrease Round: [K3, k2tog] 23 times, knit to end of round. 108 sts rem.

Shape Neck

Row 1: K4 (6, 8, 8, 8, 10, 10) sts. Wrap the next st and turn.

Row 2: P52 (56, 58, 58, 58, 64, 64) sts around the back neck. Wrap next st and turn.

Row 3: Knit to 8 sts before first wrapped st, wrap next st and turn.

Row 4: Purl to 8 sts before second wrapped st, wrap next st and turn.

Repeat Rows 3 and 4 one more time.

Knit 1 round, working the wraps together with their wrapped sts.

Neckband: Join CC1 and work in corrugated rib for 1 (1, 1, 1¼, 1¼, 1½, 1½)". Bind off with MC only.

Finishing

Weave underarm sts together with the Kitchener stitch. Weave in ends. Block to finished measurements.

Staghorn Hat

by Cheryl Burke

This hat includes the same adorable yet manly rows of oak leaves, acorns, and squirrels along with the contrasting piping of the Staghorn Pullover.

Size

One size fits most adults

Finished Measurements

Circumference: 21"

Height: 8"

Materials

Colorway 1:

Reynolds Whiskey (100% wool; 195 yd./50g per skein)

MC: #31 Ecru; 1 skein

CC1: #59 Tobacco; 1 skein

CC2: #103 Chartreuse; 1 skein

CC3: #4204 Buckwheat; 1 skein

Lining yarn: Berroco Ultra Alpaca Light (50% Super Fine Alpaca, 50% Peruvian Wool; 144 yd./50g per skein)

Colorway 2:

Reynolds Whiskey (195 yd./50g per skein)

MC: #59 Tobacco; 1 skein

CC1: #31 Ecru; 1 skein

CC2: #133 Green; 1 skein

CC3: #4204 Buckwheat; 1 skein

Lining yarn: Berroco Ultra Alpaca Light (144 yd./50g per skein)

U.S. 5 (3.75mm) circular needle, 16" length, *or size needed to match gauge*

U.S. 4 (3.5mm) double-pointed needles or longer circular for magic loop technique

U.S. 5 (3.75mm) double-pointed needles or longer circular for magic loop technique

U.S. 6 (4mm) double-pointed needles or longer circular for magic loop technique

Stitch markers

Darning needle

Gauge

24 sts × 28 rows = 4" in St st and colorwork

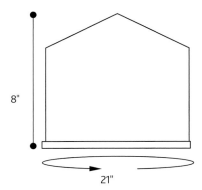

Special Stitches and Terms

I-cord cast-on: Begin by casting on 3 sts. Place these sts on left needle. Kfb, k2. *Slip the last 4 sts from right needle to left needle; kfb, k3; repeat from * until you have cast on the desired number of sts plus 3.

Slip the last 4 sts from right needle to left needle, k2tog, k2tog; slip the last 2 sts from right needle to left needle; k2tog. The cast-on is complete. When you are finished knitting the hat, use the tail of the cast-on to graft together the I-cord edge.

Pattern Notes

The row of stitches just above the I-cord cast-on will look loose. Don't panic! When you pick up stitches for the hat lining, it will tighten up these loose stitches.

Directions

I-Cord Edging

Using CC2 and largest needles, CO 128 sts with the I-cord cast-on.

Cut CC2, leaving an 8" tail.

Body

Set up rnd: Switch to size 5 circular needles and with MC, *k32, pm, rep from * 4 times. Join in round, being careful not to twist stitches.

Work Rnds 1–50 of colorwork chart, changing colors as indicated.

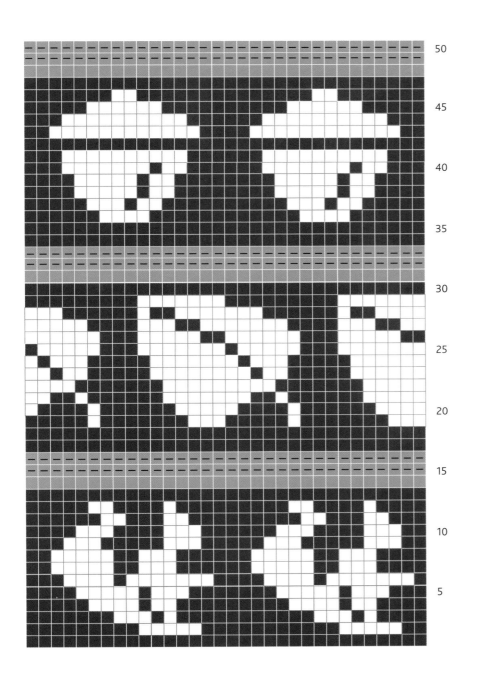

50

45

40

35

30

25

20

15

10

5

- ■ MC
- □ CC1
- ▨ CC2
- — Purl

Shape crown: Break CC2, join MC and work decrease round as follows: *ssk, work to 2 sts before marker, k2tog, rep from * to end of round. 8 sts decreased.

Repeat decrease round every round until 8 sts rem. Cut MC, leaving a 12" tail, and thread yarn through rem 8 sts. Weave in ends.

Lining

Using size 4 dpns, on the inside bottom of the hat, pick up the 128 purl bumps of CC2 from the I-cord cast-on. 128 sts on needle.

With RS facing, attach CC3 and knit all sts. Join in round and continue in St st until lining measures 2" from picked up sts. Do not bind off. Cut yarn, leaving 42" tail.

Fold lining up on the inside of hat and use the tail to sew the live sts to the inside of hat. Be sure that the lining sts are aligned with the corresponding column of sts inside the hat as you sew them down or the lining will bias.

Finishing

Weave in all ends. Block to finished measurements.

Snowmates

by Stephen Houghton and Tammy George (pattern engineered by Jackie Pawlowski)

Cozy up with Snowmates, a set of his and hers ski sweaters featuring colorful coordinating designs so you'll never lose each other in a crowd again. Matchy-matchy sweater sets were really popular in decades past, and it's time to embrace it once again in the name of solidarity on the slopes. Window panes of high-contrast color add just the right amount of brightness. Rolled hems and a band of color inside the necklines finish these classic pullovers in a most interesting way. The ladies' version features added waist shaping and three-quarter-length sleeves for an added feminine touch.

Snowmates For Him

Sizes

S (M, L, XL)

Finished Measurements

Chest: 36 (40, 44, 50)"

Materials

Cascade 220 (100% wool; 220 yd./100g per skein)

MC: Dark heathered gray; 6 (7, 8, 9) skeins

CC1: Turquoise; 1 skein for all sizes

CC2: Yellow; 1 skein for all sizes

3 U.S. 6 (4mm) circular needles, 12" length, *or size needed to match gauge*

U.S. 6 (4mm) circular needle, 24" or 36" length

U.S. G-6 (4mm) crochet hook

Waste yarn for provisional cast-on

Darning needle for finishing

Stitch markers

Measuring tape

Gauge

21 sts × 28 rows = 4" in St st

Special Stitches and Terms

JMCO (Judy's Magic Cast-On): see page 172

Provisional cast-on: see page 172

Wrap and turn (w&t): Work to the point specified in the pattern to wrap and turn. On a knit side, with yarn at back, slip the next stitch on the left hand needle purlwise to the right hand needle. Bring working yarn to front and slip stitch from right needle back to the left needle. Turn work. On a purl side, with yarn in front, slip the next stitch from the left needle to the right needle, move yarn to back and slip stitch from right needle back to the left needle. Turn work.

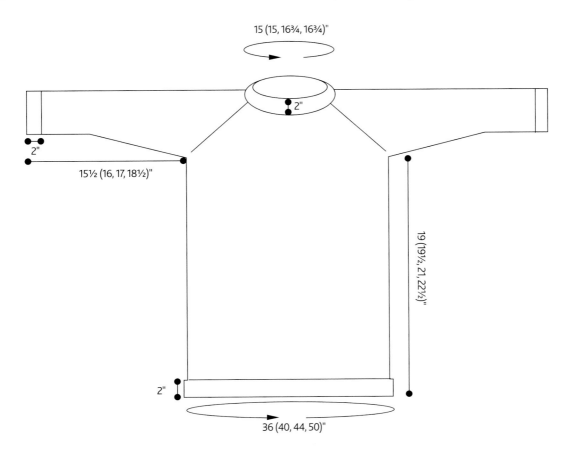

15 (15, 16¾, 16¾)"

2"

2"

15½ (16, 17, 18½)"

19 (19½, 21, 22½)"

2"

36 (40, 44, 50)"

Directions

Collar

You will start with the inside of the collar, worked in contrasting color.

Using provisional cast-on and scrap yarn, CO 80 (80, 88, 88) sts over 12" needle.

Rnd 1: K80 (80, 88, 88) with CC1, pm and join in the round, being careful not to twist.

Rnds 2–9: Knit.

Rnd 10: Change to MC and knit.

Rnd 11: Purl to create turning ridge.

Outside of Collar

Rnds 12–21: K4, p4, rep to end of round.

Join Collar

Rnd 22: Remove waste yarn from provisional cast-on, and transfer the 80 (80, 88, 88) sts to spare circular needle. Fold along the purl ridge with wrong sides touching. Holding both needles together in the left hand, with the outside of the collar facing you, knit the hem sts together with the collar sts by putting the right-hand needle through 1 st on the front needle and the corresponding st on the back needle and knitting these 2 sts together. Repeat around. 80 (80, 88, 88) sts on needle.

Raglan Shaping Set-Up

For Sizes S and M Only:

Rnd 23: K1, pm, k2, pm, k10, pm, k2, pm, k26, pm, k2, pm, k10, pm, k2, pm, k25.

For Sizes L and XL Only:

Rnd 23: K1, pm, k2, pm, k10, pm, k2, pm, k30, pm, k2, pm, k10, pm, k2, pm, k29.

Yoke Shaping

To shape the neck so that it sits comfortably, with the back higher than the front, short rows are used. You will be working back and forth over this section.

Row 24: K1, M1R, sm, k2, sm, M1L, k10, M1R, sm, k2, sm, M1L, k26 (26, 30, 30), M1R, sm, k2, sm, M1L, k10, M1R, sm, k2, sm, M1L, w&t. 8 sts added.

Row 25: Purl back to the first marker, sl first marker, p1, w&t.

Row 26 (RS): Knit to first marker, M1R, sm, k2, sm, M1L, knit to next marker (left shoulder), M1R, sm, k2, sm, M1L, knit to next marker (across back), M1R, sm, k2, sm, M1L, knit to next marker (right shoulder), M1R, sm, k2, sm, M1L, knit to wrapped st, pick up wrap and knit it together with the wrapped st tbl, w&t.

Row 27 (WS): Purl back to wrapped st by first marker, pick up wrap and purl it together with the wrapped st, w&t.

Repeat the last 2 rows 6 more times, switching to longer needle when necessary. 144 (144, 152, 152) sts.

The yoke shaping is complete; continue working in the round.

Rnd 40 (RS): Knit to first marker, M1R, sm, k2, sm, M1L, knit to next marker (left shoulder), M1R, sm, k2, sm, M1L, knit to next marker (across back), M1R, sm, k2, sm, M1L, knit to next marker (right shoulder), M1R, sm, k2, sm, M1L, knit to wrapped st and work it, continuing in the round (across front), knit to wrapped stitch and work it. 152 (152, 160, 160) sts.

Rnd 41: Knit 1 round, returning to first marker, which will indicate the beginning of round.

Raglan Increasing

Continue increasing every other round at the markers as follows:

Increase Round: Sl first marker, k2, sm, M1L, knit to next marker, M1R, sm, k2, sm, M1L, knit to next marker, M1R, sm, k2, sm, M1L, knit to next marker, M1R, sm, k2, sm, M1L, knit to beginning of round marker, M1R.

Next rnd (Plain Round): Knit.

Rep these 2 rounds 13 times more. 264 (264, 272, 272) sts.

Rnd 70: Rep the Increase Round above.

Rnd 71: Knit.

Rnd 72: Knit.

Rep these 3 rounds 2 (5, 8, 14) times more. 288 (312, 344, 392) sts.

Left Sleeve

Work the sleeve on shorter needles while the rest of the sweater is held on original needle.

Remove first marker, k2, and remove second marker. Cut yarn. Slip 60 (66, 74, 86) sts of left sleeve onto spare shorter needle. Keep third marker here.

Body and right sleeve sts should be secured/placed on a holder as they won't be worked at this time.

Using JMCO and MC, CO 10 (14, 18, 20) sts onto 2 sets of 12" circular needles. This is the underarm.

Do not turn work. Slide 10 (14, 18, 20) sts on bottom needle to center of cable to hold for later. Continue knitting the 60 (66, 74, 86) sleeve sts with the top needle from the JMCO. K5 (7, 9, 10) from the sts just cast on, and pm. This will mark beginning of sleeve rounds. 70 (80, 92, 106) sts for sleeve.

Work 8 (6, 5, 4) rounds even, then begin sleeve decreases as follows:

Next rnd (Decrease Round): K1, ssk, knit to 3 sts before marker, k2tog, k1.

Repeat the Decrease Round every 9th (7th, 6th, 5th) round 10 (15, 17, 24) times more. 48 (48, 56, 56) sts.

Continue in St st until sleeve measures 15½ (16, 17, 18½)" or 2" shorter than desired sleeve length.

Cuff

Rnds 1–10: *K4, p4, rep from * to end of round.

Rnd 11: Purl to create turning ridge.

Rnd 12: Knit.

Rnds 13–20: With CC1, knit.

Turn sleeve inside out. With spare needle, pick up 48 (48, 56, 56) sts on the WS where ribbing began at cuff Rnd 1. Fold along purl row with wrong sides touching.

Use three-needle bind-off to attach hem and bind off all sts.

Right Sleeve (with Color Arm Band)

The sleeve is worked on shorter needles while body is held on original needle. Join yarn at original third marker, at the back left underarm. Remove marker, k2, remove marker, k80 (86, 94, 106), remove marker, k2, remove marker. Cut yarn.

Slip 60 (66, 74, 86) sts of right sleeve onto spare shorter needle.

Body sts should be secured/placed on a holder as they won't be worked at this time.

Using JMCO and MC, CO 10 (14, 18, 20) sts onto 2 sets of 12" circular needles. This is the underarm.

Do not turn work. Slide 10 (14, 18, 20) sts on bottom needle to center of cable to hold for later. Continue knitting the 60 (66, 74, 86) sleeve sts with the top needle from the JMCO. K5 (7, 9, 10) from the sts just cast-on and pm. This will mark beginning of sleeve rounds. 70 (80, 92, 106) sts for sleeve.

Work 8 (6, 5, 4) rounds even, then begin sleeve decreases as follows:

Next rnd (Decrease Round): K1, ssk, knit to 3 sts before marker, k2tog, k1. Work 1 set of sleeve decreasing rounds. 68 (78, 90, 104) sts.

Begin Colorwork

During colorwork, two strands of yarn are carried for the entire round. Secure MC yarn by twisting on the 4th stitch of each color block.

Rnd 1: K2 (2, 3, 0) in CC1, *k3 in MC, k7 in CC1, rep from * to last 6 (6, 7, 4) sts, k3 in MC, k3 (3, 4, 1) in CC1.

Rnds 2–10: Maintain colorwork as set in Rnd 1, while at the same time decreasing on the 9th (7th, 6th, 5th) row. As you decrease, maintain the columns of MC and CC1 as set.

The next 10 rounds will be worked with CC2 and MC. Sts worked in CC1 previously will now be worked in CC2. The columns of stitches should be maintained as set as you continue to decrease every 9th (7th, 6th, 5th) round.

Rnd 11: K1 (1, 2, 0) in CC2, k3 (3, 3, 1) in MC, k7 in CC2, *k3 in MC, k7 in CC2, rep from * to last 5 (5, 6, 2) sts, k3 (3, 3, 2) in MC, k2 (2, 3, 0) in CC2.

Rnds 12–20: Continue with colorwork patt as set.

Work remainder of right sleeve in the same manner as left, decreasing as set until there are 48 (48, 56, 56) sts.

Continue working until sleeve measures 15½ (16, 17, 18½)" or 2" before desired sleeve length.

Cuff

Work as on left sleeve.

Body

Join yarn at back right underarm, k5 (7, 9, 10) live sts on JMCO needle, pm to indicate side seam, k5 (7, 9, 10).

K84 (90, 98, 110) across front.

K5 (7, 9, 10), pm. This is the new beginning for body rounds. 188 (208, 232, 260) sts.

Continue working until body measures 7 (7½, 9, 10½)" from underarm.

To prepare for colorwork, increase/decrease to a multiple of 10 sts as follows:

Sizes S and M only: Increase 2 sts, evenly spaced over next row.

Size L only: Decrease 2 sts evenly over next row. 190 (210, 230, 260) sts total.

Begin Colorwork

As before, during colorwork, two strands of yarn are carried for the entire round. Secure MC yarn by twisting on the 4th st of each color block.

Rnds 1–10: *K3 (3, 3, 0) in CC2, *k3 in MC, k7 in CC1, rep from * to last 7 (7, 7, 0) sts, k3 in MC, k4 (4, 4, 0) in CC1.

Rnds 11–20: *K3 (3, 3, 0) in CC1, *k3 in MC, k7 in CC2, rep from * to last 7 (7, 7, 0) sts, k3 in MC, k4 (4, 4, 0) in CC2.

Work 4 rounds even in MC only.

Repeat Rnds 1–20 once. The colorwork is complete.

Work 4 rounds even in MC.

In the next round increase/decrease to a multiple of 8 sts as follows:

Sizes S and L only: Increase 2 sts evenly spaced.

Sizes M and 1X only: Decrease 2 sts evenly spaced. 192 (208, 232, 258) sts.

Waist Hem

Rnds 1–10: *K4, p4, rep from * around.

Rnd 11: Purl to create turning ridge.

Rnd 12: Knit.

Rnds 13–20: Switch to CC1 and knit.

Turn body inside out. With spare needle, pick up 192 (208, 232, 258) sts on the WS where ribbing began. Fold along purl row with wrong sides touching.

Use three-needle bind-off to attach hem and bind off sts.

Finishing

Weave in all ends, making sure to close any gaps at underarms.

Snowmates For Her

Sizes
XS (S, M, L, 1X, 2X)

Finished Measurements
Chest: 34 (37, 40, 44, 48, 54)"

Materials
Cascade 220 (220 yd./100g per skein)

MC: #8400 Smokestack; 5 (6, 6, 7, 7, 8) skeins

CC1: #8892 Blue Jay; 1 skein for all sizes

CC2: #7828 Lemon Peel; 1 skein for all sizes

U.S. 4 (3.5mm) circular needles, 16" length

U.S. 6 (4mm) circular needles, 16" and 32" or 40", depending on bust size

U.S. 6 (4mm) double-pointed needles

Spare needle U.S. 4 or smaller for joining provisional cast-on.

U.S. G-6 (4mm) crochet hook

Stitch markers

Row counter

Darning needle

Waste yarn for provisional cast-on

Gauge
22 sts × 32 rows = 4" in St st

Special Stitches and Terms
Provisional cast-on: see page 172

Wrap and turn (w&t): see page 47

Pattern Notes
Garment is worked seamlessly from the top down with folded hems at both the collar and bottom edges. Knitting begins at the inside of the collar.

An additional 32" or 40" circular needle is helpful while knitting the body for trying on. Don't be afraid to try garment on often and make adjustments for a customized fit.

The armband can be knit on either arm. We chose to knit the his and hers sweaters on opposite arms so that when they hold hands on the chilly slopes, the bands would meet in the middle.

Directions

Collar

This sweater is seamlessly knit in one piece, starting with the inside of the collar. Knit the inside of the collar using needles two sizes smaller than for the rest of the sweater. The ribbing inside of the collar is designed to be offset from the ribbing on the outside of the collar, so that it nests inside and prevents excess bulk.

With waste yarn, provisionally cast 113 (121, 121, 129, 137, 145) sts onto the size 4 circular needles. Knit 1 row with CC2.

Join for knitting in the round (sl last stitch from right needle to left needle, pm, and k2tog). 112 (120, 120, 128, 136, 144) sts.

Row 1: *K4, p4, rep from * to end.

Rep Row 1 until piece measures 2" from cast-on edge.

Switch to MC and knit all stitches of next round.

Switch to the size 6 circular needles and purl all stitches of next round.

Row 2: *P4, k4, rep from * to end.

Rep Row 2 until piece measures 2" from turning row.

Transfer provisional stitches from waste yarn to size 4 circular needle. 112 (120, 120, 128, 136, 144) sts should be on smaller needle. Fold collar at purl ridge so that the MC is on the outside and CC2 is on the inside.

Next row: Insert right-hand needle through first st on front needle then through first st on back needle, knit these 2 sts together. Repeat with the next sts on each needle until all sts are joined, and the collar is completely closed.

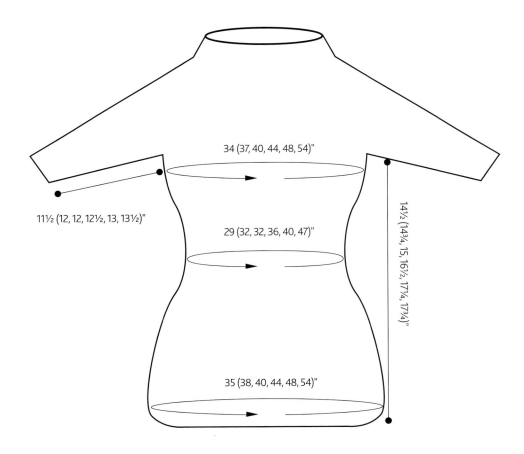

34 (37, 40, 44, 48, 54)"

11½ (12, 12, 12½, 13, 13½)"

29 (32, 32, 36, 40, 47)"

14½ (14¾, 15, 16½, 17¼, 17¾)"

35 (38, 40, 44, 48, 54)"

Yoke

First, establish raglan "seams" by placing markers to separate shoulder pieces from the front and back of sweater. Then, work short rows to shape neck. Finally, increase 8 stitches every other row to shape yoke until body stitches meet comfortably under arm.

Beginning of round is located at the center of back neck. Markers used to demarcate raglan "seams" should be different than the marker placed earlier to mark beginning of round.

Set-up row: K20 (21, 21, 22, 23, 24), pm, k2, pm, k12 (14, 14, 16, 18, 20), pm, k2, pm, k40 (42, 42, 44, 46, 48), pm, k2, pm, k12 (14, 14, 16, 18, 20), pm, k2, pm, k20 (21, 21, 22, 23, 24).

Row 1: K20 (21, 21, 22, 23, 24), sm, k2, sm, k12 (14, 14, 16, 18, 20), sm, k2, sm, k1, wrap next stitch, turn work.

Row 2: Slip wrapped st, p1, sm, p2, sm, p12 (14, 14, 16, 18, 20), sm, p2, sm, p40 (42, 42, 44, 46, 48), sm, p2, sm, p12 (14, 14, 16, 18, 20), sm, p2, sm, p1, wrap next stitch, turn work.

Row 3: Slip wrapped st, knit to marker, M1R, sm, k2, sm, M1L, knit to next marker, M1R, sm, k2, sm, M1L, knit across back stitches slipping beginning of round marker to next raglan marker, M1R, sm, k2, sm, M1L, knit to next marker, M1R, sm, k2, sm, M1L, knit to wrapped st, pick up wrap and knit together with wrapped st, wrap next st, turn work.

Row 4: Slip wrapped st, purl to marker, sm, p2, sm, purl to next marker, sm, p2, sm, purl across back stitches slipping beginning of round marker to next raglan marker, sm, p2, sm, purl to next marker, sm, p2, sm, purl to wrapped st, pick up wrap and purl together with wrapped st, wrap next st, turn work.

Repeat Rows 3 and 4 until back of neck measures 2½" from collar ribbing.

Next row: Slip wrapped st, knit to marker, M1R, sm, k2, sm, M1L, knit to next marker, M1R, sm, k2, sm, M1L, knit across back stitches slipping beginning of round marker to next raglan marker, M1R, sm, k2, sm, M1L, knit to next marker, M1R, sm, k2, sm, M1L, knit to wrapped st, pick up wrap and knit together with wrapped st, knit to next wrapped st, pick up wrap and knit together with wrapped st, knit to next marker, sm, k2, sm, knit to next marker, sm, k2, sm, knit to beginning of round marker.

Short-row neck shaping is now complete, and beginning of round is in middle of back section. Beginning of round marker is not included in row instructions to sm.

Row 1: Knit all stitches.

Row 2 (Increase Round): Knit to marker, M1R, sm, k2, sm, M1L, knit to next marker, M1R, sm, k2, sm, M1L, knit across front to next marker, M1R, sm, k2, sm, M1L, knit to next marker, M1R, sm, k2, sm, M1L, knit to end. (8 sts increased.)

Repeat Rows 1 and 2 until there are 320 (344, 376, 416, 472, 528) total sts.

[For easier checking, there should be: 92 (98, 106, 116, 130, 144) sts in each of the body sections, 64 (70, 78, 88, 102, 116) sts in each of the sleeve sections, and 8 seam sts in all sizes.]

Next rnd: Knit all stitches.

Try on piece to check length of yoke. Knit even until body sections meet comfortably under the arm.

Sleeves

For sizes XS and 1X, "seam" stitches are split between body and sleeve sections. For all other sizes, "seam" stitches are allocated to body section.

Right Sleeve

For Size XS and 1X Only:

Remove beginning of round marker. Knit across back sts to marker. Remove marker, k1, pm (this marker now denotes beginning of sleeve round), k1, remove marker, knit to next marker, remove marker, k1.

For All Other Sizes:

Knit across back sts to marker. Remove marker, k2, sm (this marker now denotes beginning of sleeve round), knit to next marker, remove marker.

All Sizes:

Transfer sleeve sts to dpns. 66 (70, 78, 88, 104, 116) sts.

Knit 1 row even.

Decrease Round: K1, k2tog, knit to last 3 sts, ssk, k1.

Work decrease row every 6 (7, 7, 6, 4, 4) rows 9 (7, 11, 12, 20, 22) times.

48 (56, 56, 64, 64, 72) sts rem.

Knit until sleeve measures 9½ (10, 10, 10½, 11, 11½)" or reaches about an inch below elbow.

Begin cuff.

Rnd 1: *K4, p4, rep from * to end.

Rep until cuff measures 2". Bind off loosely.

Left Sleeve

For Size XS and XL Only:

Join yarn at right underarm, pm, knit across front sts to marker. Remove marker, k1, pm (this marker now denotes beginning of sleeve round), k1, remove marker, knit to next marker, remove marker, k1.

For All Other Sizes:

Knit across front sts to marker. Remove marker, k2, sm (this marker now denotes beginning of sleeve round), knit to next marker, remove marker.

All Sizes:

Transfer sleeve sts to dpns. 66 (70, 78, 88, 104, 116) sts.

Knit 1 rnd even.

Work decreases while, *at the same time,* beginning colorwork band when sleeve measures 2½" from underarm.

Decrease Round: K1, k2tog, knit to last 3 sts, ssk, k1.

Knit decrease row every 6 (7, 7, 6, 4, 4) rows 9 (7, 11, 12, 20, 22) times. 48 (56, 56, 64, 64, 72) sts rem.

Knit until sleeve measures 9½ (10, 10, 10½, 11, 11½)" or reaches about an inch below elbow.

Colorwork Band

Rnd 1: K4 (4, 4, 4, 5, 5), *(K5 in CC1, K2 in MC), rep from * 7 (8, 9, 11, 12, 14) times, using MC knit to end.

Rep Rnd 1, 6 times.

Rnd 2: Knit to first colorblock, *(K5 in CC1, K2 in MC), rep from * 7 (8, 9, 11, 12, 14) times, using MC knit to end.

Rep Rnd 2, 6 times.

Continue knitting in MC, completing decrease rows as instructed. 48 (56, 56, 64, 64, 72) sts rem.

Knit until sleeve measures 9½ (10, 10, 10½, 11, 11½)" or reaches about an inch below elbow.

Begin cuff.

Rnd 1: *K4, p4, rep from * to end.

Rep until cuff measures 2". Bind off loosely.

Body

Work hourglass waist shaping from underarms to hips. When hip increases are completed, begin colorwork blocks. Bind off using a turned hem.

Set-up row: Join yarn at left underarm, pm, knit across 94 (102, 110, 120, 132, 148) back sts, place beginning of round marker.

Knit 2" from underarm.

Begin Waist Shaping

Decrease Round: K1, k2tog, knit to 3 sts before marker, ssk, k1, sm, k1, k2tog, knit to last 3 sts, ssk, k1.

Work Decrease Round every 3 (3, 2, 3, 3, 3) rnds 7 (7, 11, 10, 11, 10) times. 160 (176, 176, 200, 220, 256) waist sts.

Work even for 3 (3, 3, 2½, 2½, 2½)".

Increase Round: K1, M1L, knit to 3 sts before marker, M1R, k1, sm, k1, M1L, knit to last 3 sts, M1R, k1.

Knit Increase Round every 3 (4, 3, 4, 3, 4) rnds 10 (8, 11, 10, 12, 11) times.

For Size S and XL Only:

Work 1 rnd even.

Next rnd: Knit across front sts, sm, k1, M1L, knit to last 3 sts, M1R, k1. 200 (210, 220, 240, 270, 300) hip sts.

Work even for 3 (3, 3, 2½, 2½, 2½)".

Colorwork Band

Rnd 1: * (K7 in CC1, K3 in MC), rep from * to end.

Rep Row 1, 8 times.

Rnd 2: * (K7 in CC1, K3 in MC), rep from * to end.

Rep Rnd 2, 8 times.

End colorwork.

Knit 10 rnds even. Insert an extra circular needle through the back of the sts on the last knit round.

Hem

Knit 6 rnds even.

Purl 1 round.

Knit 6 rounds even, fold at purl ridge inwards and work a three-needle bind-off to join sts on both needles and bind off.

Finishing

Weave in all ends, close any holes at underarms, and block garment to desired measurements.

Après Ski Skirts

by Kelly Bridges

We've decided that it's time to bring back the knitted skirt in a big way! One of the most versatile pieces in this book is our Après Ski Skirt. Use any of the three charts included, modify an old favorite, or knit it up in a solid color, and you'll wonder why you've been wearing pants this whole time. Three variations for clever edge finishing and optional shaping (what we like to call the "butt gusset") will let you customize your skirt even further. And knitted skirts aren't just for winter! The charted skirts featured are knit using wool, but you can lighten things up for summer by working the same pattern in linen or hemp yarn for another twist on a new favorite.

Sizes

S (M, L, 1X, 2X).

Finished Measurements

Waist: 27½ (31, 35, 38½, 42)"

Hips (without gussets): 38 (42, 46, 49½, 53)"

Bottom Edge (without gussets): 40½ (48, 51½, 55, 59)"

Materials

Chamonix version (shown in size L without gussets):

Reynolds Whiskey (100% wool; 195 yd./100g per skein)

    Color A: #053 Teal; 2 (3, 3, 3, 4) balls

    Color B: #103 Light Olive; 1 (1, 2, 2, 2) balls

    Color C: #059 Charcoal; 1 (2, 2, 2, 2) balls

    Color D: #131 Dark Pink; 1 ball

    Color E: #102 Dark Orange; 1 ball

Beignets version (shown in size S without gussets):

Reynolds Whiskey (100% wool; 195 yd./100g per skein)

    Color A: #101 Orange; 4 (4, 5, 5, 6) balls

    Color B: #131 Dark Pink; 1 ball

    Color C: #016 Burgundy; 1 ball

U.S. 3 (3.25mm) and U.S. 4 (3.5mm) 24" or 32" circular needles, *or size needed to match gauge*

U.S. 4 (3.5mm) short double-pointed needles for braid edging only

1" wide elastic, cut to your waist circumference plus 2"

Needle and thread

Gauge

26 sts × 33 rows = 4" in St st on larger needles.

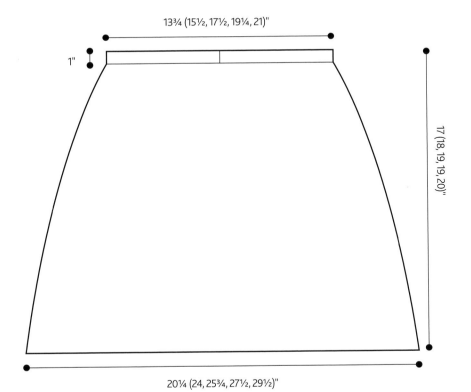

13¾ (15½, 17½, 19¼, 21)"

1"

17 (18, 19, 19, 20)"

20¼ (24, 25¾, 27½, 29½)"

Special Stitches and Terms

Kfb: Increase by knitting into the front and back of the next st.

2-st nupp: Insert the right needle between the second and third st on the left needle from front to back, wrap yarn around needle clockwise, and pull the loop through. Wrap yarn around needle counter-clockwise and pull this loop through previously made loop (1 loop on the right needle). Sl 2 sts pwise from the left needle to the right needle and lift loop over these sts as if to bind off to complete the nupp.

1-st nupp: Work as above, but insert the right needle between first and second st on the left needle and sl only one st from the left needle to the right needle.

yo2: see page 171

Pattern Notes

This versatile skirt pattern can be varied to suit your fancy. We show it here in two versions done in colorwork and wool. If you'd like to add gussets, follow the instructions given within the pattern. In addition to the color variations, you can also choose from three different edging options to finish your skirt. Read through the whole pattern before you begin, and highlight the options you've chosen to use to guide you as you create your skirt.

Directions

Waist Casing: For All Versions

Take the elastic and overlap the ends to form a circle that fits comfortably at your waist, remembering that the knitted fabric will make the fit feel slightly tighter. With needle and thread, sew the ends together.

With smaller needles and Color A, CO 180 (204, 228, 252, 276) sts. Place marker and join into the round, being careful not to twist the sts. Work in St st for 1¼".

Change to larger needles and purl 1 round to create turning ridge.

Work in St st for 1¼". Fold knitting over elastic band and join as follows: *Insert right needle into next st on left needle, then into corresponding st from cast-on edge. Knit these 2 sts together. Rep from * to last 7 sts. K7 sts without joining to CO edge (this leaves a gap for adjusting elastic if needed).

Body

For the Chamonix or Beignets version: Continue in St st and place markers as follows: K90 (102, 114, 126, 138) sts, pm, knit to end of rnd. This marker and the beginning of rnd marker indicate side seams.

For the Chamonix version only: Begin colorwork now. See "Colorwork Patterns" on page 58.

For Gussetless version: Next rnd (Increase Round): Kfb, knit to 1 st before marker, kfb, sm, kfb, knit to last st, kfb.

Rep the Increase Round every other round 11 times more.

Then rep the Increase Round every 4th (4th, 5th, 5th, 5th) rnd 15 times total. 288 (312, 336, 360, 384) sts on needle.

Continue at edging.

Gusseted Version Only

The optional gussets add about 3½" to hip and finished hem measurements to create a fuller skirt.

K22 (25, 28, 31, 34), place gusset marker, k46 (52, 58, 64, 70), place gusset marker, k22 (25, 28, 31, 34), place side seam marker, k22 (25, 28, 31, 34), place gusset marker, k46 (52, 58, 64, 70), place gusset marker, knit to end of rnd. Shape side seams and gussets at the same time as follows:

Next rnd (Increase Round 1): *Kfb, **knit to 1 st before gusset marker, kfb, sm, kfb, rep from ** once, knit to 1 st before side seam marker, kfb, sm, rep from *.

Work 1 rnd even.

Next rnd (Increase Round 2): Kfb, knit to 1 st before side seam marker, kfb, sm, kfb, knit to last st, kfb.

Work 1 rnd even.

Rep these 4 rounds twice more.

Rep Increase Round 2 every other round 9 times more. Then rep Increase Round 2 every 4th (4th, 5th, 5th, 5th) rnd 15 times total. 312 (336, 360, 384, 408) sts on needle.

For single-color or Chamonix: Work even in St st until skirt measures 16 (17, 18, 18, 19)" from the bottom of waist casing.

For Beignets: Work even in St st until skirt measures 11½ (12½, 13½, 13½, 14½)" from the bottom of waist casing, then begin colorwork. See "Colorwork Patterns" on page 58.

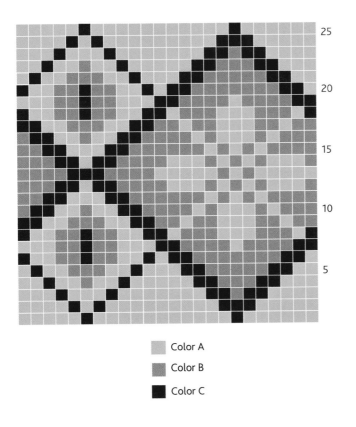

Color A

Color B

Color C

Flocon de Neige Chart

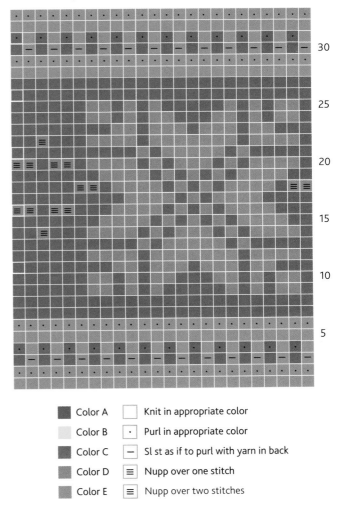

	Color A		Knit in appropriate color
	Color B	·	Purl in appropriate color
	Color C	−	Sl st as if to purl with yarn in back
	Color D	≡	Nupp over one stitch
	Color E	≡	Nupp over two stitches

Edgings

When the skirt measures 16 (17, 18, 18, 19)" from the bottom of the waist casing, or desired length, finish your skirt with one of the following three edgings.

Basic edging: Purl 1 round to create turning ridge. Change to smaller needles and work 6 rounds in St st. Bind off loosely. Fold at turning ridge and whipstitch bound-off edge to body of skirt.

Picot edging: Work 3 rounds in St st. On next rnd: *K1, yo2, k2tog, rep from * to end of rnd. Knit 1 round, letting second wrap of yo2 fall off the needle without working it. Knit 1 round, working into yo hole instead of the st above it on needle, allowing the stitch on the needle to fall as you work. Knit 2 rounds. Bind off loosely knitwise. Whipstitch bound-off edge to body of skirt at first round of picot edge.

Braid edging: Bind off loosely in purl. Directions are written for two colors. If working with just one color, you will need two separate balls to work the braid. Consider color A as ball A and color B as ball B.

With RS facing, color A and two dpns, CO 3 sts. Work 3 rows as follows: Slide sts to opposite end of dpn, k2, sl 1, yo, pick up and knit 1 st from bound-off edge of skirt, pass yo and sl st over. Work 6 rows as follows: Slide sts of opposite end of dpn. K3. With color B and another dpn, CO 3 sts. Work 6 rows as follows: Slide sts of opposite end of dpn. K3. *Bring B cord over A cord, skip 1 st from bound-off edge of skirt, then work 3 rows as follows: Slide sts to opposite end of dpn, k2, sl 1, yo, pick up and k1 st from bound-off edge of skirt, pass yo and sl st over. Work 6 rows as follows with color B: Slide sts to opposite end of dpn. K3. Bring A cord over B cord, skip 1 st from

La Montagne Chart

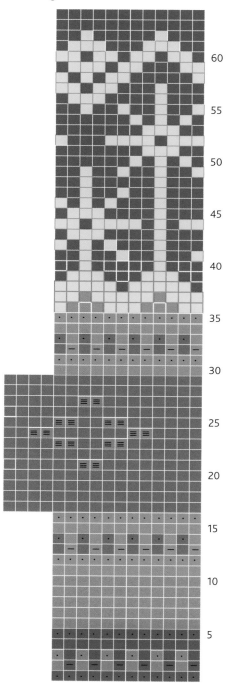

bound-off edge of skirt, then work 3 rows as follows with A: Slide sts to opposite end of dpn, k2, sl 1, yo, pick up and k1 st from bound-off edge of skirt, pass yo and sl st over. Work 6 rows as follows with A: Slide sts to opposite end of dpn. K3. Rep from * across entire bottom of skirt. Graft live sts to corresponding sts on the cast-on edge of the same color cord.

Colorwork Patterns
Chamonix

Work Rnds 1–40 of La Montagne chart, incorporating increases into the patt. Continue repeating Rnd 40 only until the skirt measures 10½ (11, 12, 12, 13)" from the bottom of the waist casing.

Work Rnds 41–64 of La Montagne chart.

Work Rnds 1–33 of Flocon de Neige chart.

If needed, continue to work even in Color C until skirt measures 16 (17, 18, 18, 19)" from the bottom of the waist casing.

Beignets

When skirt measures 11½ (12½, 13½, 13½, 14½)" from waist casing, work the 25 rows of Beignets Chart, then work even with Color A until skirt measures 16 (17, 18, 18, 19)".

Finishing

To finish the Beignets skirt as shown, use the basic edging. Make a whole bunch of pom-poms of desired size and color, and attach to turning ridge at desired spacing (for the size Small skirt shown in the photo, there are 30 pom-poms).

To finish the Chamonix skirt as shown, work the picot edge with Color C.

Make your own charted version: The number of stitches you begin with will support a 12-st colorwork repeat. The number of sts you have on the needle after the increases are complete will support a 24-st colorwork repeat. Any denominator thereof can also be used (2, 4, 6, 8, 12), so make Chamonix your own! Use blank graph to create a stunning colorwork pattern all your own. Keep in mind that any increases will need to be worked into this pattern, so design the main increase section as a simple 2–4 st repeat—like stripes, dots, crosses, or Xs. This will also keep the focus on a highly designed, gorgeous bottom band, instead of on your hips!

St. Moritz

by Snowden Becker

Wrap yourself up for the holidays in the ultra-feminine St. Moritz pullover. Its deeply scooped neck and flattering fit will dazzle you out of the winter doldrums. The diamond stitch pattern adds lots of depth without extra bulk, so the flattering lines and added waist shaping will hug you just right. The asymmetrical button closure at the garter-stitch border is echoed in the collar and sleeve edging for some Jazz-age flair. Three-quarter-length sleeves and buttery soft yarn make this sweater the perfect addition for an evening of wintertime celebration.

Sizes

S (M, L, 1X, 2X)

Finished Measurements

Chest: 34 (38, 41, 45, 50)"

Materials

Knit One, Crochet Too Babyboo (55% nylon, 45% bamboo, 115 yd./50g per skein); #423 Lemon Ice; 8 (8, 9, 10, 11) skeins

U.S. 6 (4mm) circular needles, 24–32" length, *or size needed to match gauge*

U.S. 6 (4mm) double-pointed needles, or a second circular needle to work on two needles in the round

Locking stitch markers or safety pins

Darning needle

6 buttons, ½–¾" diameter

Waste yarn

Gauge

19 sts × 27 rows = 4" in St st

Special Stitches and Terms

M1: see page 171

Pfb: see page 170

Knitted cast-on: see page 172

Pattern Notes

Ill-fitting armholes and upper arms are a common problem for top-down raglans, especially at the upper end of a pattern's size range. Special instructions are provided here for working extra body increases on wrong-side rows to keep the finished proportions correct in sizes L, 1X, and 2X, resulting in a much better fit. This method can also be adapted to improve the fit of nearly any top-down raglan pattern for those who are larger in the bust, smaller in the arms, or fall between sizes for these measurements.

Use the knitted cast-on when directed to cast-on new stitches for the underarm and neck.

Want to experiment a little? Work the edging in a contrasting color, or try a different textured stitch for the body. The purl-stitch mock

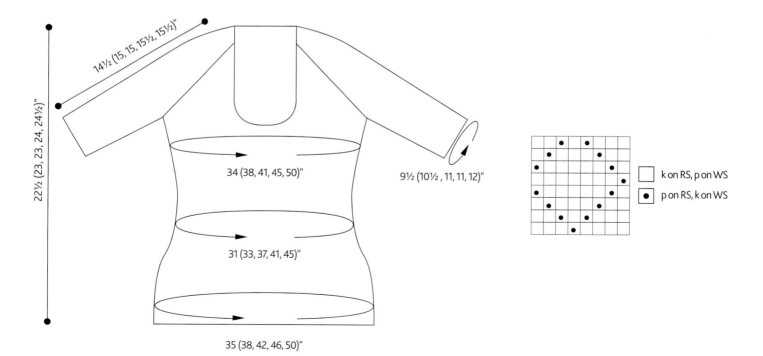

14½ (15, 15, 15½, 15½)"

22½ (23, 23, 24, 24½)"

34 (38, 41, 45, 50)"

9½ (10½ , 11, 11, 12)"

31 (33, 37, 41, 45)"

35 (38, 42, 46, 50)"

☐ k on RS, p on WS

⦁ p on RS, k on WS

seams at the sides and sleeves provide a visual break that conveniently eliminates the need for an exact match on stitch counts.

Directions

Yoke

CO 45 (51, 57, 57, 63) sts.

Row 1 (set-up row; WS): P1, pm on next st and knit it, p5 (7, 9, 9, 11), pm on next st and knit it, p29 (31, 33, 33, 35), pm on next st and knit it, p5 (7, 9, 9, 11), pm on next st and knit it, p1.

Increases will be worked on either side of these marked sts, which will always be worked in reverse St st (purl on RS rows, knit on WS rows). You may wish to move the markers as you knit, to keep them close to your working row.

Row 2 (first increase row; RS): K1; M1, p1, M1; k2 (3, 4, 4, 5), p1, k2 (3, 4, 4, 5); M1, p1, M1; k6 (7, 0, 0, 1), (p1, k7) to last st before next marked st, k1; M1, p1, M1; k2 (3, 4, 4, 5), p1, k2 (3, 4, 4, 5); M1, p1, M1; k1. (8 sts increased.)

Row 3 (WS): P2, k1; p2 (3, 4, 4, 5), k1, p1, k1, p2 (3, 4, 4, 5); k1; p6 (7, 8, 8, 1), (k1, p1, k1, p5) three times, p0 (1, 2, 2, 3); k1, p2 (3, 4, 4, 5), k1, p1, k1, p2 (3, 4, 4, 5); k1, p2.

The last two rows correspond to Rows 1 and 2 of the chart on page 60, centering the diamond pattern on each of the back and sleeve sections. Continue following the chart, beginning with Row 3, and work increased sts into the patt as you proceed, being especially careful to match the pattern placement at front and back. (It's easier than it sounds—just make sure you're working the same number of knit sts in patt before and after the sleeve increases on the back and the fronts.)

For Sizes S and M Only:

Next row (RS): *K1, work in patt as set to last st before marker, k1, M1, p1, M1; rep from * 3 times; work in patt as set to last st, end k1. (8 sts increased.)

Next row (WS): P1, *follow patt as set to last st before marked st, p1, k1, p1; rep from * 3 times; end p1.

Rep these 2 rows 23 (25) times. 245 (267, –, –, –) sts on needles. Continue to "Separate Sleeves" section.

For Sizes L, 1X, and 2X Only:

RS row: *K1, work in patt as set to last st before marker, k1, M1, p1, M1; rep from * 3 times; work in patt as set to last st, end k1. (8 sts increased.)

WS increase row: *Work in patt as set to st before marked st, pfb, k1, work in patt as set to next marked st, k1, pfb; rep from * once; work in patt as set to end. (4 sts increased.)

Work these 2 rows – (–, 4, 9, 11) times.

Continue increasing on RS rows as set: *K1, work in patt as set to last st before marker, k1, M1, p1, M1; rep from * 3 times; work in patt as set to last st, end k1. (8 sts increased.)

Work WS rows without further increases as follows: P1, *follow patt as set to last st before marked st, p1, k1, p1; rep from * 3 times; end p1.

Repeat these 2 rows until a total of – (–, 54, 54, 58) rows have been worked and there are – (–, 289, 309, 339) sts on needles.

Separate Sleeves

Next row (RS): Work in patt as set to the first marked st. Transfer the sleeve sts plus the two marked sts to waste yarn, then cast on 3 sts (all sizes) at the underarm, transferring one of the sleeve markers to the center cast-on st; Work in patt across back sts to next marked st; transfer marked sts and sleeve sts to waste yarn. Cast on 3 sts (all sizes) at underarm, again marking the center st, and work rem sts in patt.

Increase for Neckline

You will continue working all front and back sts in patt as set. Work the 3 center underarm sts as k1, p1, k1 on RS rows and p1, k1, p1 on WS rows all the way down to the hem, creating a purl gutter or false seam.

CO 1 st at the beg of the next 2 rows, then work across in patt.

CO 2 sts at the beg of the next 2 rows, then work across in patt.

Next row (WS): CO 3 sts, work in patt across.

Next row (RS): CO 18 (20, 22, 22, 24) sts, work to end of row in patt. Do not turn. Place marker and join to begin working in the round. The new start of the round will be at the lower-right corner of the neckline. Be careful working the first and last sts of the patt here, as the slight jog may make it look strange; however, it will be invisible in the finished garment.

There are 164 (176, 196, 216, 236) live sts, equally divided between front and back. The diamond patt should also be centered on both the front and the back.

Shape Waist

Work 8 rounds in patt as set.

Next rnd: *Work to last 2 sts before the "side seam," k2tog, p1, ssk; rep from * once, then work to end of round. (4 sts decreased.)

Work 3 rounds in patt without shaping.

Rep these 4 rounds 3 (4, 4, 4, 4) more times. 148 (156, 176, 196, 216) sts.

Work 10 rounds without shaping.

Next rnd: *Work to last 2 sts before the "side seam," M1, k1, p1, k1, M1; rep from * once, then work to end. (4 sts increased.)

Work 3 rounds in patt without shaping.

Rep these 4 rounds 4 (5, 5, 5, 5) times. 168 (180, 200, 222, 240) sts.

Work even in patt until work measures 18 (18½, 18½, 19, 19)" from center back neck, or 3½" less than desired length.

Hem

The bottom border is worked back and forth in garter st.

Next row: Turn and knit across all 168 (180, 200, 222, 240) sts; cast on 5 sts and turn.

Next row (RS): Knit.

Continue knitting all rows for 35 rows, working buttonholes on Rows 5, 17, and 29 as follows: k3, yo, ssk, knit to end of row.

Bind off all sts loosely on a WS row.

Sleeves

Work both sleeves the same to hem.

Using dpns or two circular needles, with RS of work facing and the garment right way up, join yarn and pick up and knit 1 st in the left-most of the 3 cast-on sts at one underarm; this will be the 1st st of the new round. Work all of the held sts in patt as set to end, removing waste yarn, then pick up and knit 2 more sts in the cast-on sts at the underarm to finish the round. 60 (66, 68, 68, 74) sts on needles. The three picked-up sts will always be worked as k1, p1, k1 to create a false seam, as for the body sts. Join and work in the round as follows.

Next rnd: Ssk, work in patt to last 3 sts, k2tog, p1. (2 sts decreased.)

Work 3 rounds without shaping.

Rep these 4 rounds until 46 (50, 54, 54, 58) sts rem.

Work without further shaping until sleeve measures 12 (12½, 12½, 13, 13)" from cast-on edge (or 1½" less than desired length).

Left Sleeve

Next rnd: K23 (25, 27, 27, 29) sts, turn.

The cuff is now worked back and forth.

Next row (WS): Knit all 46 (50, 54, 54, 58) sts, CO 5 sts. Turn.

Knit 15 more rows, working a buttonhole on Row 7 as k3, yo, ssk, knit to end of row.

Bind off all sts loosely on a WS row.

Right Sleeve

Next rnd: K23 (25, 27, 27, 29) sts, CO 5 sts, turn.

Next row (WS): Knit all sts.

K15 more rows in garter st, working buttonhole on Row 7 as for hem and other sleeve.

Bind off all sts loosely on a WS row.

Collar

Using circular needles and starting at lower-right corner (opposite side from the overlap in hem) with WS facing, pick up and knit 1 st in each st cast on at front of neckline; pick up and knit 2 sts for every 3 rows up left side of neckline; pick up and knit 1 st in every cast-on st across top of sleeves and back neck; and pick up and knit 2 sts for every 3 rows down the right side of the neckline to the starting point; cast on 5 sts to create neckline tab.

Place 6 markers as follows: 1 at each of the back raglan seams, and 2 pairs—each 10 sts apart—at the bottom corners of the neckline. (Place 1 marker 7 sts from the button tab end and another 7 sts from the start of the picked-up sts, then match their placement on the opposite side.)

Next row (RS): Turn and (k to marker, ssk) twice; then (k to 2 sts before next marker, k2tog) three times; knit to last marker, ssk; knit to end.

Work 3 rows even.

Rep these 4 rows twice.

Bind off all sts loosely on the next WS row.

Finishing

There are no seams to work! Just weave in all your ends, reinforcing the joins at the underarms if desired, and sew on some fabulous sparkly buttons opposite the buttonholes.

Peppermint Lounge Set

by Adrian Bizilia

We're in love with Peppermint Lounge, a stylish candy-striped hat-and-mitten set. They're almost sweet enough to eat! Almost. It's amazing how something as simple as a hat and mittens can add an instant 1960s look to an outfit, but this set does just that with its bright stripes, full-bodied pom-poms, and a simple chinstrap. Who doesn't love a hat with a chinstrap? This is the perfect time to use that single vintage button you've been holding onto for just the right project.

Size

One size fits most adults.

Finished Measurements

Hat circumference: 20", unstretched

Hat length: 7"

Mitten circumference: 9"

Mitten length: 9¼"

Materials

Harrisville New England Shetland (100% wool; 217 yd./50g per skein)

MC: #44 White; 2 skeins

CC: #2 Red; 1 skein

U.S. 2 (2.75mm) straight or circular needles

Note: For the edging on the hat, you can use a 16" circular needle or double-pointed needles according to your preference. For the edging and thumbs on the mittens, use double-pointed needles.

U.S. D-3 (3.25mm) crochet hook for provisional cast-on

Thin, smooth cotton yarn or string for provisional cast-on and thumbs

Stitch markers

Safety pin

Darning needle

Pom-pom maker or breath mint tin

1 small button

Gauge

25 sts × 13 rows = 4" in garter st

Special Stitches and Terms

Provisional cast-on: see page 172

Wrap and turn (w&t): see page 47

Stretchy bind-off: K2, sl these 2 sts back to left needle pwise, k2tog, *k1, slip 2 sts back to left needle pwise, k2tog, rep from * until all sts are bound off. Repeat second line around.

Garter Stitch Grafting: Be sure that the front needle has purls up against it and the back needle has knits against it. You'll have to turn your work around to orient it in this manner.

Insert a tapestry needle into the first stitch on the front needle as if to purl and then into the first stitch on the back needle as if to purl again.

**Insert the tapestry needle into the first stitch on the front needle as if to knit and slip it off the end of the knitting needle.

Insert the tapestry needle into the next stitch on the front needle as if to purl, but this time, leave it on the needle. Gently pull the yarn through.

Insert the tapestry needle into the first stitch on the back needle as if to knit and slip it off the end of the knitting needle.

Insert the tapestry needle into the next stitch on the back needle as if to purl, leave the stitch on the needle, and gently pull the yarn through. Repeat from ** until all the stitches have been grafted together.

Pattern Notes

This pattern is knit side to side in garter stitch using short rows for shaping, then the first and last rows are grafted together. Both mittens are identical.

Short rows are used to shape the mitten cuff. The CC ridges never enter this area, so the cuff is narrower than the hand portion of the mitten.

Trim is picked up and knit down from bottom edges and the neck strap is knit separately and sewn on for stability. Be sure to use the stretchy bind-off for the mittens and hat. But use the long-tail cast-on and regular bind-off for the strap for stability.

Do not cut yarns when changing colors. Bring the new color under the old color when decreasing with short rows, but bring the new color over the old color when increasing with short rows to keep the carried yarn best hidden. When changing colors, pull things nice and snug to prevent holes.

Do not slip the first stitch of the row at the bottom edge of mittens and hat. We want things to be nice and stretchy.

Directions for Mittens (Make 2)

With provisional cast-on and MC, CO 59 sts.

Decrease Rows

Set-up row (WS): Knit to last st, w&t. The stitch you just wrapped is the point at the top of the mitten.

Change to CC, do not cut MC.

Row 1 (RS): Knit to last 12 sts, pm, w&t.

Row 2 (WS): Knit to 1 st before wrapped st, w&t. (2 wrapped sts on the right needle.)

Change to MC, do not cut CC.

Row 3: Knit to wrapped st, pick up wrap and knit it together with the stitch it wraps, knit to end of row.

Row 4: Knit to 1 st before last wrapped st, w&t. (3 wrapped sts on the right needle.)

Row 5: Knit to end of row.

Row 6: Knit to 1 st before last wrapped st, w&t. (4 wrapped sts on the right needle.)

Rep Rows 1–6 of the patt 3 more times, then work Rows 1–4 once more. You will have 15 wrapped sts at the top of the mitten.

Next row (RS): Knit.

Increase Rows

Row 1 (WS): Knit to wrapped st; knit it without knitting the wrap; w&t.

Row 2 (RS): On MC rows: Knit to end. On CC Rows: Knit to marker, w&t.

Repeat these 2 rows 14 times, then Row 1 once more. You will have wrapped the last stitch again.

Knit 1 RS row.

You have finished half the mitten.

Repeat decrease rows again until you have 15 wrapped sts at the mitten point, ending with a WS row.

Create Thumbhole

Next row (RS): K18, knit next 11 sts with cotton waste yarn for thumb, slip these 11 sts pwise back to left needle, knit them with working yarn, and continue to end of row.

Repeat increase rows until second-to-last wrapped stitch at mitten tip is wrapped again, ending on WS row.

Knit 1 RS row.

Cut yarn, leaving a yard-long tail in MC for grafting.

Remove provisional crochet chain and place sts on needle. Be sure both needle points face the bottom of the mitten.

Graft first row to last, following instructions at beginning of patt. Weave in ends.

Make a second mitten in the same manner.

Thumbs

Put needles through all sts on both sides of the waste yarn: 11 sts on one side and 12 on the other. Remove waste yarn.

Attach MC at crotch of thumb and knit 1 round, picking up 1 st at the ends and knitting it together tbl with the last st, to close any gaps.

Purl 1 round to create 1 MC ridge.

Change to CC and work 1 ridge (knit 1 round; purl 1 round).

Change to MC.

Decrease Ridge

Rnd 1: K2tog, knit to last 2 sts, k2tog. 21 sts.

Rnd 2: Purl.

Work 1 ridge plain with MC.

Switch to CC and work 1 decrease ridge. 19 sts.

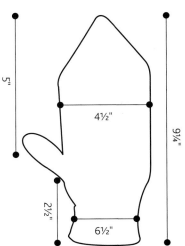

Continue in garter st maintaining stripe patt, until 16 ridges are completed, ending with 2 MC ridges.

Switch to CC.

Next rnd: Knit.

Next rnd: *K2tog, rep from * to last st, k1. 10 sts.

Cut yarn, leaving 6" tail. Thread yarn through rem sts, pull to tighten and secure end.

Edging

With CC and RS facing, pick up 1 st for each ridge at mitten cuff. 40 sts.

Knit 8 rows.

Bind off using stretchy bind-off. Weave in ends.

Finishing

Wash and block mittens.

Pom-poms shown have 5" circumference and were created by wrapping yarn 50 times around the short length of a breath mint tin. Remove wrapped yarn, tie with MC, leaving 6" tails. Pom-pom was trimmed to round shape, hand washed and air dried, then trimmed to perfection with very sharp scissors.

Attach to mitten where cuff meets trim. Tie securely on inside and weave in ends.

Directions for the Hat

With provisional cast-on and MC, cast on 48 sts.

Begin Short Row Decreases

In this section, you will knit 1 st less each WS row before wrapping and turning.

Row 2 (WS): Knit to last st, w&t.

The stitch you just wrapped is only wrapped, never knit. This stitch is the point at the crown of the hat.

Change to CC.

Row 3 (RS): Knit.

Row 4 (WS): Knit to 1 st before wrapped st at end of row, w&t.

Change to MC and rep Rows 3 and 4 twice to create 2 MC ridges.

Continue repeating these 2 rows in the stripe patt established (1 ridge CC, 2 ridges MC) until you have 14 wrapped sts on right needle, ending on a WS row. 28 rows, including cast-on row, have been worked.

Begin earflap and, ***at the same time,*** continue with short row shaping. In this section, you will knit 1 more stitch each WS row before wrapping and turning. Read the sections on the hat shaping and earflap shaping entirely before you continue knitting, as you will be working these sections simultaneously. Begin with Row 1 of Short Row Increases and Row 1 of the earflap on the next row.

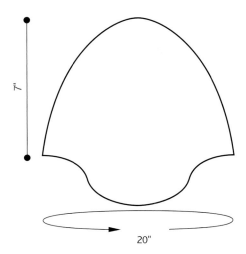

7"

20"

Earflaps

Earflaps are created by increasing at bottom edge of hat, while maintaining short rows in patt at crown of hat. Please read through entire patt and refer to diagram to understand placement beforehand.

**Increases for Earflaps:

Row 1 (RS): Knit to last st, yo, k1, turn.

Row 2 (WS): K1, knit the yarn over tbl, continue row, short row shaping as instructed in patt. Repeat these 2 rows 7 more times, until you have increased 8 sts.

Knit 4 ridges (8 rows) even, ending on WS row.

Decreasing for Earflaps:

Row 1 (RS): Knit to last 3 sts, k2tog, k1.

Row 2 (WS): Knit across, short row shaping as instructed in patt.

Repeat these 2 rows 7 more times. You have decreased 8 sts and worked a total of 40 rows for the earflap.**

Short-Row Increases:

Row 1 (RS): Knit to end of row, working earflap as specified.

Row 2 (WS): Knit to wrapped stitch. Knit it without knitting the wrap, w&t.

Repeat these 2 rows until you wrap the last wrapped st again, ending with a WS row. (54 rows, including cast-on row, have been worked.)

Knit 1 RS row.

You have finished one-fifth of the hat.

Repeat short-row decrease and increase crown-shaping sections, while finishing the first earflap, then continue with short-row shaping.

At Row 128, instead of wrapping 14th st, wrap 13th again. This is center front of hat (you're halfway there!) and wrapping the 13th st twice will preserve striping patt for second half of hat.

Continue increasing and decreasing at crown until you get to Row 168.

Next row (RS): Begin earflap shaping, maintaining crown short-row shaping as before.

After finishing second earflap, continue knitting, following crown short-row shaping, until you have completed 261 rows, ending with a RS row.

Cut yarn, leaving a yard-long tail in MC for grafting.

Remove provisional cast-on, placing sts on needle. Be sure both needle points face the bottom of the hat. Graft as for mittens. Weave tail through all the wraps around the crown stitch, cinching tight. Weave in ends.

Edging

With MC and RS facing, pick up and knit 1 st in each ridge at hat edge. 131 sts.

Knit 7 rows.

Bind off using stretchy bind-off. Weave in ends.

Neck Strap

CO 60 sts, leaving 8" tail.

Rows 1–3: Knit.

Row 4: K3, yo, k2tog, knit to end.

Rows 5–7: Knit.

Bind off, leaving 8" tail.

Finishing

Wash and block hat and strap separately. Attach the button to center of earflap, where edging begins. Button strap onto hat, and place the hat on your head. Pull the strap under your chin to check the length of strap. Pin free end to other earflap at a comfortable length. Sew strap to inside of earflap, using tails. Weave in ends.

Café Apron

You'll be twirling around your kitchen with a fresh-baked cake and a demented grin in no time with our easy-peasy apron made from a vintage café curtain. Whether it's mid-century barkcloth, cotton with pom-pom fringe, or sheer polyester with Swiss dots and a funky ruffle, chances are it will work. It's up to you to determine whether this apron is going to be a workhorse or a show pony. If it's going to get dirty, make sure the fabric is sturdy and can withstand the washer. If you'll just be wearing it for fancy, a light hand-washing will suffice for more delicate fabrics and trim. Pre-washing is always a good idea if the fabric has been marinating in the stale air of decades gone by. If your curtain is cotton or something that won't melt under an iron, go ahead and press it, too. If it's something sheer and polyester-y, give it a spritz of water and hang it to get rid of the wrinkles.

Depending on the curtain panel you're working with, you may be just a couple of simple steps away from an amazing, one-of-a kind apron. If the width and length are just right, you only need to attach a sturdy piece of twill tape, grosgrain, or fabric ribbon to tie it on—go directly to Step 9 or 10.

But chances are you'll need to do some alterations to make your apron fit just right. The length is entirely up to you: short and flirty, long and lanky, whatever you please. To determine the width you'll need, measure across your front from hip to hip.

What You'll Need

- 1 café curtain that is at least as wide as your hip-to-hip measurement.
- Coordinating twill tape, grosgrain, or fabric ribbon. It should measure at least 1" wide and four times your hip-to-hip width to tie in the back.
- Matching thread
- Sewing machine

What to Do

1. Scour the earth looking for the most amazing vintage café curtain ever. Make sure it's at least as wide as your hip-to-hip measurement. (Extra perfection points if it's exactly right!)
2. Stand befuddled in the ribbon aisle of the craft store laboring over the momentous decision and rows of ribbon before you. Bring snacks—this could take a while.
3. If you need to trim the length, make sure you cut from the boring end. Don't you dare snip off those ruffles! Better to lose the rod pocket than a pretty, frilly edge. Trim for length before you tackle the width. The "waistline" of your curtain can change considerably if you trim the top portion. Leave an extra 1" seam allowance when you measure.
4. If you need to trim the width, determine if you want the apron to be straight or flared for some added flippiness. Either way, the best approach for matching edges is to fold the curtain in half and pin the top portion together to prevent slipping.
5. Halve your hip-to-hip measurement plus 1" for a seam allowance. So if your hip-to-hip measurement is 20", measure 11" from the fold toward the outer edge and mark the fabric.
6. For a straight apron, simply cut straight down the fabric from your mark all the way to the bottom. For a flared apron, decide how much of an angle you want and cut from your mark to the bottom of the fabric.

7. At this point, you may have as many as three unfinished edges. Finish the edge you made while trimming for length first. Make a ½" fold toward the back of the fabric and press. (If it's not fabric you can iron, a cold iron is fine; you just need to make a crease.) Fold in same direction another ½" and press. Topstitch with a ⅜" seam allowance.

8. Finish the sides in a similar fashion. If you have an intact rod pocket, do not fold, and seam it closed. Sew the edges right up to the opening of the rod pocket and stop. Snip ½" of the edge of the opening, and fold inward and press so it all looks nice and even. If there is no rod pocket, sew right to the edge.

9. If there is a rod pocket, insert the ribbon and pull through to the other side. Make sure that the same amount is left hanging out of either end. Stitch the opening closed, and backstitch over the ribbon to make sure it's really in there. Repeat at the other end of the rod pocket.

10. If there is no rod pocket, fold ribbon in half lengthwise and mark the center. Line it up with the center of the apron and pin it in place. Starting at one edge of the apron, sew it to the back of the apron's waist. Sew along the top edge of the ribbon and sew another line along the bottom of the ribbing to make sure it's secure.

11. Put on your apron and go bake yourself the fluffiest, rummiest cake ever!

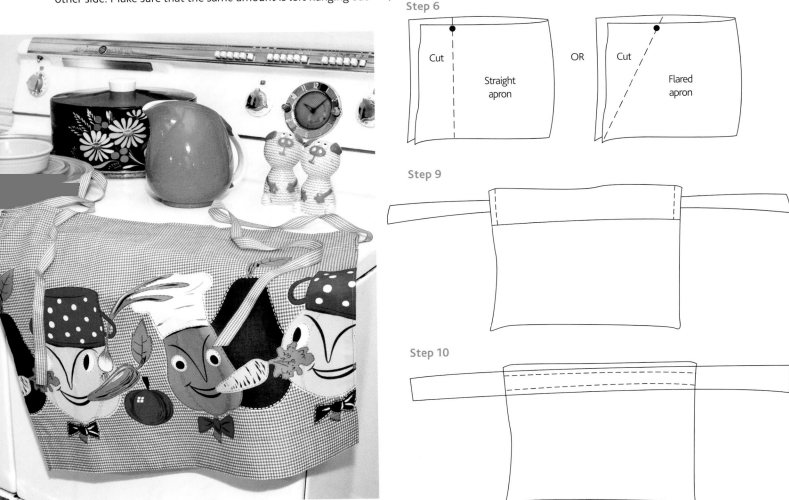

Step 6

Cut — Straight apron — OR — Cut — Flared apron

Step 9

Step 10

chapter **3**

Vrrrrooom!

For the last century, cars have been the quintessential accessory for folks who have someplace to be, even if that place is a strip of road downtown where the sole destination is the other end and back again. Cities have been built around them; most people very fondly name them (and know whether they're male or female), and someone even invented a way to allow them to watch movies with us. Truly our love of cars goes beyond the convenience of getting from Point A to Point B. In fact, if the ride is good enough, who really cares about Point B? They've brought people together and allowed them to get even further apart. They've even inspired culture and fashion with their continuously updated styles providing instantly recognizable icons of their day. Sturdy and functional, curvaceous and opulent, outrageous and futuristic, sporty and fun, muscular and sexy. That is the history of the automobile, and it can be argued that these phrases could also describe the fashions and trends of the decades in which they were manufactured. It is those fashions that inspired us to create this homage to car culture made almost entirely out of yarn.

Pump Jockey

by Jodi Green

Pump Jockey is a men's cardigan fashioned after a classic gas station jacket. Customize it with your favorite fella's name for added vintage appeal. This sweater features a sturdy zip front, a turned hem, and the mother of all cardigan accoutrements—a side pocket! From the color to the embroidery, this is an instant favorite that any fan of retro fashion will love.

Sizes

XS (S, M, L, XL, XXL)

Finished Measurements

Chest: 41 (44, 46, 48½, 51, 53)"

Materials

Valley Yarns Northampton (100% wool; 247 yd./100g per skein)

MC: #09 Lizard Green; 6 (6, 7, 7, 8, 8) skeins

CC: #06 Dark Gray; 1 skein for all sizes

U.S. 6 (4mm) circular needles, 24" length or longer, *or size needed to match gauge*

Stitch holders or waste yarn

Darning needle

22" metal separating zipper

Sewing needle and thread (to match main color)

A small amount of a third contrasting yarn for knitted patch (optional)

1 skein of embroidery floss or a small amount of contrasting yarn for embroidery (optional)

Gauge

22 sts × 32 rows = 4" in St st

Special Stitches and Terms

Twisted Purl cast-on: Holding work on your left-hand needle, insert right needle into first stitch purlwise through the back loop. Wrap yarn as you normally would to purl. Pull the loop through and place it onto the left needle.

Pattern Notes

Instructions are given for optional inseam pockets.

Directions

Back

With CC, CO 112 (120, 126, 132, 138, 144) sts. Starting with a WS row, work 7 rows in St st. Break yarn.

Next row (RS): Join MC and knit all sts.

Work even in St st until piece measures 15 (15½, 15½, 16, 16½, 17)" from color change, ending with a WS row.

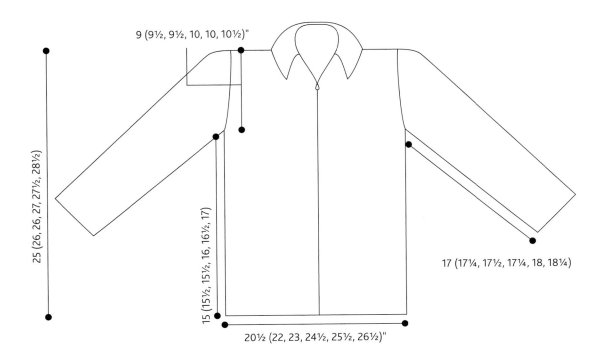

9 (9½, 9½, 10, 10, 10½)"

25 (26, 26, 27, 27½, 28½)

15 (15½, 15½, 16, 16½, 17)

20½ (22, 23, 24½, 25½, 26½)"

17 (17¼, 17½, 17¼, 18, 18¼)

Armhole Shaping

Continuing in St st, bind off 3 sts at the beginning of next 4 (4, 4, 4, 8, 8) rows, then bind off 2 sts at the beginning of the next 2 (4, 4, 4, 2, 4) rows.

Next row (RS): K1, ssk, knit to last 3 sts, k2tog, k1.

Next row: Purl.

Rep the last 2 rows 1 (2, 3, 5, 3, 3) times more. 92 (94, 98, 100, 102, 104) sts.

Work even until armhole measures 9 (9½, 9½, 10, 10, 10½)" from initial bind-off, ending with a WS row.

Next row (RS): K32 (32, 34, 34, 35, 36) sts. Put next 28 (30, 30, 32, 32, 32) sts on holder for back neck. Put rem 32 (32, 34, 34, 35, 36) sts on a second holder or spare needle for left shoulder. Turn work and continue on the 32 (32, 34, 34, 35, 36) sts for right shoulder only.

Next row (WS): P1, p2tog, purl to end.

Next row (RS): Bind off 5 sts, knit to last 3 sts, k2tog, k1.

Next row (WS): Purl.

Bind off 5 sts at beg of next 2 RS rows.

Next row (WS): Bind off rem 15 (15, 17, 17, 18, 19) sts.

With RS facing, join yarn at neck edge to work left shoulder.

Next row (RS): K1, ssk, knit to end.

Next row (WS): Bind off 5 sts, purl to last 3 sts, p2tog tbl, p1.

Next row (RS): Knit.

Bind off 5 sts at beg of next 2 WS rows.

Next row (RS): Bind off rem 15 (15, 17, 17, 18, 19) sts.

Right Front

With CC, CO 58 (61, 64, 68, 71, 74) sts.

Work 6 rows in St st beginning with a WS row.

Next row (WS): Purl to end, CO 2 sts using twisted purl cast-on. Break yarn. This contrast hem will later be turned under. 60 (63, 66, 68, 71, 74) sts.

Next row (RS): Join MC and knit.

Continue even in St st until work measures 15 (15½, 15½, 16, 16½, 17)" from color change, ending with a RS row.

Armhole Shaping

Bind off 3 sts at beg of next 2 (2, 2, 2, 4, 4) WS rows.

Bind off 2 sts at beg of next 1 (2, 2, 2, 1, 2) WS rows.

Next row (RS): Knit to last 3 sts, k2tog, k1.

Next row: Purl.

Rep the last 2 rows 1 (2, 3, 5, 3, 3) times more. 50 (50, 52, 52, 53, 54) sts.

Work even until armhole measures 7 (7½, 7½, 8, 8, 8½)" from initial bind-off, ending with a RS row.

Next row (WS): Work to last 16 (16, 16, 16, 16, 18) sts and place these sts on holder, turn and continue on the rem 34 (34, 36, 36, 37, 38) sts only.

Next row (RS): K1, ssk, knit to end.

Next row (WS): Purl to last 3 sts, p2tog tbl, p1.

Work even until armhole measures 9 (9½, 9½, 10, 10, 10½)" from initial bind-off, ending with a WS row.

Next row (RS): K1, ssk, knit to end.

Next row (WS): Bind off 5 sts, purl to last 3 sts, p2tog tbl, p1.

Next row (RS): Knit.

Bind off 5 sts at beg of next 2 WS rows.

Next row (RS): Bind off rem 15 (15, 17, 17, 18, 19) sts.

Left Front

With CC, CO 58 (61, 64, 68, 71, 74) sts.

Work 6 rows in St st beginning with a WS row.

Next row (WS): Purl to end, CO 2 sts using twisted purl cast-on. Break yarn. This contrast hem will later be turned under. 60 (63, 66, 68, 71, 74) sts.

Next row (RS): Join MC and knit.

Continue even in St st until work measures 15 (15½, 15½, 16, 16½, 17)" from color change, ending with a WS row.

Armhole Shaping

Bind off 3 sts at beg of next 2 (2, 2, 2, 4, 4) RS rows.

Bind off 2 sts at beg of next 1 (2, 2, 2, 1, 2) RS rows.

Next row (RS): K1, ssk, knit to end of row.

Next row: Purl.

Rep the last 2 rows 1 (2, 3, 5, 3, 3) times more. 50 (50, 52, 52, 53, 54) sts.

Work even until armhole measures 7 (7½, 7½, 8, 8, 8½)" from initial bind-off, ending with a WS row.

Next row (RS): Work to last 16 (16, 16, 16, 16, 18) sts and place these sts on holder, turn and continue on the rem 34 (34, 36, 36, 37, 38) sts only.

Next row (WS): P1, p2tog, purl to end.

Next row (RS): Knit to last 3 sts, k2tog, k1.

Work even until armhole measures 9 (9½, 9½, 10, 10, 10½)" from initial bind-off, ending with a RS row.

Next row (WS): P1, p2tog, purl to end.

Next row (RS): Bind off 5 sts, knit to last 3 sts, k2tog, k1.

Next row (WS): Purl.

Bind off 5 sts at beg of next 2 RS rows.

Next row (WS): Bind off rem 15 (15, 17, 17, 18, 19) sts.

Sleeve (Make 2)

With CC, CO 56 (60, 62, 66, 68, 72) sts. Work 7 rows in St st, ending with a WS row. Break yarn.

Next row (RS): Join MC and continue in St st until piece measures 4 (4¼, 4¼, 4½, 4½, 5)" from first green row, ending with a WS row.

Next row (Increase Row; RS): K1, M1, knit to last st, M1, k1.

Work 5 rows even.

Rep these 6 rows 13 times more.

Rep the Increase Row.

Work 7 rows even.

Rep these 8 rows once more. 88 (92, 94, 98, 100, 104) sts.

Work even until piece measures 17 (17¼, 17½, 17¾, 18, 18¼)" from first MC row, ending with a WS row.

Continuing in St st, bind off 3 sts at the beginning of next 4 (4, 4, 4, 8, 8) rows, then bind off 2 sts at the beginning of the next 2 (4, 4, 4, 2, 4) rows. 72 (72, 74, 78, 72, 72) sts.

Next row (RS): K1, ssk, knit to last 3 sts, k2tog, k1.

Next row: Purl.

Rep these 2 rows 9 (9, 10, 11, 11, 12) times. 54 (54, 54, 56, 50, 48) sts.

Bind off 5 sts at beg of next 4 rows.

Bind off rem 34 (34, 34, 36, 30, 28) sts.

Optional Inseam Pocket (Make 1 or 2)

With MC, CO 19 sts.

Next row (WS): Purl.

Next row (RS): Knit, M1, knit to end.

Next row (WS): Purl to last st, M1 pwise, p1.

Next row (RS): K1, M1, knit to end.

Next row (WS): Purl.

Rep these 2 rows 14 times more.

Work even in St st until pocket measures 5" from the cast-on edge, ending with a WS row.

Next row (RS): K1, ssk, knit to end.

Next row (WS): Purl.

Rep these 2 rows once more.

Next row (RS): K1, ssk, knit to last 3 sts, k2tog, k1.

Next row (WS): P1, p2tog, purl to end.

Rep these 2 rows 3 times more.

Next row (RS): K1, ssk, knit to last 3 sts, k2tog, k1.

Next row (WS): Purl.

Rep these 2 rows twice more.

Bind off rem sts.

With RS facing, pick up and knit 19 sts along the cast-on edge.

Next row (WS): Purl.

Next row (RS): Knit to last st, M1, k1.

Next row (WS): P1, M1 pwise, purl to end.

Next row (RS): Knit to last st, M1, k1.

Next row (WS): Purl.

Rep these 2 rows 14 more times.

Work even in St st until piece measures 5" from CO row, ending with a WS row.

Next row (RS): Knit to last 3 sts, k2tog, k1.

Next row (WS): Purl.

Rep these 2 rows once more.

Next row (RS): K1, ssk, knit to last 3 sts, k2tog, k1.

Next row (WS): Purl to last 3 sts, p2tog, p1.

Rep these 2 rows 3 times more.

Next row (RS): K1, ssk, knit to last 3 sts, k3tog, k1.

Next row (WS): Purl.

Rep these 2 rows twice more.

Bind off rem sts.

Finishing
Attach Sleeves

Wet-block sweater pieces before joining.

Using MC and mattress st, join right front to right back at shoulder and left front to left back at shoulder.

If inseam pockets are being included, fold each pocket in half along the line of picked-up stitches, RS together, and whip st pieces together around the curved edge, leaving the 5"-long straight edge open. Place sweater fronts against back with WS together and, beginning at the hem, mattress st side seams together to 4" from the first row of MC. Starting at this point, with the folded pocket edge toward the top of the sweater and the reverse St st side of the pocket against the WS of the sweater front, sew one side of the pocket opening along the front side seam of the sweater using mattress st. Stitch the other side of the pocket along the side edge of the sweater back in the same manner, then continue to join sweater fronts to back along the side seam. If desired, the top edge of the pocket can be whip stitched down on the inside front of the sweater for stability.

Stitch the inside sleeve seam. Pin the sleeve cap into armhole and sew in.

Fold hems up along the color change line and whip st closed on the inside, using MC.

Along front opening edge, fold two-stitch selvedge to inside. Pin zipper to opening edge so that the folded edge abuts the edge of the zipper teeth. Using sewing needle and matching sewing thread, stitch the zipper to sweater along selvedge.

Collar

Start at right front opening with the RS of work facing. Transfer 16 (16, 16, 16, 16, 18) held sts to circular needle. Join MC and knit these stitches. Pick up and knit 10 (10, 12, 12, 14, 14) sts along right front edge. Pick up and knit 7 sts along back right neck edge. Knit 28 (30, 30, 32, 32, 32) held sts at back neck. Pick up and knit 7 sts along back left neck edge. Pick up and knit 10 (10, 12, 12, 14, 14) sts along left front edge. Knit 16 (16, 16, 16, 16, 18) held sts from front left neck.

Next row (WS): Knit.

Next row (RS): Knit.

Continue working even in garter st until collar measures 3" from neck edge.

Bind off all sts loosely.

Optional Embellishment
Name Embroidered on a Knitted Patch

To determine the size of your knitted patch, first chart or draw your desired lettering to scale using knitter's graph paper. Count the total number of sts and rows your charted name takes up.

With the background color of the patch, CO the number of sts you counted across your chart.

Working in St st, increase at the beginning and end of the next 2 rows (4 sts increased).

Work even the number of rows you counted on your chart.

Decrease at the beginning and end of the next 2 rows. Bind off.

Using embroidery floss or contrasting yarn, stitch your name on the center of the patch using desired stitch method.

Pin patch to left front of sweater with the left edge of the patch about 2" in from the front opening edge. Make sure the placement is low enough that the patch isn't hidden behind the folded-down collar. To stitch the patch in place invisibly, use sewing thread to match the patch and whip st just beneath patch edge. For a decorative sewn edge, use the same yarn or floss as the embroidery and sew patch in place with a whip st, blanket st.

Name Embroidered Without a Patch

To embroider your name directly on the sweater, first chart or draw your desired lettering to scale. For example, the name "Bob" was charted on knitters' graph paper at 5½ sts x 8 rows per inch scale. For perfect placement, cut around the name and pin the paper in place on the sweater until you like the way it looks. Using embroidery floss or contrasting yarn, stitch the name using the desired stitch method. In general, duplicate stitch will look better for blocky letters, while chain stitch embroidery will look better for cursive letters. The jacket sample was done using six strands of embroidery floss and chain stitch. For duplicate stitch, start in a corner and follow your chart. For chain stitch, you may wish to transfer your lines to the sweater first using chalk or lines of basting thread. The sample sweater was embroidered freehand by marking out the boundaries of the letters with pins and frequently laying the original drawing over the embroidery to ensure the lines were still close to the original design.

Double Decker

by Cirila Rose

Take a trip around old London with Double Decker, a truly swingin' set featuring an innovative snap-front cardigan and matching hat using your favorite fabric. The sweater is chock full of clever detailing, such as an applied I-cord bind-off, fabric-covered buttons and knit-in button band facings. A hidden button placket can be used to wear the sweater closed, or you can remove the snap-in panel to wear it as an open jacket. It's got a trim fit with a slightly swingy silhouette that looks neatest when knit with little to no ease. The matching hat adds an extra touch of fanciness. You'll only need about a quarter of a yard of fabric, so splurge and buy something really special.

Cardigan

Sizes

S (M, L, 1X, 2X)

Finished Measurements

Chest: 36 (38, 40, 42, 44)"

Materials

Berroco Lustra (50% Peruvian wool, 50% Tencel Lyocell; 197 yd./100g per skein)

MC: #3159 Provence 5 (6, 7, 7, 8) skeins

CC: #3102 Aioli 1 skein for all sizes

U.S. 6 (4mm) straight or circular needles, 24" length, *or size needed to match gauge*

U.S. 6 (4mm) double-pointed needles

Locking ring stitch markers

8 snaps

Tapestry needle

14 buttons ⅞" diameter or a Dritz Cover Button kit with refills to make 14 buttons

¼ yd. of cotton fabric to cover buttons (if needed)

Sewing needle and thread

Gauge

20 sts × 26 rows = 4" in St st

Special Stitches and Terms

Seed stitch (over an even number of sts): Row 1: *K1, p1, rep from *. All following rows: Purl all knit sts and knit all purl sts.

Pattern Notes

Sweater pieces can be knit on a straight needle but a circular needle is easiest for neckband.

Directions

Back

The lower back is knit first. Stitches are bound off and then picked up across the top of this piece to provide structure and detailing before working the upper back.

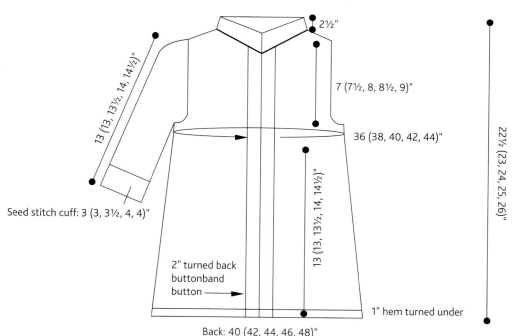

13 (13, 13½, 14, 14½)"

2½"

7 (7½, 8, 8½, 9)"

36 (38, 40, 42, 44)"

22½ (23, 24, 25, 26)"

Seed stitch cuff: 3 (3, 3½, 4, 4)"

13 (13, 13½, 14, 14½)"

2" turned back buttonband button

1" hem turned under

Back: 40 (42, 44, 46, 48)"

Using CC, CO 100 (106, 110, 116, 120) sts. Work in St st for 1", ending with a WS row.

Next row (RS): Join MC and work set-up row: K33 (35, 36, 38, 40) sts, sl 1 pwise, pm, work next 32 (34, 36, 38, 38) sts in seed st, pm, sl 1 st pwise, k33 (35, 36, 38, 40) sts to end.

Next row (WS): Purl to marker, sm, work in seed st to next marker, sm, purl to end.

Work in patt as established until piece measures 3 (3, 3½, 4, 4½)" from CO edge, ending with a WS row.

Row 1 (Decrease Row; RS): Knit to 1 st before marker, sl next st pwise, p1, k2tog, maintain seed st to 3 sts before marker, p2tog, k1, sm, sl 1 st pwise, knit to end. Mark 1 of the just worked decreases with a locking stitch marker.

Rows 2–12: Work 11 rows even in patt.

Row 13 (Decrease Row; RS): Knit to 1 st before marker, sl next st pwise, k1, p2tog, maintain seed st to 3 sts before marker, k2tog, p1, sm, sl 1 st pwise, knit to end.

Rows 14–24: Work 11 rows even in patt.

Rep Rows 1–24 one time more, then rep Row 1 once more. 90 (96, 100, 106, 110) sts.

Work even in patt until piece measures 13 (13, 13½, 14, 14½)" from cast-on edge, ending with a RS row. Bind off.

With WS facing, start at right end of the bound-off edge and pick up and k90 (96, 100, 106, 110) sts.

Next row (RS): Knit.

Work 3 more rows in St st.

Armhole Shaping

Bind off 4 (4, 4, 5, 5) sts at beg of the next 2 rows.

Bind off 3 (3, 3, 3, 3) sts at beg of the next 2 rows.

Next row (RS): K2, ssk, knit to last 4 sts, k2tog, k2.

Purl 1 row.

Rep these 2 rows 1 (3, 2, 3, 3) more times. 72 (76, 80, 82, 86) sts.

Continue in St st until armhole measures 7 (7½, 8, 8½, 9)".

Shoulders Shaping

Bind off 7 (8, 9, 6, 7) sts at beg of next 2 rows.

Bind off 7 (7, 9, 6, 6) sts at beg of next 2 rows.

For 1X and 2X only: Bind off 6 sts at beg of next 2 rows.

Bind off rem 44 (46, 44, 46, 48) sts.

Right Front

Using CC, CO 60 (63, 65, 68, 70) sts. Work St st for 1".

Switch to MC and continue in St st for 3 (3, 3½, 4, 4½)" working the first 10 sts of every RS row as follows: K9, sl 1 pwise, knit to end (these stitches will be folded back to form button band hem facing).

Next RS row: Knit to last 4 sts, k2tog, k2.

Work 11 rows even.

Rep these 12 rows 4 times. 55 (58, 60, 63, 65) sts.

Work even until piece measures 13 (13, 13½, 14, 14½)", ending with a WS row.

Next row (RS): Work small dart decrease as follows: Work 10 button band sts as set, k21 (22, 24, 24, 26) sts, k2tog, k1, ssk, knit to end. 53 (56, 58, 61, 63) sts.

Next row (WS): Knit to form a purl ridge to last 10 sts, p10.

Next row (RS): Sl 10 button band sts to a spare dpn. Fold inward to the WS at slipped stitch, forming button band facing and a double thickness of fabric. Cut working yarn and rejoin at slipped stitch edge, now the first stitch of the row. Join the body stitches and the hem facing sts by knitting the first 10 sts tog with new working yarn.

Next row (WS): Purl to last 10 sts, work 10 sts in seed st.

Next row (RS): Work 10 sts in seed st, k to end of row.

Rep these 2 rows for 1", ending with a RS row.

Shape Armhole

Next row (WS): Bind off 4 (4, 4, 5, 5) sts, purl to last 10 sts, seed st to end of row.

Next row (RS): Seed st over 10 sts, knit to end of row.

Next row (WS): Bind off 3 (3, 3, 3, 3) sts, purl to last 10 sts, seed st to end of row.

Next row (RS): Seed st over 10 sts, knit to last 4 sts, ssk, k2.

Next row: Purl.

Rep these 2 rows 1 (3, 2, 3, 3) times. 34 (35, 38, 39, 41) sts.

Work in St st, maintaining seed st button band, until armhole measures 5½ (6, 6½, 7, 7½)" ending with a WS row.

Shape Neck

Next row (RS): Bind off 8 sts, knit to end.

Next row (WS): Purl.

Next row (RS): Bind off 3 sts, knit to end.

Dec 1 st at neck edge every RS row 3 times as follows: K2, ssk, knit to end of row.

Work even until armhole measures 7 (7½, 8, 8½, 9)".

Bind off rem 20 (21, 24, 25, 27) sts.

Left Front

Using CC, CO 60 (63, 65, 68, 70) sts. Work St st for 1".

Switch to MC and continue in St st for 3 (3, 3½, 4, 4½)" working every RS row as follows: Knit to last 10 sts, sl 1 pwise, k9 (these stitches will be folded back to form button band hem facing). End with a WS row.

Next row (RS): K2, ssk, knit to last 10 sts, sl 1, k9.

Work 11 rows even.

Rep these 12 rows 4 times. 55 (58, 60, 63, 65) sts.

Work even until piece measures 13 (13, 13½, 14, 14½)" ending with a WS row.

Next row (RS): Work small dart decrease as follows: K31 (33, 33, 36, 36) sts, k2tog, k1, ssk, knit to end. 53 (56, 58, 61, 63) sts.

Next row (WS): P10 button band sts, knit to end to form purl ridge.

Next row (RS): Knit to last 20 sts, sl the last 10 sts to a spare dpn and fold inward toward the WS at slipped st, forming button band facing and a double thickness of fabric. Knit these sts together with last 10 body sts to join.

Next row: Begin seed st over first 10 sts, purl to end of row.

Continue as set for 1", ending with a WS row.

Shape Armhole

Next row (RS): Bind off 4 (4, 4, 5, 5) sts, knit to last 10 sts, work seed st to end.

Next row and following WS rows: Seed st over 10 sts, purl to end.

Next row (RS): Bind off 3 (3, 3, 3, 3) sts, work in patt to end.

Next row (RS): K2, k2tog, work in patt to end.

Work 1 WS row.

Rep the last 2 rows 1 (3, 2, 3, 3) times. 34 (35, 38, 39, 41) sts.

Work even until armhole measures 5½ (6, 6½, 7, 7½)", ending with a RS row.

Shape Neck

Next row (WS): Bind off 8 sts, work to end.

Knit 1 row.

Next row (WS): Bind off 3 sts, work to end.

Dec 1 st at neck edge every RS row 3 times as follows: Knit to last 4 sts, k2tog, k2.

Work even until armhole measures 7 (7½, 8, 8½, 9)".

Bind off rem 20 (21, 24, 25, 27) sts.

Sleeves (Make 2)

Using MC, CO 50 (50, 50, 54, 54) sts.

Work in seed st for 3 (3, 3½, 4, 4)".

Next row (Increase Row; RS): Switch to St st and inc 1 st at each end as follows: K2, M1, knit to last 2 sts, M1, k2.

Rep this Increase Row every 6th row 5 (5, 8, 10, 12) more times. 62 (62, 68, 76, 80) sts.

Work even until sleeve measures 13 (13, 13½, 14, 14½)" from CO edge, ending on a WS row.

Bind off 4 (5, 6, 8, 9) sts at beg of next 2 rows.

Next row (Decrease Row; RS): K2, ssk, knit to last 4 sts, k2tog, k2.

Rep this Decrease Row every 4th row 0 (0, 1, 2, 1) times, then every RS row 14 (13, 11, 9, 11) times.

Work 1 WS row.

Bind off 3 sts at beg of the next 2 rows.

Bind off rem 24 (24, 30, 36, 36) sts.

Finishing

Sew shoulder seams, and set in sleeve caps. Sew side and sleeve seams. Fold contrast color hem facings approximately in half and tack to WS. Sew button band facings to WS.

Neckband

Using MC, with RS facing, begin at right front neck edge at button band and pick up and knit 64 (64, 68, 68, 72) sts. Work in seed st for 4 rows.

Next row: Place markers as follows, continuing in seed st: work 16 (16, 17, 17, 18) sts, pm, work 16 (16, 17, 17, 18) sts, pm, work 16 (16, 17, 17, 18) sts, pm, work in seed st to end.

Next row (RS): *Work in seed st to 2 sts before marker, ssk, sm, k2tog, rep from * 2 times, continue in seed st to end.

Work even in seed st until neckband measures 2½", ending with a WS row. Break yarn.

Next row (RS): Join CC and knit.

Purl next row.

Bind off using I-cord bind-off as follows: Using cable cast-on, CO 3 sts. *K2, k2tog tbl, then sl these 3 sts pwise back to the left needle and rep from * until all sts have been worked.

Buttons

If you're using a button cover kit, follow directions on the package to cover 14 buttons with fabric. Sew two buttons to each sleeve at corners of turned back cuffs, sewing through both layers of fabric. Sew two buttons above back pleat to match picture. Sew 8 remaining buttons onto button bands, spacing them evenly about 2" apart, starting with neckband and ending above purl ridge.

Hidden Button Placket

Using MC, CO 36 sts. Work 1½" in seed st.

Next row: Work 5 sts in seed st, pm, k26, pm, work 5 sts in seed st. Keeping edge sts in seed st and center sts in St st, work until piece measures 5" from cast-on edge. Work for 1½" in seed st, then bind off all sts. Sew one half of snaps to this placket piece, spaced to match the placement of the 8 buttons on cardigan fronts. Sew corresponding snap pieces to button band facing, underneath buttons.

Finishing

Block the cardigan, paying special attention to hem facings.

Hat

Size

One size fits most adults

Finished Measurements

Circumference: 21"

Height: 7½"

Materials

Berroco Lustra (50% wool, 50% Tencel Lyocell; 197 yd./100g per skein); #3159 Provence; 1 skein

U.S. 6 (4mm) circular needles, 16" length, *or size needed to match gauge*

U.S. 6 (4mm) double-pointed needles

22" × 6" strip of Liberty fabric and sewing thread to match

Stitch markers

Tapestry needle

Sewing needle

¼ yd. cotton fabric for headband

Gauge

20 sts × 28 rows = 4" in St st

22 sts × 27 rows = 4" in seeded rib

Special Stitches and Terms

Seeded Rib: Rnd 1: K1, P1 around. **Rnd 2:** Knit all sts. Rep these 2 rounds.

Wrap and turn (w&t): see page 47

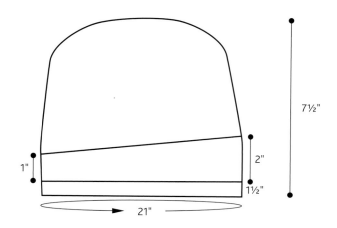

7½"

1"

2"

1½"

21"

Directions

Before you begin knitting, wind off approximately 20 yd. of yarn and reserve it to knit the tab.

Using circular needle, CO 100 sts. Join, being careful not to twist, pm to indicate beg of round.

Working in seeded rib, knit until hat measures 1½" from cast-on edge.

Switch to St st and begin short-row shaping.

Next row: K94 (6 sts before marker), w&t.

Next row: P88 (6 sts before marker), w&t.

Next row: Knit to 1 st before previously wrapped st, w&t.

Next row: Purl to 1 st before previously wrapped st, w&t.

Rep the last 2 rows once more.

With RS facing, knit 8 rounds. Hat will measure 2" from the end of ribbing on the longer side.

Make Tab

Next rnd: Knit to last 5 sts; using a dpn and the reserved yarn, pick up and knit 10 sts (5 on each side of marker) in the first stockinette row of hat.

Work back and forth in St st on these 10 sts for 5 more rows, or until it is even with the opposite side of the hat, ending with a WS row.

With RS facing and using original working yarn, with dpn held in front of the left needle, knit the 10 sts on the dpn together with the first 10 sts of the hat to join them; knit to end of round.

Work in seeded rib for 3½" (for a more eye-shielding cloche, knit for 4"), ending with Rnd 1 of seeded rib.

Shape Crown

Note: On Rnds 5, 9, and 13, you will have to shift the marker to work the last decrease of the round. Work the decrease, then replace the marker after it.

Rnd 1: *K7, s2kp, rep from * to end of round. 80 sts.

Rnd 2: *(K1, p1) 3 times, k2, rep from * around.

Rnd 3: Knit.

Rnd 4: Rep Rnd 2.

Rnd 5: K1, *k5, s2kp, rep from * around. 60 sts.

Rnd 6: *P1, k1, rep from * to end of round.

Rnd 7: Knit all sts.

Rnd 8: Rep Rnd 6.

Rnd 9: K1, *k3, s2kp, rep from * around. 40 sts.

Rnd 10: *K1, p1, k2, rep from * around.

Rnd 11: Knit.

Rnd 12: Rep Rnd 10.

Rnd 13: K1, *k1, s2kp, rep from * around. 20 sts.

Rnd 14: *P1, k1, rep from * to end of round.

Rnd 15: Knit all sts.

Rnd 16: Rep Rnd 14.

Rnd 17: *S2kp, k1, rep from *. 10 sts.

Rnd 18: K2tog 5 times. 5 sts.

Cut yarn, leaving a 10" tail. Thread tail onto tapestry needle, and pass yarn through 5 rem sts twice, drawing hole shut and weaving in end.

Finishing

Weave in ends and block if desired.

Make Fabric Band

Placing the hat on a bowl or hat form will make attaching the fabric band easier. Make the band using a piece of fabric approximately 22" long and 6–8" tall. Loosely pleat the fabric lengthwise, tapering the edges to match the widths of the stockinette portion of the hat: the widest part in the center should be 2–3" and the edges should be 1–2". Iron the pleats and baste at the ends if desired with needle and thread. Wrap fabric band around the stockinette part of the hat and thread the two ends through the knitted tab at the back of the hat. Overlap edges and sew them together, then hide the join underneath the tab. If desired, tack the fabric embellishment in place with needle and thread.

Rally

By Pamela Wynne

Rally will get your heart racing with its streamlined fit and variable skirt design. The skirt can be knit at three different angles to allow for three different looks, ranging from slim to swingy. The neck and sleeves are edged with a high-contrast detail, and the ribbed waistline adds shaping and support. The houndstooth stitch pattern has a mod look with timeless appeal. Prepare to stop traffic in this dress.

Sizes

XS (S, M, L, 1X, 2X, 3X)

Finished Measurements

Chest: 29½ (33, 37½, 41, 45½, 49, 53½)"

Note: The dress is meant to have a close fit. Measure your chest circumference so that the tape measure is even with your armpits and choose your size based on this measurement. Use the optional bust dart and hip shaping for a perfect fit.

MATERIALS

Cascade 220 (100% wool, 220 yd./100g per skein)

Note: The yardage for the following colors is in the table below.

MC: Gray

CC1: Black

CC2: Yellow

U.S. 7 (4.5mm) circular needle, 24" length, *or size needed to obtain gauge*

U.S. 8 (5mm) circular needle, 24" length

U.S. 5 (3.75mm) circular needle, 24" length

U.S. 7 (4.5mm) double-pointed needles or 12" circular needle

4 stitch markers

Tapestry needle

Waste yarn

Gauge

18 sts × 26 rows = 4" in St st, after blocking

Special Stitches and Terms

Provisional cast-on: see page 172

Pattern Notes

Measurement at the hip (approx 10" below waist) will depend on the skirt angle:

- 5°: adds 6¼" to waist measurement
- 10°: adds 11½"
- 15°: adds 20"

The yardage will vary quite a lot based on what skirt angle and length you choose. The estimates in the table are for a 26" skirt at a 10° angle. Longer skirts and/or the 15° option will need more of colors MC and CC1; shorter skirts and/or the 5° option might be able to get away with less.

Directions

Provisionally cast-on 94 (94, 94, 94, 108, 108, 108) sts, pm, and join for knitting in the round.

Waist Size	Yardage			Skirt Opening Circumference at 26" Length		
	MC	CC1	CC2	5°	10°	15°
29½"	880	220	220	44½"	60½"	75½"
33"	880	220	220	48"	64"	79"
37½"	1,100	220	220	52½"	68½"	83½"
41"	1,320	440	220	56"	72"	87"
45½"	1,540	440	220	60½"	76½"	91½"
49"	1,760	440	220	64"	80"	95"
53½"	1,980	440	220	68½"	84½"	99½"

Collar

Using CC2, Work in St st (knit all rounds) for 2".

Purl 1 round. Break yarn.

Switch to MC and work in St st for 2".

Divide For Raglan Increases

K33 (33, 33, 33, 37, 37, 37) sts for front, pm, k14 (14, 14, 14, 17, 17, 17) sts for left sleeve, pm, k33 (33, 33, 33, 37, 37, 37) sts for back, pm, k14 (14, 14, 14, 17, 17, 17) sts for right sleeve.

Raglan Increases

Rnd 1: *Kfb, knit to 1 st before marker, kfb, sm. Rep from * 3 more times to end of round.

Rnd 2: Knit.

Rep these 2 rounds 14 (18, 23, 27, 30, 34, 39) more times. [214 (246, 286, 318, 356, 388, 428) sts on needles, 44 (52, 62, 70, 79, 87, 97) sts for each sleeve and 63 (71, 81, 89, 99, 107, 117) sts each for front and back.]

Separate Sleeves

Knit to marker, remove marker, place the next 44 (52, 62, 70, 79, 87, 97) sts onto scrap yarn for sleeve (you will come back to these stitches later), CO 1, pm to mark side seam, CO 2, knit to marker, place the next 44 (52, 62, 70, 79, 87, 97) sts onto scrap yarn for sleeve, CO 2, pm to mark side seam, CO 1. 132 (148, 168, 184, 204, 220, 240) body sts on needle.

Work even in St st for 2". If desired, add bust darts and/or waist shaping as follows:

Optional Bust Darts

Worked back and forth across front stitches.

Note: The directions below are for bra cup sizes A (B, C, D, E, DD). They do not correspond to the overall garment size.

Row 1: Knit to 3 sts before marker, w&t.

Row 2: Purl to 3 sts before marker, w&t.

Row 3: Knit to 2 sts before previous wrap, w&t.

Row 4: Purl to 2 sts before previous wrap, w&t.

Rep the last 2 rows 1 (3, 5, 7, 9, 11) more times.

Return to knitting in the round, knitting across all stitches. When you come to a wrapped st, pick up the wrap and knit it together with the wrapped st.

Waist Shaping

Continue knitting in the round until the bodice measures 7" from underarm.

Next row: K2tog, knit to 2 sts before marker, ssk, sm, k2tog, knit to 2 sts before marker, ssk. [128 (144, 164, 180, 200, 216, 236) sts.]

Work even until bodice measures 8" from underarm, or until you'd like the 2¼" waistband to begin.

Waistband

Using smallest needles and CC1, knit 1 row.

Work in k1, p1 rib for 2¼".

Skirt

Houndstooth Chart

Change to largest needles to begin working houndstooth color chart.

Rnd 1 (Set-up rnd): *Work in houndstooth patt to m, sm, M1 in CC1, pm, rep from *

Rnds 2–4: Work in houndstooth patt, maintaining 1-stitch column of CC1 between markers.

As you begin to increase, incorporate increased sts into houndstooth patt.

Rnd 5 (Increase Round): *K in houndstooth patt to m, M1 in patt, sm, k1 in CC1, sm, M1 in patt, rep from *.

Continue to work in houndstooth patt, working increase rounds at the interval indicated for the desired skirt angle:

5° angle: work increase round every 10th round

10° angle: work increase round every 5th round

15° angle: *work increase round on 3rd round, then following 4th round, rep from *

Continue in houndstooth patt, with increases and 1-st column of CC1, until the skirt reaches 26", or desired length.

Using CC2, knit 3 rounds. Do not bind off. Break yarn, leaving a tail twice as long as the circumference of the skirt. Using a tapestry needle, tack live sts down to inside of skirt, along the first row of CC2 purl bumps.

Sleeves

Transfer the live sleeve sts from scrap yarn to size 7 dpns or 12" circular needles. Using MC, pick up and knit 1 st to the right of the 3 sts cast on under the arm, then pick up and knit the 3 cast-on sts, then 1 st to the left of those 3, for a total of 5 underarm sts.

Place marker and join for knitting in the round. Knit to the last 5 (underarm) sts, ssk, k1, k2tog.

Using CC2, knit 3 rounds. Do not bind off. Break yarn, leaving a tail twice as long as the circumference of the sleeve. Using a tapestry needle, tack live sts down to inside of sleeve, along the first row of CC2 purl bumps.

Rep for second sleeve.

Collar

Remove your provisional cast-on and, using a tapestry needle, tack live sts down to the inside of the collar, along the row of purl bumps just above the first raglan increase round.

Finishing

Weave in ends. Block.

Fast Lane

By Caryn Lantz (pattern adapted for Lady Speedway by Amy Herzog)

Get revved up with a pair of his and hers sweaters for the speed demons out there. Based on the classic hot rod jackets from the 1960s, the Speedway and Lady Speedway cardigans feature sporty stripes and zip fronts for some souped-up 8-cylinder matchy-matchy action. Instructions for an optional button tab on the waistline add a dash of extra detail. The ladies' version features added waist shaping to hug your curves.

Speedway

Size

S (M, L, XL, XXL)

Note: Since this is a slim sweater, choose a size 2–4" larger than your chest measurement.

Finished Measurements

Chest: 36 (40, 44, 48, 52)"

Materials

Louet Gems Sport Weight (100% Merino Wool; 225 yd./100g per skein)

MC: #2563 Blue; 6 (8, 9, 11, 12) skeins

CC1: #2113 Cherry Red; 1 skein for all sizes

CC2: #2703 White; 1 skein for all sizes

U.S. 2 (2.75mm) straight or circular needles

U.S. 3 (3.25mm) straight or circular needles, *or size needed to match gauge*

All-purpose or sport separating plastic zipper to match main color yarn; size to fit finished length.

Sewing needle and thread to match zipper

2 buttons of your choice, ¾" diameter

Darning needle

Row counter

Gauge

24 sts × 36 rows = 4" in St st using larger needles

Pattern Notes

All sweater pieces have a turned-up hem. Shoulders are joined using three-needle bind-off.

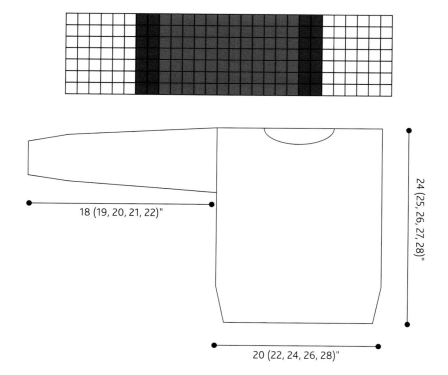

18 (19, 20, 21, 22)"

24 (25, 26, 27, 28)"

20 (22, 24, 26, 28)"

Directions

Back

With smaller needle and MC, CO 108 (120, 130, 140, 152) sts.

Work in St st for 2", ending with a RS row.

Knit 1 WS row to create turning ridge.

Change to larger needle, and work in St st for 2".

Increase 1 st at each side every 8 (8, 8, 6, 6) rows a total of 6 (6, 8, 10, 10) times on RS rows as follows: Kfb, knit to last 2 sts, kfb, k1. 120 (132, 144, 156, 168) sts.

Work in St st until piece is 24 (25, 26, 27, 28)" from hem fold line, ending with WS row.

Next row (RS): K42 (45, 50, 54, 59) sts, attach a second ball of yarn, and bind off 36 (42, 44, 48, 50) sts for neck, k42 (45, 50, 54, 59) sts.

Left Side of Neck

Next row: Purl.

Next row: K1, ssk, knit to end of row.

Rep the last 2 rows once more.

Work 3 more rows in St st and put rem 40 (43, 48, 52, 57) sts on holder.

Right Side of Neck

Next row (WS): Begin at neck edge and purl.

Next row: Knit to last 3 sts, k2tog, k1.

Rep the last 2 rows once more.

Work 3 more rows in St st and put rem 40 (43, 48, 52, 57) sts on holder.

Right Front

With MC and smaller needles, CO 54 (60, 65, 70, 76) sts. Work in St st for 2", ending with a RS row.

Knit 1 WS row to create turning ridge.

Change to larger needle, and work in St st for 2", ending with a WS row.

Increase 1 st at the end of row every 8 (8, 8, 6, 6) rows a total of 6 (6, 8, 10, 10) times on RS rows as follows: Knit to last 2 sts, kfb, k1. 60 (66, 72, 78, 84) sts.

Continue in St st until piece measures 22 (23, 24, 25, 26)" from hem fold line, ending with WS row.

Shape Neck

Next row: Bind off 11 (13, 13, 14, 15) sts, knit to end of row.

Next row: Purl.

Next row: K1, ssk, knit to end of row.

Rep the last 2 rows 8 (9, 10, 11, 11) times. 40 (43, 48, 52, 57) sts.

Continue in St st until piece measures 25 (26, 27, 28, 29)" from hem fold line. Put rem sts on stitch holder.

Left Front

With MC and smaller needles, CO 54 (60, 65, 70, 76) sts.

Work in St st for 2", ending with a RS row.

Knit 1 WS row to create turning ridge.

Change to larger needle, k2 (5, 7, 10, 13) sts in MC, work 28 sts of intarsia chart (on page 88) beginning with Row 1, k24 (27, 30, 32, 35) sts in MC. Continue with chart as set and work even in St st until piece measures 2" from turning ridge.

While continuing intarsia chart, increase 1 st at the beginning of row every 8 (8, 8, 6, 6) rows a total of 6 (6, 8, 10, 10) times on RS rows as follows: Kfb, knit to end of row. 60 (66, 72, 78, 84) sts.

Continue with intarsia in St st until piece measures 22 (23, 24, 25, 26)" from hem fold line, ending with RS row.

Next row (WS): Bind off 11 (13, 13, 14, 15) sts, purl to end of row.

Next row: Knit to last 3 sts, k2tog, k1.

Next row: Purl.

Rep the last 2 rows 8 (9, 10, 11, 11) times. 40 (43, 48, 52, 57) sts.

Continue in St st until piece measures 25 (26, 27, 28, 29)" from hem fold line. Put rem sts on holder.

Sleeves

With smaller needles and MC, CO 52 (54, 60, 66, 68) sts. Work in St st for 2", ending with a RS row.

Knit 1 WS row to create turning ridge.

Change to larger needles, and work in St st for 2", ending with a WS row.

Next row (Increase Row; RS): Kfb, knit to last 2 sts, kfb, k1.

Rep this Increase Row every 4th row 33 (35, 38, 38, 40) times more. 120 (126, 138, 144, 150) sts. Continue until sleeve measures 18 (19, 20, 21, 22)", or desired length to underarm. This will create the same upper-arm ease for all sizes.

Bind off all sts.

Sweater Assembly

Join back to right front at shoulder with right sides together using three-needle bind-off. Repeat for left shoulder. Sew sleeves to body, centering the top of the sleeves with the shoulder seams. Sew underarm seams and side seams. Fold hem of cuffs to the inside and stitch in place. *Do not* fold up the hem on the body quite yet . . . . Refer to the "Button Tabs at Waist" section for further assembly instructions.

Collar

With MC and smaller needle, pick up and knit 120 (126, 136, 142, 158) sts as follows: Beginning at bound-off neckline sts at right front edge, pick up and knit 39 (40, 44, 45, 52) sts along right front neckline, 42 (46, 48, 52, 54) sts along back neckline, and 39 (40, 44, 45, 52) sts along left front neckline.

Work 7 rows in seed st.

Next row (RS): Ssk, work in patt to last 2 sts, k2tog.

Next row (WS): P2tog, work in patt to last 2 sts, p2tog tbl.

Next row (RS): Ssk, work in patt to last 2 sts, k2tog.

Next row (WS): P3tog, work in patt to last 2 sts, p3tog tbl.

Bind off rem sts in patt.

Zipper Facing
Right Front

With RS facing, use smaller needles and MC to pick up and knit 3 sts for every 4 rows (write down number of stitches you picked up). Knit 1 WS row. Work 5 rows in St st, then work 5 rows in reverse St st. Bind off.

Left Front

Pick up and knit the same number of stitches and work as for right front. Fold facings to inside along picked-up edge and steam lightly, then fold back toward the front edge at the line where stockinette changes to reverse stockinette stitch. Pin zipper between the two facings, and hand-sew zipper in place.

Button Tabs at Waist

These tabs at the bottom are *faux* . . . merely a decoration to make you look badass.

On the left front, 3 sts in from side seam and 3 rows up from hem fold, pick up 9 sts vertically. Work in seed st for 3", ending with a WS row.

Next row: K2tog, work 5 sts, ssk.

Next row: K2tog, k3tog.

Bind off last 2 sts.

Fold tab toward the back and over the side seam. Position button over the tab, and sew it through both the tab and the sweater. Repeat for button tab on right side. Fold up hem and stitch in place.

Finishing

Weave in ends, block, throw sweater on, and rebel without a cause.

Lady Speedway

Sizes
XS (S, M, L, XL)

Finished Measurements
Chest: 34 (38, 40, 42, 46)"

Materials
Louet Gems Sport Weight (100% wool; 225 yd./100g per skein)

MC: #11 Cherry Red; 5 (6, 7, 7, 8) skeins

CC1: #80 Black; 1 skein for all sizes

CC2: #70 White; 1 skein for all sizes

U.S. 4 (3.5mm) straight or circular needles, *or size needed to match gauge*

U.S. 3 (3.25mm) straight or circular needles

Openable stitch markers or safety pins

Darning needle

Row counters

Zipper, size to fit finished length

Sewing needle and thread to match zipper

Gauge
24 sts × 36 rows = 4" in St st using larger needles

Pattern Notes
All sweater pieces have a turned-up hem. Shoulders are joined using three-needle bind off.

Directions
Back
With smaller needles, CO 102 (114, 120, 126, 138) sts in MC. Work in St st for 2",

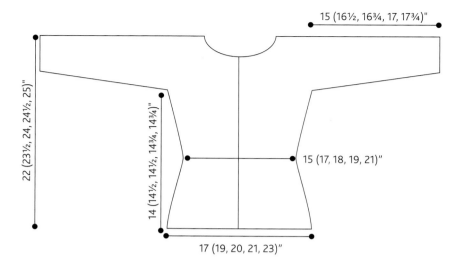

15 (16½, 16¾, 17, 17¾)"

22 (23½, 24, 24½, 25)"

14 (14½, 14½, 14¾, 14¾)"

15 (17, 18, 19, 21)"

17 (19, 20, 21, 23)"

ending with a RS row. Knit 1 WS row to create turning ridge. Switch to larger needles, and work in St st for 3½", ending with a WS row.

Shape Waist

Decrease Row: K1, ssk, knit to last 3 sts, k2tog, k1.

Work 3 rows even.

Rep these 4 rows 5 times more—a total of 6 decrease rows have been worked, and 90 (102, 108, 114, 126) sts rem.

Work 1½" even.

Increase Row: K1, M1, knit to last st, M1, k1. Work 3 rows even.

Rep these 4 rows 5 times more—a total of 6 increase rows have been worked, and there are 102 (114, 120, 126, 138) sts.

Work even until the piece measures 14 (14½, 14½, 14¾, 14¾)" from hem fold line, ending with a WS row.

Shape Armholes

Bind off 5 (6, 6, 6, 6) sts at beg of the next 2 rows.

Bind off 4 sts at beg of the next 2 rows.

Next Row: K1, ssk, knit to last 3 sts, k2tog, k1. Work 1 row even. Rep these 2 rows 1 (4, 5, 5, 6) times more. 80 (84, 88, 94, 104) sts. Work even until the armhole measures 8 (9, 9½, 9¾, 10¼)" ending with WS row. The Back will measure 22 (23½, 24, 24½, 25)" from hem fold line.

Shape Neck and Shoulders

The shoulders are worked one at a time and shaped with short rows.

Next row (RS): K22 (23, 24, 27, 30) sts, attach a second ball of yarn and bind off 36 (38, 40, 40, 44) sts for neck, k22 (23, 24, 27, 30) sts.

Next row (WS): Purl across 22 (23, 24, 27, 30) sts for left shoulder.

Next row (RS): K14 (15, 16, 18, 20) sts, bring yarn to front, sl next st pwise, bring yarn to back, turn.

Next row (WS): Purl to end.

Next row (RS): K7 (8, 8, 9, 10) sts, bring yarn to front, slip next st pwise, bring yarn to back, turn.

Next row (WS): Purl to end.

Next row (RS): Knit across row, knitting the wraps along with the wrapped sts to prevent gaps.

Place 22 (23, 24, 27, 30) shoulder sts on holder. Return to the 22 (23, 24, 27, 30) sts held for right shoulder.

Next row (WS): P14 (15, 16, 18, 20) sts, bring yarn to back, slip next st pwise, bring yarn to front, turn.

Next row (RS): Knit to end.

Next row (WS): P7 (8, 8, 9, 10) sts, bring yarn to back, slip next st pwise, bring yarn to front, turn.

Next row (RS): Knit to end.

Next row (WS): Purl across row, purling the wraps with the wrapped sts through the back loop to prevent gaps. Place 22 (23, 24, 27, 30) shoulder sts on holder.

Right Front

With smaller needles, CO 51 (57, 60, 63, 69) sts in MC. Work in St st for 2", ending with a RS row. Knit 1 WS row to create turning ridge. Switch to larger needles, and work in St st for 3½", ending with a WS row.

Decrease Row: Knit to last 3 sts, k2tog, k1.

Work 3 rows even.

Rep these 4 rows 5 times more—a total of 6 decrease rows have been worked, and 45 (51, 54, 57, 63) sts rem. Work 1½" even.

Increase Row: Knit to last st, M1, k1.

Work 3 rows even.

Rep these 4 rows 5 times more—a total of 6 increase rows have been worked, and there are 51 (57, 60, 63, 69) sts.

Work even until the piece measures 14 (14½, 14½, 14¾, 14¾)" from hem fold line, ending with a RS row.

Shape Armholes

Next row (WS): Bind off 5 (6, 6, 6, 6) sts, purl to end.

Knit 1 row even.

Next row (WS): Bind off 4 sts, purl to end.

Next row (RS): Knit to last 3 sts, k2tog, k1.

Rep this row every RS row 1 (4, 5, 5, 6) times more. 39 (42, 44, 47, 52) sts.

Continue in St st until piece measures 20 (21½, 22, 22¼, 23)" from hem fold line, ending with WS row.

Shape Neck

Next row (RS): Bind off 10 (12, 13, 13, 14) sts, knit to end.

Purl 1 row even.

Next row: K1, ssk, knit to end of row.

Next row (WS): Purl.

Rep these 2 rows 6 (6, 6, 6, 7) times more. 22 (23, 24, 27, 30) sts rem.

Continue even until the armhole measures 8 (9, 9½, 9¾, 10¼)". Piece should measure 22 (23½, 24, 24½, 25)" from hem fold line, ending with WS row.

Next row (RS): K14 (15, 16, 18, 20) sts, bring yarn to front, sl next st pwise, bring yarn to back, turn.

Next row (WS): Purl to end.

Next row (RS): K7 (8, 8, 9, 10) sts, bring yarn to front, sl next st pwise, bring yarn to back, turn.

Next row (WS): Purl to end.

Next row (RS): Knit across row, knitting the wraps along with the wrapped sts to prevent gaps.

Place 22 (23, 24, 27, 30) shoulder sts on holder.

Left Front

With smaller needles, CO 51 (57, 60, 63, 69) sts in MC. Work in St st for 2", ending with a RS row. Knit 1 WS row to create turning ridge.

Switch to larger needles, and set up stripes using the intarsia method: You will need 2 balls of CC2, each with approximately 30 yd., 1 ball of CC1 (approximately 60 yd.), 2 bobbins or small balls of MC, each with approximately 15 yd., plus larger balls of MC for the body of the sweater. K12 (15, 19, 19, 20) sts with MC; with CC2, k4; with small ball of MC, k2; with CC1, k8; with small ball of MC, k2; with CC2, k4; with MC, knit the rem 19 (22, 21, 24, 29) sts.

Continue to work in St st, maintaining vertical intarsia stripes as set for 3½", ending with a WS row.

Note: You will continue working stripes as set through all waist, armhole, and neck shaping—the stripes fall entirely within the portion of the sweater that continues to the shoulder. You will work the last purl row of the shoulder stitches in MC to simplify the three-needle bind-off.

Decrease Row (RS): K1, ssk, knit to end.

Work 3 rows even.

Rep these 4 rows 5 times more—a total of 6 decrease rows have been worked, and 45 (51, 54, 57, 63) sts rem. Work 1½" even.

Increase Row (RS): K1, M1, knit to end of row.

Work 3 rows even.

Rep these 4 rows 5 times more—a total of 6 increase rows have been worked, and there are 51 (57, 60, 63, 69) sts.

Work even until the piece measures 14 (14½, 14½, 14¾, 14¾)" from hem fold line, ending with a WS row.

Shape Armholes

Next row (RS): Bind off 5 (6, 6, 6, 6) sts, knit to end.

Next row (WS): Purl.

Next row: Bind off 4 sts, knit to end.

Next row: Purl.

Next row: K1, ssk, knit to end of row.

Rep this row every RS row 1 (4, 5, 5, 6) times more. 39 (42, 44, 47, 52) sts.

Continue in St st until piece measures 20 (21½, 22, 22¼, 23)" from hem fold line, ending with RS row.

Shape Neck

Next row (WS): Bind off 10 (12, 13, 13, 14) sts, purl to end.

Next row (RS): Knit to last 3 sts, k2tog, k1.

Next row: Purl to end.

Rep these 2 rows 6 (6, 6, 6, 7) times more. 22 (23, 24, 27, 30) sts rem.

Work even until the armhole measures 8 (9, 9½, 9¾, 10¼)", ending with a RS row. *Keep stripes as set through short rows.*

Next row (WS): P14 (15, 16, 18, 20) sts, bring yarn to back, sl next st pwise, bring yarn to front, turn.

Next row (RS): Knit to end.

Next row (WS): P7 (8, 8, 9, 10) sts, bring yarn to back, sl next st pwise, bring yarn to front, turn.

Next row (RS): Knit to end.

Next row (WS): Purl across row with MC, purling the wraps with the wrapped sts through the back loop to prevent gaps.

Place 22 (23, 24, 27, 30) shoulder sts on holder.

Sleeves (Make 2)

With smaller needles and MC, CO 48 (52, 54, 56, 60) sts. Work in St st for 2", ending with a RS row. Knit 1 WS row to create turning ridge.

Change to larger needles and work in St st for 2", ending with a WS row.

Increase Row (RS): K1, M1, knit to last st, M1, k1.

Rep this Increase Row every 4th row 13 (15, 17, 19, 16) times, then every 6th row 6 (6, 5, 4, 7) times to 88 (96, 100, 104, 108) sts. Work even until the piece measures desired length to armhole or 15 (16½, 16¾, 17, 17¾)", ending with a WS row.

Shape Cap

Bind off 5 (6, 6, 6, 6) sts at beg of the next 2 rows.

Bind off 4 (4, 4, 4, 4) sts at beg of the next 2 rows.

Next row: K1, ssk, knit to last 3 sts, k2tog, k1.

Next row: Purl to end.

Rep these 2 rows 1 (4, 5, 5, 6) times more. 66 (66, 68, 72, 74) sts.

Decrease 1 st at each end of needle every 4 rows 0 (0, 0, 1, 4) times, then decrease 1 st at each end of needle every RS row 9 (8, 9, 8, 1) times to 48 (50, 50, 54, 64) sts.

Bind off 2 sts at beg of next 8 (10, 10, 10, 4) rows.

Bind off 3 sts at beg of next 4 (4, 4, 4, 12) rows.

Bind off rem 20 (18, 18, 22, 20) sts.

Finishing

With RS together, use the three-needle bind-off to join fronts to back at shoulder.

Sew sleeves to body. Sew underarm and side seams. Fold cuff hems to the inside and stitch in place. *Do not* fold up the hem on the body quite yet.

Collar

With MC and smaller needle, pick up and knit 92 (98, 102, 102, 108) sts as follows: Beginning at bound-off neckline sts at right front edge, pick up and knit 28 (30, 31, 31, 32) sts along right front neckline to shoulder, 36 (38, 40, 40, 44) sts along back neckline, and 28 (30, 31, 31, 32) sts along left front neckline.

Work 7 rows in seed st.

Next row (RS): Ssk, work in patt to last 2 sts, k2tog.

Next row (WS): P2tog, work in patt to last 2 sts, p2tog tbl.

Next row (RS): Ssk, work in patt to last 2 sts, k2tog.

Next row (WS): P3tog, work in patt to last 2 sts, p3tog tbl.

Bind off rem sts in patt.

Zipper Facing

On the right front: With RS facing, use smaller needles and MC to pick up and knit 3 sts for every 4 rows from cast-on edge to bottom of collar. Note the number of sts you picked up. Knit 1 WS row. Work 5 rows in St st, then work 5 rows in reverse St st. Bind off all sts.

On the left front: Pick up and knit the same number of sts and work as for right front.

Fold facings to inside along picked-up edge and steam lightly, then fold back toward the front edge at the line where St st changes to reverse St st. Pin zipper between the two facings, and hand-sew zipper in place. Fold up hem and stitch in place. Throw sweater on, and rebel without a cause.

Saucy Convertible

by Marnie MacLean

Get ready to take the top down with Saucy Convertible, a truly amazing little sweater that is every bit as fun as your favorite summer ride. The top portion of the sweater creates a versatile silhouette designed to be worn a multitude of ways. You can wear it as is, or embellish with vintage jewelry for a V-neck, off-the-shoulder, square neck, or jaunty asymmetrical look. Short-row shaping and darts are used to make this slim-fitting top a flattering addition to any wardrobe.

Sizes

XS (S, M, L, XL, 1X, 2X, 3X)

Finished Measurements

Chest: 32 (34, 36, 38, 40, 42, 44, 46)"

Materials

Rowan Calmer (75% cotton, 25% microfiber; 175 yd./50g per skein); #493 Plum 5 (5, 5, 5, 6, 6, 6, 6) skeins

U.S. 7 (4.5 mm) circular needle, 24" or longer, *or size needed to match gauge*

Spare U.S. 7 needle to work yoke

U.S. G-6 (4mm) crochet hook

Stitch markers

Tapestry needle

Gauge

22 sts × 31 rows = 4" in St st

Special Stitches and Terms

Provisional cast-on: see page 172

Wrap and turn (w&t): see page 47

Pattern Notes

This simple garment is knit in pieces from the bottom up and shaped with flattering body darts. You will knit the body and sleeves up to the yoke before joining them together. The yoke is knit sideways, from the center back, and you join it to the live stitches from the body and sleeves as you work your way around.

Directions

Back

CO 83 (88, 93, 98, 103, 108, 114, 118) sts.

Begin Waist Shaping

Place markers for darts as follows: K28 (29, 31, 33, 34, 36, 38, 39) sts, pm, k27 (30, 31, 32, 35, 36, 38, 40) sts, pm, knit to end of row.

Decrease every 8th row 0 (0, 0, 0, 0, 1, 1, 5) times, then every 6th row 4 (4, 5, 5, 7, 6, 6, 1) times, then every 4th row 3 (3, 2, 2, 0, 0, 0, 0) times as follows on RS rows: Knit to 2 sts before marker, k2tog, sm, knit to next marker and sm, ssk, knit to end of row. 69 (74, 79, 84, 89, 94, 100, 106) sts.

Shape Waist and Bust

Work 9 rows even for waist, then begin increasing for bust as follows:

Next row (RS): Knit to marker, M1R, sm, knit to next marker and sm, M1L, knit to end of row.

Rep the increase row every 6th row 2 (2, 1, 1, 0, 0, 0, 0) times, then every 4th row 8 (8, 9, 9, 10, 9, 9, 7) times, then every other row 0 (0, 0, 0, 0, 1, 1, 3) times. 91 (96, 101, 106, 111, 116, 122, 128) sts.

Work even until piece measures 15".

Front

CO 83 (88, 93, 98, 103, 108, 114, 118) sts.

Next row: K21 (22, 23, 25, 26, 27, 29, 30) sts, pm, k41 (44, 47, 48, 51, 54, 56, 58) sts, pm, knit to end of row.

Work waist and bust shaping as for back.

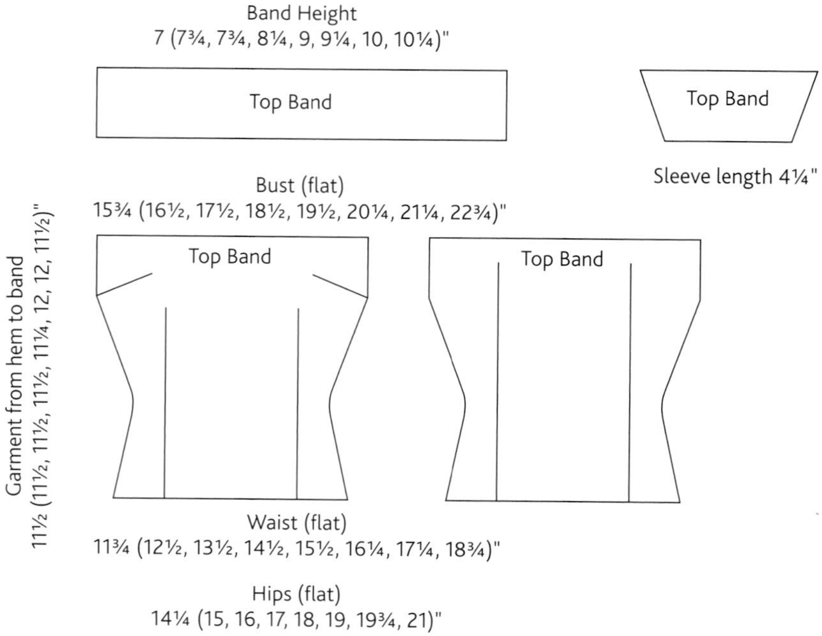

Band Height
7 (7¾, 7¾, 8¼, 9, 9¼, 10, 10¼)"

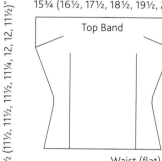
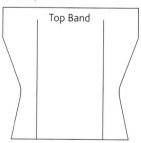

Top Band

Top Band

Sleeve length 4¼"

Garment from hem to band
11½ (11½, 11½, 11½, 11¼, 12, 12, 11½)"

Bust (flat)
15¾ (16½, 17½, 18½, 19½, 20¼, 21¼, 22¾)"

Top Band

Top Band

Waist (flat)
11¾ (12½, 13½, 14½, 15½, 16¼, 17¼, 18¾)"

Hips (flat)
14¼ (15, 16, 17, 18, 19, 19¾, 21)"

Work 8 rows even, then begin optional short-row bust darts as follows:

Next row (RS): Knit to last st, w&t.

Next row (WS): Purl to last st, w&t.

Next row: Work to 4 (4, 4, 5, 5, 4, 4, 4) sts before last wrapped st, w&t.

Rep the last row 7 (7, 7, 7, 7, 11, 11, 11) times more, or as desired. 91 (96, 101, 106, 111, 116, 122, 128) sts.

Note: For best results, try on garment and check that short rows fit properly. You may work fewer or more to suit your personal shape.

Work even until the front measures the same as the back.

Place all live sts on waste yarn or spare needles and sew the side seams together.

Sleeves (Make 2)
CO 41 (43, 45, 45, 47, 50, 53, 56) sts.

Begin working in St st.

Increase every 12th row, 3 times as follows on RS rows: K1, M1R, knit to last st, M1L, k1. 47 (49, 51, 51, 53, 56, 59, 62) sts.

Sew sides of sleeve together to form tube. Keep live sts on stitch holder or waste yarn.

Join the Pieces
With sleeve seam and side seam of body touching and RS facing, graft 8 (8, 10, 10, 10, 10, 12, 12) sts of sleeve to corresponding 8 (8, 10, 10, 10, 10, 12, 12) sts of body (half on each side of the seam) for the underarm. Place rem 244 (258, 264, 274, 288, 304, 314, 326) sts onto circular needle.

Yoke
CO 39 (43, 43, 45, 49, 51, 55, 57) sts to spare needle using a provisional cast-on. Neckband is worked sideways attached to the body as you work.

Find the center back of the garment. Place the garment so the hem is to the left, center back is up, and the live sts are to the right. (Reverse if you knit left-handed.)

Every RS row, you will knit the last st of the band with 1 st of the body, regardless of any other shaping that happens.

Begin attaching the yoke to the body at the center of the back with RS facing.

Row 1 (RS): Sl 1, p1, *k1, p1, rep from * to last st, knit last st together with 1 st from body.

Row 2 (WS): Sl 1, work sts as they appear to end of row.

Rep these 2 rows until you reach the sleeve sts. Find the center st on the sleeve and mark it.

Next row (RS): Sl 1, *k1, p1, rep from * to last st, knit last st together with 1 st from body.

Next row (WS): Sl 1, k1, w&t.

RS rows: Work in patt ending with k2tog with last st and 1 st from sleeve.

WS rows: Sl 1, work in patt to wrapped st, pick up the wrap, and work it and the wrapped st together in patt, w&t.

Continue as set until you reach the marked st.

RS rows: Work in patt ending with k2tog with last st and 1 st from sleeve.

WS rows: Sl 1, work in patt to 1 st before wrapped st, w&t (each WS row is 1 st shorter than previous row).

When you have completed the sleeve sts, go back to working as for the back, across entire front, picking up all wraps on the first row.

Rep the short-row section for the second sleeve. Work the remaining half of the back as you did the first half. Remove the provisional cast-on and join center back of the yoke by grafting or with a three-needle bind-off.

Finishing
Using a crochet hook, sc along the bottom edge of garment.

Weave in all ends. Block as desired.

Sunday Drive

by Annie Modesitt

Break out the pillbox hat and giant sunglasses for our swingy car coat; it's a Sunday Drive you can enjoy any day. Dress it up for a night out or make it your everyday errand coat. Made from luxurious Merino and cashmere yarn, it will soon become an all-time favorite. Three-quarter-length sleeves and a slightly pointed collar are a nod to the amazing style of our foremothers, who really knew how to put an outfit together.

Sizes

S/M (L/1X)

Finished Measurements

Chest: 26¼" (33½")

Materials

Handmaiden Casbah (81% Superwash Merino, 10% nylon, 9% cashmere; 356 yd./115g per skein)

CA: Smoke; 3 (5) skeins

CB: Wine; 3 (5) skeins

U.S. G-6 (4mm) crochet hook, *or size needed to match gauge*

Openable stitch markers or safety pins

Tapestry needle

Gauge

17 sts × 16 rows = 4" in stitch pattern

Special Stitches and Terms

Gr (Group): Worked over 14 sts: sc, 2 hdc, 2 dc, 3 tr, 2 dc, 2 hdc, 2 sc.

Rev Gr (Reverse Group): Worked over 14 sts: tr, 2 dc, 2 hdc, 3 sc, 2 hdc, 2 dc, 2 tr.

Directions

Wave Pattern

Row 1: With CA, skip first 2 ch, [1 Gr over next 14 ch] rep to end of ch, turn.

Row 2: Ch 1 (counts as 1 sc) skip first st, sc evenly to end, working last st into top of t-ch, turn.

Row 3: Attach CB, drop CA. Ch 4 (counts as 1 tr), skip first st, [1 Rev Gr over next 14 sts] rep to end of row, turn.

Row 4: With CB rep Row 2.

Note: The yarn is not cut; it is carried up the side of the work and will be covered by the edging during finishing. This garment begins at the neckline and proceeds downward.

Jacket Yoke

With CA, ch 60 loosely.

Work Rows 1–4 of Wave Patt, then begin raglan shaping as follows:

Mark (**M**) the 8th, 22nd, 36th, and 50th sts in row: these **M** sts are increase points for the raglan shaping. Move these markers up as you work each row. Continue in patt as established and at the same time increase at each **M** as follows:

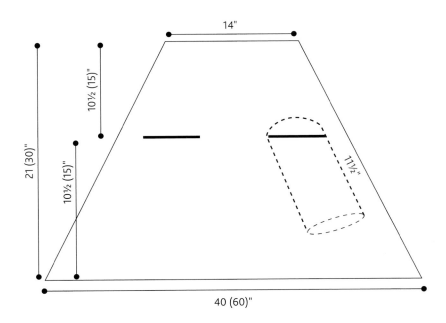

Row 5: With CA, [patt to next **M**, 3tr in **M**]. Rep to end of row—66 sts total.

Row 6 and all WS rows: Ch 1, skip first st, sc to end, working last st in top of t-ch.

Row 7: With CB, [patt to 2 sts before next **M**, 2sc, 3sc in **M**, 2sc]. Rep to end of row—74 sts total.

Row 9: With CA, [patt to 3 sts before next **M**, 3tr, 3tr in **M**, 3tr]. Rep to end of row—82 sts total.

Row 11: With CB, [patt to 4 sts before next **M**, 4sc, 3sc in **M**, 4sc]. Rep to end of row—90 sts total.

Row 13: With CA, [patt to 5 sts before next **M**, 5tr, 3tr in **M**, 5tr]. Rep to end of row—98 sts total.

Row 15: With CB, [patt to 6 sts before next **M**, 6sc, 3sc in **M**, 6sc]. Rep to end of row—106 sts total.

Row 17: With CA, [patt to 7 sts before next **M**, 7tr, 3tr in **M**, 7tr]. Rep to end of row—114 sts total.

Row 19: With CB, work in established patt, incorporating groups of trs from previous row into patt—114 sts total.

Row 20: Work as Row 6.

Rep Rows 5–20 1 (2) times, 36 (52) rows—170 (226) sts total in final row.

Create Opening for Sleeve

Next Row (RS): [Work in established patt to next **M**. Ch 14 (14) sts, skip to next **M**] twice. Work in established patt to end of row.

Next row (WS): Ch 1, skip first st, sc across with last st in top of t-ch. Move st markers up as you work, marking increase points on both sides at sleeve opening.

Body

Continue in established patt, increase in each **M** as before, rep Rows 5–20 of
raglan shaping to create the body of the jacket.

Work a total of 36 (52) rows past sleeve opening—170 (254) sts in final row.

Sleeve

There should be 3 (4) Gr repeats on the shoulder edge and 14 (14) sts on the underarm edge of the sleeve opening worked in CA, a total of 56 (70) sts around the entire opening.

Position work so that RS of work is facing.

Attach CA at the bottom edge of the sleeve. Work in established patt with 1(1) 14-st motif across 14 (14) bottom edge sts.

Sl st in first st of top edge, turn work and sc back across 14 (14) sts of bottom edge. Sl st in next st (last st of top edge) and turn work, joining top to bottom.

Attach CB and work established patt in rnds rep Rows 1–4 of Wave Patt, alternating 2 rows of CB, 2 rows of CA. Work sleeve for a total of 40 rows from join or desired length, ending with CA.

Cuff

Rnd 1: With RS facing and CB, hdc evenly around sleeve—56 (70) sts.

Rnd 2: With CA and RS facing, hdc fl evenly around.

Rnd 3: With CB, rep last rnd.

Rep last 2 rnds twice, then work one last rnd in CA.

Front Facings

Beg at lower Right Front edge, with RS facing, attach CB and hdc 52 (84) sts up Right Front to neck edge. 3 hdc in corner st, 56 hdc across neck edge, 3 hdc in corner st. Hdc 52 (84) sts down Left Front edge—166 (230) sts.

Mark (**M**) center st of each group of 3 at neck corners.

Next row (WS): [Hdc fl to **M**, 3 hdc in **M**] twice, hdc fl to end of row—170 (234) sts.

Next row (RS): With CA [Hdc bl to **M**, 3 hdc in **M**] twice, hdc fl to end of row—174 (238) sts.

Next row: With CB [Sc fl to 1 st before **M**, sc3tog] twice, sc fl to end of row—178 (242) sts.

Rep last row 3 times, decreasing at each corner in previous increases—166 (230) sts.

Finishing

Steam-block garment. Fasten in all ends neatly on the wrong side.

Turn cuff back at first hdc rnd and tack in place. Turn the Front Facing back at last hdc row in CA, and with CB sew facing edge to wrong side of garment. Steam-block cuffs and facings.

Repeat Rows 5–20 for a 14-stitch increase every 16 rows.

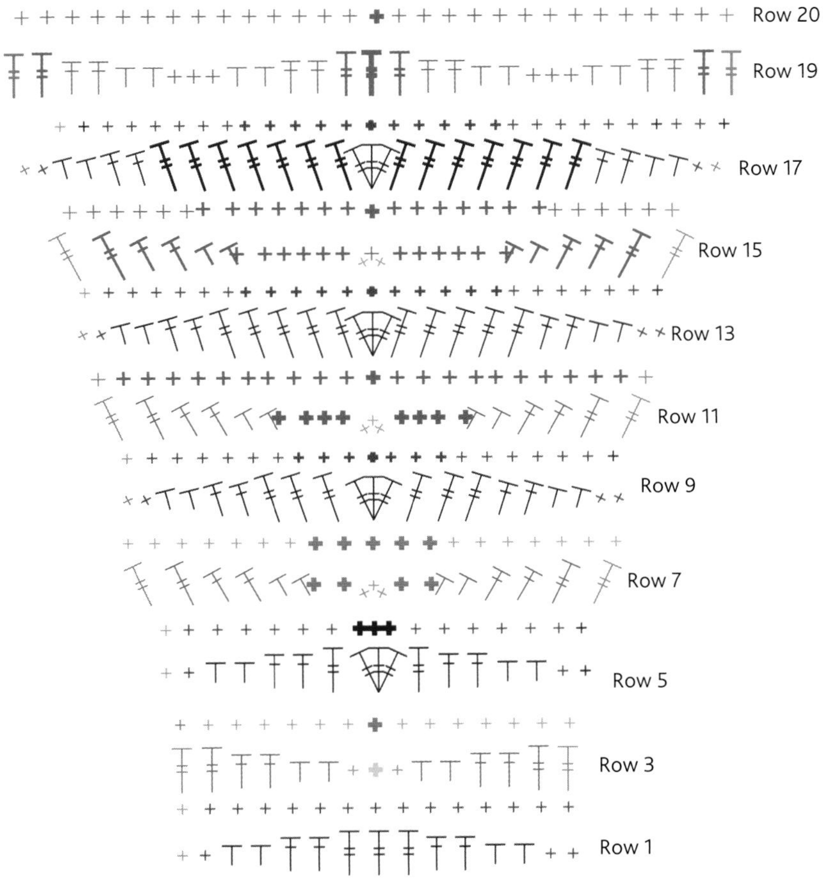

Row 20
Row 19
Row 17
Row 15
Row 13
Row 11
Row 9
Row 7
Row 5
Row 3
Row 1

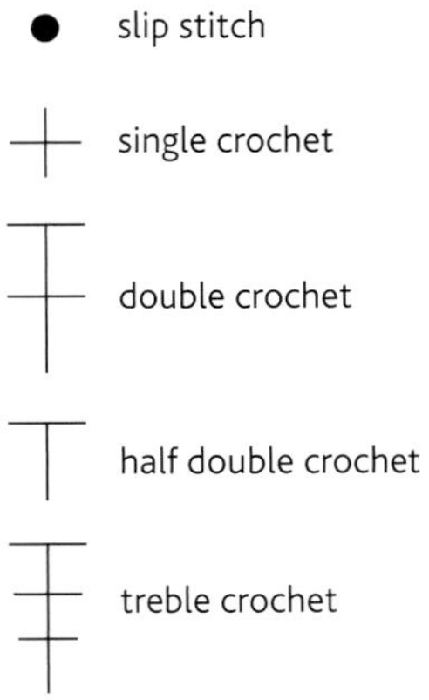

● slip stitch

+ single crochet

double crochet

half double crochet

treble crochet

chapter 4

Shake a Tail Feather

The Mashed Potato. Salsa. The Funky Chicken. The Jerk. No, this is not a list of things we saw at the local buffet restaurant last night. They're just a few in a long list of dance names that make us want to jump up and shake a tail feather! We would rather do the Monkey than most things, and we would never, ever step on a Jitterbug. We can Bump and Swim and Bunny Hop all night long, then Hustle and Twist into the morning. We'll Cha-Cha and Boogaloo until the cows come home, and then we'll make the cows do the Pony with us. We'll even do an Achy Breaky/Electric Slide in a Cabbage Patch, if you'll indulge us.

Of course, we will only do these things in the privacy of our homes, preferably in our pajamas, and most likely while singing into a hairbrush. So when our chance to express our fondness for dance without actually having to, you know, dance, came up, we were thrilled. Part of the joy of dancing is the styles that go with them. One of the rules of going out dancing is to lose the pajamas and get all gussied up, so get your glam on!

Swing Time

by Kirsten Kapur

Release your inner Ginger Rogers (she's cowering behind your inner Joan Crawford) with Swing Time, our shapely pull-over featuring 1940s-inspired shoulder shaping and swell button details. Sumptuous fine-gauge yarn in a wool/bamboo blend knits up into a soft, pretty sweater that will make you feel like a starlet, so get ready for your close-up. Then set off to find perfect buttons for the nifty closure at the neck in back and to accent the sleeve cuffs. The slight puff at the shoulder and short length at the waist go nicely with vintage-inspired, high-waisted pants or skirts for a really authentic look and an exquisite silhouette.

Sizes

S (M, L, 1X, 2X)

Finished Measurements

Chest: 32 (36, 40, 44, 48)"

Materials

Blue Moon Fiber Arts Woobu (60% merino wool, 40% bamboo; 620 yd./226g per skein); Spinel; 2 skeins for all sizes

U.S. 5 (3.75mm) straight or circular needles, *or size needed to obtain gauge*

U.S. 4 (3.5mm) straight or circular needles

Openable stitch markers or safety pins

Darning needle

4 buttons, ¾" diameter

2 buttons, 1¼" diameter

Gauge

24 sts × 34 rows = 4" in k4, p2 rib on larger needles, blocked

Pattern Notes

This pattern is meant to fit with zero ease. Choose your size accordingly.

For the front and back pieces, the first row is a WS row. For the sleeve pieces, the first row is a RS row. This will allow the correct edge to show when the sleeve cuff is folded up.

A long tail cast-on was used throughout.

Directions

Back

Using smaller needles, CO 98 (110, 122, 134, 146) sts.

Beginning with a WS row, work in k1, p1 rib for 4". End with a WS row.

Next row (RS): Switch to larger needles and k3, (p2, k4) to last 5 sts, p2, k3.

Next row (WS): P3, (k2, p4) to last 5 sts, k2, p3.

Rep these 2 rows until the back measures 11½ (12, 12, 12, 12)" from the cast-on edge, ending with a WS row.

Shape Armholes

Bind off 4 (5, 6, 9, 12) sts at the beginning of the next 2 rows, maintaining the rest of the sts in established patt.

Next row (RS): K2, ssk, work in patt to the last 4 sts, k2tog, k2.

Next row (WS): Work sts as they appear.

Rep these 2 rows 5 (5, 8, 9, 11) more times. 78 (88, 92, 96, 98) sts rem.

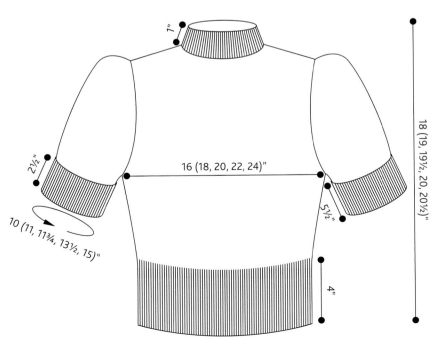

7"

2½"

10 (11, 11¾, 13½, 15)"

16 (18, 20, 22, 24)"

5½"

18 (19, 19½, 20, 20½)"

4"

Continue to work in established patt until the back measures 3½ (4, 4½, 5, 5½)" from the beg of armhole shaping, ending with a WS row.

Create Back Placket and Buttonholes

Next row (RS): Work 37 (42, 44, 46, 47) sts in patt, (k1, p1) twice, put the rem 37 (42, 44, 46, 47) sts on a holder. Turn work.

Right Back
Placket Rows

Work the 37 (42, 44, 46, 47) sts on the needle as follows:

WS rows: (P1, k1) twice, work in established patt to end.

RS rows: Work in established patt to last 4 sts (k1, p1) twice.

Work as above for 17 rows.

Buttonhole Rows

Next row (RS): Work in established patt to last 4 sts, k1, p1, yo, k1, p1.

Next row (WS): P1, k2tog, p1, k1, work in established patt to end.

Work 7 more placket rows as established above.

Shape Neck and Shoulder

Next row (WS): Bind off 14 (14, 16, 16, 18) sts, work in established patt to end.

Next row (RS): Bind off 8 (10, 10, 10, 10) sts, work in established patt to the last 4 sts, k2tog, k2.

Next row (WS): K3, work in established patt to end.

Rep the last 2 rows once more.

Bind off rem 9 (10, 10, 12, 11) sts.

Left Back

Transfer the 37 (42, 44, 46, 47) sts held for left back to working needles. With the RS facing, fold the right back down to reveal the WS. With the right needle, working from right to left, pick up and knit 1 st in each of the 4 purl bumps from the row below the first placket row. These will be the first 4 stitches of the row. Continue the row by working the 37 (42, 44, 46, 47) sts from the left needle in established patt.

Next row (WS): Work in established patt to the last 4 sts, (p1, k1) twice.

Next row (RS): (K1, p1) twice, work in established patt to end.

Rep these 2 rows a total of 12 times more (26 rows total). Work the WS row once more.

Shape Neck and Shoulder

Next row (RS): Bind off 14 (14, 16, 16, 18) sts, work in established patt to end.

Next row (WS): Bind off 8 (10, 10, 10, 10) sts, work in established patt to end.

Next row (RS): K2, ssk, work in established patt to end.

Next row (WS): Bind off 8 (10, 10, 10, 10) sts, work in established patt to last 3 sts, p3.

Next row (RS): K2, ssk, work in established patt to end.

Bind off the rem 9 (10, 10, 12, 11) sts.

Front

Work the same as for back through the armhole shaping.

Continue to work in established patt until the armhole measures 5½ (6, 6½, 7, 7½)", ending with a WS row.

Next row (RS): Work 29 (34, 34, 36, 35) sts in established patt, and place these sts on a holder, bind off 20 (20, 24, 24, 28) sts, work rem 29 (34, 34, 36, 35) sts in established patt.

Right Front

Next row (WS): Work in established patt.

Next row (RS): K2, ssk, work in established patt to end.

Rep these last 2 rows 3 more times. 25 (30, 30, 32, 31) sts rem.

Work 4 rows even in established patt.

Next row (WS): Bind off 8 (10, 10, 10, 10) sts, work in established patt to end.

Next row (RS): Work in established patt.

Rep these 2 rows once more.

Next row (WS): Bind off rem 9 (10, 10, 12, 11) sts.

Left Front

Transfer the sts held for left front to the working needles. With WS facing, attach yarn at the neck edge.

Next row (WS): Work in patt.

Next row (RS): Work in established patt to last 4 sts, k2tog, k2.

Next row (WS): Work in established patt to end.

Rep the last 2 rows 3 more times. 25 (30, 30, 32, 31) sts rem.

Work 4 rows in established patt.

Next row (RS): Bind off 8 (10, 10, 10, 10) sts, work in established patt to end.

Next row (WS): Work in established patt.

Rep these 2 rows once more.

Bind off rem 9 (10, 10, 12, 11) sts.

Sleeves (Make 2)

Using smaller needles, CO 61 (66, 71, 81, 91) sts.

Beginning with a RS row, work in k1, p1 rib for 5", ending with a WS row.

Switch to larger needles.

Next row (RS): K4, (kfb, p1, k3) to last 2 sts, k2. 72 (78, 84, 96, 108) sts.

Next row (WS): P5, (k2, p4) to the last st, p1.

Continue in established patt, working the sts as they appear, until piece measures 7" from cast-on edge. End with a WS row.

Shape Sleeve Cap

Bind off 4 (5, 6, 9, 12) sts at the beginning of the next 2 rows.

Next row (RS): K2, ssk, work in established patt to last 4 sts, k2tog, k2.

Next row (WS): P3, work in established patt to last 3 sts, p3. Rep the last 2 rows 5 (5, 8, 9, 11) more times. 52 (56, 54, 58, 60) sts rem.

Continue to work in established patt, knitting the knit sts and purling the purl sts, until sleeve measures 11 (11, 11¾, 12¼, 12½)" from cast-on edge. End with a WS row.

Next row (RS): K2, ssk, work in patt to last 4 sts, k2tog, k2.

Next row (WS): Work in established patt.

Rep these last 2 rows 1 (3, 2, 2, 3) more times. 48 (48, 48, 52, 52) sts rem.

Next row (RS): Ssk 12 (12, 12, 13, 13) times, k2tog 12 (12, 12, 13, 13) times. 24 (24, 24, 26, 26) sts rem.

Next row (WS): Bind off rem sts.

Finishing

Block all pieces. Sew shoulder seams together.

Neck Band

With the RS facing, and starting at the placket at the left back neck, use smaller needles to pick up and knit 83 (83, 91, 91, 99) sts around neck edge. Do not join.

Next row (WS): P1, (k1, p1) to end of round.

Next row (RS): K1, (p1, k1) to end of round.

Rep these 2 rows once more.

Next row (WS): To create buttonhole p1, k1, yo, k2tog, p1, (k1, p1) to end of row.

Continue in rib for 4 more rows.

Bind off loosely.

Finish Sewing

Sew the sleeves into place.

Sew side and underarm seams, stitching the bottom 4" of the sleeve edge so that the seam is on the RS. This will give a clean edge when the cuff is turned up.

Sew smaller buttons in place at back neck under buttonholes.

Sleeve Cuff

Fold lower edges of sleeves up so that the cast-on edge meets the top of the 1 × 1 ribbing. Stitch the cuff in place at the underarm seam. Stitch the buttons in place on the sleeve cuff using the photo as a guide. Be sure to stitch the button through both layers of fabric to secure the cuff.

Sock Hop

by Erin Slonaker, a.k.a. Mintyfresh

Sock Hop is a kicky little number featuring a striped turtleneck sweater and matching knee socks. Easy-fitting ribbing on both the sweater and socks make for a forgiving fit that will flatter lots of shapes, and the worsted weight yarn makes both a quick knit. Pair the sweater with shorts or a short skirt for an instant boost in retro style. Or if you're feeling extra sassy, knit it long enough to be a micro mini-dress and forgo pants altogether!

Sweater

Size

S (M, L, 1X)

Note: This sweater is designed with 2" of negative ease.

Finished Measurements

Chest: 32 (36, 38, 42)"

Materials

Valley Yarns Valley Superwash (100% superwash merino wool; 98 yd./50g per skein)

CA: #436 Wild Rose 6 (6, 7, 8) balls

CB: #545 Brownie 6 (6, 7, 8) balls

U.S. size 8 (5mm) needles, *or size needed to obtain gauge*

U.S. size 8 (5mm) double-pointed needles or preferred needles for working in the round for neck

U.S. size 5 (3.75mm) double-pointed needles or preferred needles for working in the round for neck

Stitch holder

Darning needle

Gauge

22 sts × 25 rows = 4", in ribbing patt, slightly stretched on larger needles

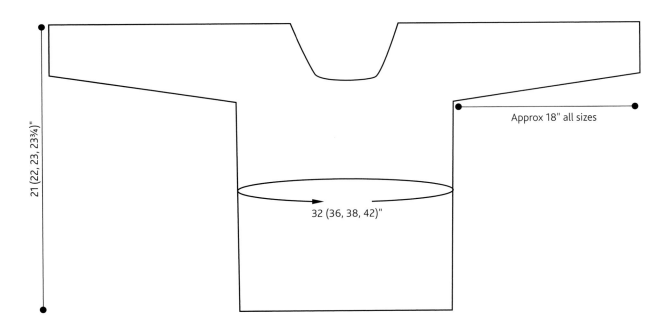

21 (22, 23, 23¾)"

Approx 18" all sizes

32 (36, 38, 42)"

Pattern Notes

The ribbing is worked with transitional knit rows to ensure clean color transitions.

Directions

Back

With CB, CO 90 (98, 106, 114) sts.

Row 1 (WS): (P2, k2) to last 2 sts, p2.

Row 2 (RS): (K2, p2) to last 2 sts, k2.

Rows 1 and 2 establish the rib patt. Continue ribbing in CB until 20 rows total have been worked.

Transition Row (WS): With CA, knit.

Next row (RS): With CA, work ribbing as established. Continue working in ribbing for 9 rows—10 rows worked with CA.

Transition Row (WS): With CB, knit.

Next row (RS): With CB, work ribbing as established. Continue for 9 more rows—10 rows worked.

Continue as established, changing colors every 10 rows and working a Transition Row at each color change until back measures 13½ (14, 14½, 15)" from cast-on edge, ending with a WS row. Note how many rows of the current stripe have been completed, to ensure front will match.

Shape Armhole

Maintaining rib and stripe patt, bind off 4 sts at the beginning of the next 2 rows.

Bind off 3 sts at the beginning of the next 2 rows.

Decrease 1 st at each edge every RS row 5 times—66 (74, 82, 90) sts rem.

Continue ribbing and stripes as established until armhole measures 7½ (8, 8½, 8¾)". Back measures 21 (22, 23, 23¾)" from cast-on edge.

Shape Shoulders

Working in ribbing and stripes as established, bind off 9 (10, 11, 12) sts at the beginning of the next 2 rows.

Bind off 8 (9, 11, 11) sts at the beginning of the next 2 rows.

Cut yarn and pull through last bound-off st to secure. Place rem 32 (36, 38, 44) sts on a holder for the back neck.

Front

With CB, CO 90 (98, 106, 114) sts. Work as for back until armhole measures 5 (5½, 6, 6½)", ending with a WS row.

Divide for Neck

Next row (RS): Work 25 (27, 30, 32) sts, place center 16 (20, 22, 26) sts on a stitch holder, join a second ball of yarn, and work to end.

Right Neck

Work 1 WS row in ribbing and stripes as established to neck edge.

Next row: Bind off 2 sts at neck edge, work to end of row.

Rep these 2 rows 3 times more—17 (19, 22, 24) sts rem.

Work even until armhole measures 7½ (8, 8½, 8¾)", ending with a RS row.

Shape Shoulder

Next row: Bind off 9 (10, 11, 12) sts, work to end of row.

Next row (RS): Work in patt.

Rep these 2 rows once more.

Bind off rem 8 (9, 11, 11) sts.

Left Neck

Return to yarn at neck edge on left side.

Next row (WS): Bind off 2 sts at neck edge, work to end of row.

Next row (RS): Work in patt.

Rep these 2 rows 3 times more—17 (19, 22, 24) sts rem.

Work even until armhole measures 7½ (8, 8½, 8¾)", ending with a WS row.

Shape Shoulder

Next row (RS): Bind off 9 (10, 11, 12) sts, work to end of row.

Next row (WS): Work in patt.

Rep these 2 rows once more.

Bind off rem 8 (9, 11, 11) sts.

Sleeves (Make 2)

With CB, CO 46 (46, 50, 50) sts.

Row 1 (WS): (P2, k2) to last 2 sts, p2.

Row 2 (RS): (K2, p2) to last 2 sts, k2.

Rows 1 and 2 establish ribbing. Continue until 20 rows have been worked in CB. Piece measures approximately 3" from cast-on edge.

Increase Row (WS): With CA, knit, increasing 1 st at each side: K1, kfb, knit to last 3 sts, kfb, k2.

With CA, work ribbing as established for 9 rows—10 rows worked with CA.

Switch to CB and rep the last two lines.

Continue as established, changing colors every 10 rows and working an Increase Row at each color change a total of 10 times. There are 66 (66, 70, 70) sts and sleeve measures approximately 18" from beginning. End with same row of current stripe as on body.

Sleeve Cap

Throughout sleeve cap, maintain ribbing and color stripes as established, working Transition Rows as on body of sweater (knit; do not increase).

All sizes: Bind off 4 sts at the beginning of the next 2 rows.

Dec 1 st at each edge on the next 10 (6, 9, 5) rows.

Dec 1 st at each edge every 3rd row 7 (9, 9, 10) times.

Dec 1 st at each edge on the next 5 (7, 5, 8) rows.

Bind off 4 sts at the beginning of the next 2 rows.

Bind off rem 6 (6, 8, 8) sts.

Finishing

Sew shoulder seams.

Turtleneck

Transfer 32 (36, 38, 44) held sts for back neck to larger double-pointed needles. With CA, pick up and knit 14 (16, 18, 20) sts along left front neck, k16 (20, 22, 26) held sts for the front neck, pick up and knit 14 (16, 18, 20) sts along right front neck. 76 (88, 96, 110) sts. Place marker to note beginning of the round.

Work k2, p2 ribbing for 1 round.

Change to smaller needles.

Continue in k2, p2 ribbing until turtleneck measures 6". Bind off loosely.

Sew side seams. Sew sleeve caps into armholes, easing in and matching stripes. (Use the appropriate color to sew each stripe so the seams are not visible.)

Weave in ends.

Knee Socks

Size

Women's 7–8 (9–10)

Finished Measurements

Foot Length: 9 (9½)"

Sock Height from Heel: 21"

Materials

Valley Yarns Valley Superwash (100% merino wool; 98 yd./50g per ball)

CA: #436 Wild Rose; 2 balls

CB: #545 Brownie; 1 ball

U.S. 7 (4.5mm) double-pointed needles, *or size needed to match gauge*

U.S. 5 (3.75mm) double-pointed needles

Stitch marker, if desired

Stitch holder

Yarn needle

Gauge

22 sts × 25 rows = 4" in ribbing patt, slightly stretched, on larger needles

Directions

Leg

With larger needles and CA, CO 56 (60) sts. Join to work in the round.

Rnd 1: (K2, p2) to end.

Rnds 2–29: Work in rib as established.

Rnd 30: With CB, knit around.

Rnds 31–43: With CB, work in k2, p2 rib to end.

Rnd 44: With CA, knit around.

Rnds 45–57: With C, work in k2, p2 rib to end.

Continue as established, changing colors after working 13 rounds in k2, p2 ribbing and working a knit round at the color change. Work until end of second stripe in CB; the leg measures approximately 11½".

Change to smaller needles, and continue in stripe patt as established for three more stripes, ending with a completed CA stripe. You can adjust the sock length by adding or subtracting stripes here.

Heel

Row 1: With CB, k26 (30) sts, turn. These are the heel sts; place rem sts on stitch holder.

Row 2 (WS): Sl 1, p1, (k2, p2) to end.

Row 3 (RS): Sl 1, k1, (p2, k2) to end.

Rep last 2 rows 11 (13) times more. Do not cut CB.

Next row (WS): With CA, purl.

Turn Heel

The sole of the foot is worked in stockinette.

Row 1: With CA, sl 1, k14 (16) sts, k2tog, k1, turn.

Row 2: Sl 1, p5, p2tog, p1, turn.

Row 3: Sl 1, knit to last st before gap, k2tog, k1, turn.

Row 4: Sl 1, purl to last st before gap, p2tog, p1, turn.

Rep Rows 3 and 4 until all sts are worked and 16 (20) sts rem.

Gusset

Pick up CB at right corner of sock, and pick up and knit 15 (17) sts along side of heel flap (2 at top of gusset and 13 (15) along edge of flap); sl 1, knit to end of heel sts; pick up and knit 15 (17) sts along other side of flap. These sts are the heel sts.

Move the held instep sts to working needles. Place a marker to indicate beginning of instep. With CB, knit across instep sts (or work in pattern if not at a color change). Place a marker to indicate beginning of sole. Knit to center of heel; this is now the beginning of the round; place a contrasting marker.

Rnd 1: Knit to 2 sts before first marker, ssk, sm, work in patt to second marker, sm, k2tog, knit to end.

Rnd 2: Work even, knitting the sole stitches and working instep in pattern as established.

Rep Rnds 1 and 2, maintaining stripe patt, until there are 26 (30) sts for the sole; 56 (60) sts total.

Foot

Continue working as established for foot, maintaining stripe pattern and keeping sole stitches in stockinette and instep in pattern. Work until sock measures approximately 7½ (8)" or 1½" shorter than desired total foot length.

Toe

The toe is worked in stockinette. Discontinue rib and stripe pattern. Work the remainder of the sock with one color only.

Smaller Size Only

Set-up rnd: Knit to end of sole, ssk, knit to last 2 sts of instep, k2tog, knit to end of round.

Both Sizes

Rnd 1: Knit even.

Rnd 2: Knit to last 2 sts of sole, k2tog, ssk, knit to last 2 sts of instep, k2tog, ssk, knit to end of round.

Rep Rnds 1 and 2 until there are 8 sts for the instep and 8 sts for the sole. Cut yarn, leaving a yard for seaming the toe.

Use Kitchener stitch to graft the toe closed. Weave in ends.

Watusi

*by Staci Perry and
Melissa LaBarre*

Do the Watusi with this hip-shaking little dress featuring an ultra mod look and bold color combination. The empire waist sits naturally and offers a truly flattering silhouette that will make you want to dance the night away. Hopefully in go-go boots. The sweet Peter Pan collar is a simple yet important detail that really nudges this dress into Brady territory. A column of small buttons pushes it right into the AstroTurf backyard that someone is always mowing. The Watusi Topper is the perfect companion for your new dress, it's got that Jiffy Pop look that all the kids are crazy for nowadays! The visor looks adorable when tilted at a jaunty angle. Wear it short and slouchy for your new pixie cut, or puff it up high to make room for your beehive.

Dress

Sizes

S (M, L, 1X, 2X)

Finished Measurements

Chest: 34 (38, 42, 46, 50)"

Materials

Cascade Sierra (80% pima cotton, 20% merino wool; 191 yd./100g per hank)

MC (top): #409 Light Green; 2 skeins for all sizes

CC1 (skirt): #66 Navy; 3 (3, 4, 4, 4) skeins

CC2 (trim): #13 Teal; 1 skein for all sizes

U.S. 7 (4.5mm) 24" or 32" circular needles, *or size needed to match gauge*

U.S. 7 (4.5mm) 16" circular needles

U.S. G-6 (4mm) crochet hook

Stitch markers

Tapestry needle

3 buttons to match CC1, ⅝" diameter

Gauge

16 sts × 24 rows = 4" in St st, blocked

Pattern Notes

Changing up the colors or knitting it in a single color will change the look of this dress dramatically, so who knows how many of these will boogie their way into your wardrobe.

Directions

Begin at the hem of the skirt, working in the round.

Skirt

Using CC1 and longer circular needles, CO 164 (184, 204, 224, 248) sts. Pm and join in the round. K86 (92, 102, 112, 118) sts, pm for side seam, knit to end of round.

Knit 6 rounds.

Purl 1 round for turning ridge.

Begin Shaping Skirt

Rnds 1–7: Knit.

Rnd 8: K1, k2tog, knit to 3 sts before marker, ssk, k1, sm, k1, k2tog, knit to 3 sts before end, ssk, k1 (4 sts decreased).

Rep these 8 rounds 14 (15, 16, 17, 19) times more, 104 (120, 136, 152, 168) sts.

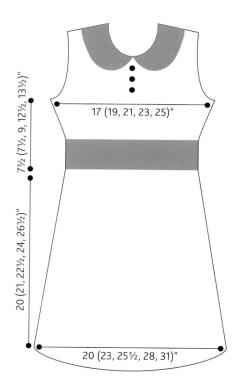

Waistband

Switch to CC2, and knit in St st for 2½ (2½, 3, 3½, 3½)".

Bodice

Switch to MC.

Rnd 1: K1, M1, knit to 1 st before marker, M1, k1, sm, k1, M1, knit to 1 st before end, M1, k1 (4 sts increased).

Rnds 2–6: Knit.

Rep these 6 rounds 4 times more, then work Rnd 1 once more—128 (144, 160, 176, 192) sts.

Work 0 (0, 6, 8, 10) rounds even.

Next rnd: Knit to 3 (3, 4, 4, 5) sts from the end. Do not complete this round.

Begin Armhole Shaping

Bind off 6 (6, 8, 8, 10) sts removing marker, k58 (66, 72, 80, 86) sts and transfer to holder or scrap yarn for front, bind off 6 (6, 8, 8, 10) sts removing marker, k58 (66, 72, 80, 86) sts.

Continue working back and forth on the sts for back only:

Row 1 (WS): Purl.

Row 2 (RS): K1, ssk, knit to last 3 sts, k2tog, k1.

Rep these 2 rows 8 times more. 40 (48, 54, 62, 68) sts.

Continue working in St st without shaping until work measures 9½ (10, 10¼, 10½, 11)" from color change at beginning of bodice, ending after a WS row.

Back Neckline Shaping

K14 (15, 16, 17, 18) sts and place on holder, bind off 12 (18, 22, 28, 32) sts, k14 (15, 16, 17, 18) sts.

Continue on left shoulder only:

Row 1: Purl.

Row 2: K1, ssk, knit to end.

Rep these 2 rows twice more, 11 (12, 13, 14, 15) sts.

Work 12 (12, 12, 18, 24) more rows in St st, put sts on hold for three-needle bind-off, break yarn.

Right Shoulder

Reattach yarn to right back to work a WS row.

Row 1: Purl.

Row 2: Knit to last 3 sts, k2tog, k1.

Rep these 2 rows twice more, 11 (12, 13, 14, 15) sts.

Work 12 (12, 12, 18, 24) more rows in St st, put sts on hold for three-needle bind-off, break yarn.

Front

Transfer sts held for front to working needles and reattach yarn to start a WS row.

Row 1: Purl.

Row 2: K1, ssk, knit to last 3 sts, k2tog, k1.

Rep these 2 rows 8 more times, 40 (48, 54, 62, 68) sts.

Purl 1 row.

Shape Front Neck

K14 (15, 16, 17, 18) sts and place on holder, bind off 12 (18, 22, 28, 32) sts, k14 (15, 16, 17, 18) sts.

Right Shoulder and Neck

Rows 1 and 3: Purl.

Row 2: Knit.

Row 4: K1, ssk, knit to end.

Rep these 4 rows twice more, 11 (12, 13, 14, 15) sts.

Work 8 (8, 12, 14, 20) more rows in St st. Break yarn and put these sts on holder.

Left Shoulder and Neck

Reattach yarn to work a WS row.

Rows 1 and 3: Purl.

Row 2: Knit.

Row 4: Knit to last 3 sts, k2tog, k1.

Rep these 4 rows twice more, 11 (12, 13, 14, 15) sts.

Work 8 (8, 12, 14, 20) more rows in St st. Break yarn and put on scrap yarn.

Finishing

Using three-needle bind-off, attach front and back straps together.

Peter Pan Collar

Using 16" circular needle and CC2, with WS facing, start at the center of the front neck and pick up and knit 6 (9, 11, 14, 16) sts across left neck, k15 (15, 18, 20, 24) sts up left front strap to seam, k12 (12, 12, 18, 22) sts down left back strap, k12 (18, 22, 28, 32) sts across back, k12 (12, 12, 18, 22) sts up right back strap to seam, k15 (15, 18, 20, 24) sts down right front strap, k6 (9, 11, 14, 16) sts back to center front. 78 (90, 104, 132, 156) sts. Turn work; do not join.

Set-up row (WS): Sl 3 wyif, p1, pm, p29 (32, 37, 48, 58) sts, pm, p12 (18, 22, 28, 32) sts, pm, p29 (32, 37, 48, 58) sts, pm, p4.

Row 1: Sl 3 wyib, knit to end.

Row 2: Sl 3 wyif, purl to end.

Collar Increases

Row 1 (RS): Sl 3 wyib, knit to marker, M1R, sm, k1, M1L, *knit to 1 st before marker, M1R, k1, sm, k1, M1L, rep from * once, knit to 1 st before marker, M1R, k1, sm, M1L, knit to end. (8 sts increased.)

Row 2: Sl 3 wyif, purl to end.

Rep these 2 rows 4 times more—118 (130, 144, 172, 196) sts.

Collar Shaping

Row 1 (RS): Sl 3 wyib, ssk, knit to marker, M1R, sm, k1, M1L, *knit to 1 st before marker, M1R, k1, sm, k1, M1L, rep from * once, knit to 1 st before marker, M1R, k1, sm, M1L, knit to last 5 sts, k2tog, k3.

Row 2: Sl 3 wyif, purl to end.

Rep these 2 rows once more.

I-Cord Bind-Off

*K2, k2tog, slip these 3 sts back to left-hand needle, rep from * until 3 sts rem unworked on the left needle. Graft these 3 sts to the 3 sts on the right needle.

Single crochet around armholes.

Weave in ends and block to measurements.

Topper

Size

One size fits most adult women

Finished Measurements

Circumference: Hat band measures 20"

Materials

Cascade Sierra (80% pima cotton, 20% merino wool; 191 yd./100g per skein)

MC: #66 Dark Blue; 1 skein

CC1: #409 Lime Green; 1 skein

CC2: #13 Teal; 1 skein

U.S. 3 (3.25mm) straight needles, *or size needed to obtain gauge*

U.S. 3 (3.25mm) circular needle, 16" length

Darning needle

Gauge

24 sts × 34 rows = 4" in St st

Pattern Notes

The main portion of the hat is worked in 6 separate sections and seamed to give the hat some stability.

Special Stitches and Terms

Wrap and turn (w&t): see page 47

Wedges

Make a total of 6 wedges: 3 with MC and 3 with CC1.

CO 22 sts.

Row 1 (RS): Knit.

Row 2 (WS): Purl.

Rep these 2 rows 4 times more.

Row 11 (RS): Purl to create a folding ridge.

Row 12: Purl.

Increase Row (RS): K1, M1, knit to last st, M1, k1.

Work in St st for 9 more rows, then rep this Increase Row once more.

Continue in St st for 2½", ending with a WS row. Piece measures approximately 5" from the cast-on edge.

Continue in St st and begin decreasing to shape crown as follows:

Decrease Row (RS): K1, k2tog, knit to last 3 sts, ssk, k1.

Rep this Decrease Row every 4th row 3 more times. 18 sts.

Rep this Decrease Row every RS row 7 times to 4 sts.

Purl 1 WS row.

Finish Top

Row 1 (RS): K2tog, ssk.

Row 2: Purl.

Row 3: K2tog.

Break yarn and pull through last st to fasten off. Set aside.

Finishing

Sew Wedges Together

Seam the wedges together along the sides, with points to the top, alternating colors. With CC2 and dpn, pick up 1 st from the top of each wedge and work a 6-stitch I-cord for 4 rows, break yarn and thread through all 6 sts, and fasten off. Weave in end.

Fold bottom edge of hat at purl ridge and sew the facing down on inside of hat. With CC2, pick up 120 sts along purl bumps at fold and work in garter st in the round for 4 rows. Bind off.

Brim

The brim uses short rows.

With MC, pick up 40 sts from bottom garter ridge across front 2 wedges.

Rows 1 and 2: Knit.

Row 3: Knit to last 2 sts, w&t; knit to last 2 sts, w&t; *knit to 1 st before wrapped st, w&t; work to 1 st before last wrapped st, w&t. Rep from * until there are 4 wrapped sts at each side.

Knit 2 rows on all 40 sts. Do not pick up wraps; knit wrapped sts normally. Bind off. Weave in ends.

Go-Go Granny

by Maryse Roudier

Until now, the idea of granny squares has existed mostly in the realm of comfy afghans and unfortunate pantsuits. Well, we're about to change all that. It's time to breathe new life into a folksy classic with Go-Go Granny, a sweater dress that would surely put the twinkle back in your saucy old grandma's eyes. The yarn used comes in a dizzying array of colors, so the possibilities are endless, from eye-piercing Technicolor to a more subdued tone-on-tone and everywhere in between. No two granny squares on our version share the same color combination, so the sky's the limit!

Sizes

S (M, L, 1X)

Finished Measurements

Chest: 34 (38, 42, 46)"

Length of dress: 34½" for all sizes

Length of top: 22" for all sizes

Note: Sizing is as simple as adding and subtracting squares, so adjusting the fit and length is a breeze.

Materials:

Tahki Stacy Charles Cotton Classic (100% mercerized cotton; 108 yd./50g per skein)

For Dress:

  Yarn A: #3818 Medium Blue; 7 (8, 8, 9) skeins

  Yarn B: #3001 White; 6 (7, 7, 8) skeins

For Top:

  Yarn A: #3818 Medium Blue; 6 (6, 6, 7) skeins

  Yarn B: #3001 White; 5 (5, 5, 6) skeins

For Dress or Top: 1 skein each of the following contrast colors:

  Yarn C: #3995 Red

  Yarn D: #3459 Hot Pink

  Yarn E: #3540 Tangerine

  Yarn F: #3402 Orange

  Yarn G: #3702 Citron

  Yarn H: #3449 Pink

  Yarn I: #3724 Green

  Yarn J: #3947 Dark Purple

  Yarn K: #3928 Lavender

  Yarn L: #3747 Burgundy

  Yarn M: #3932 Medium Purple

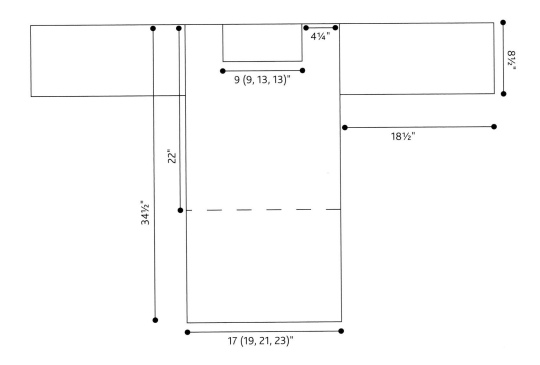

Note: You don't need to use as many colors as shown, and since only small amounts of the contrast colors are used, this is a great way to use up your leftovers from other projects.

U.S. G-6 (4mm) crochet hook, *or size needed to obtain gauge*

Openable stitch markers or safety pins

Darning needle

Gauge

19 sts × 24 rows = 4" in sc

1 granny square = 4¼" × 4¼"

Special Stitches and Terms

Traditional Granny Square: For the foundation ring: With one of the contrast colors, form a loose slipknot on the hook.

Rnd 1: Ch 3 (counts as 1 dc) 2 dc into slipknot ring, ch 3, *3 dc in slipknot ring, ch 3; rep from * two more times, join with a sl st into 3rd chain. Sl st into next 2 dc to the next 3 ch sp. Tighten slipknot by pulling free end of yarn.

Rnd 2: Join a second contrast color to 3 ch sp, holding Rnd 1 yarn in back. Ch 3 (counts as 1 dc), [2 dc, ch 3, 3 dc] into same space, *ch 1, [3 dc, ch 3, 3 dc] into next ch 3 sp; rep from * two more times, ch 1, join with slip st into 3rd ch of ch 3. Sl st into next 2 dc to the next 3 ch sp.

Rnd 3: Join a third contrast color to next 3 ch sp, holding Rnd 2 yarn in back. Ch 3 (counts as 1 dc), [2 dc, ch 3, 3 dc] into same sp, *ch 1, 3 dc into ch 1 sp, ch 1, [3 dc, ch 3, 3 dc] into next corner sp; rep from * twice, ch 1, 3 dc into ch 1 sp, ch 1, join with sl st into 3rd ch of ch 3. Sl st into next 2 dc to the next 3 ch sp.

Rnd 4: Join Yarn B to next 3 ch sp, holding Rnd 3 yarn in back. Ch 3, [2 dc, ch 3, 3 dc] into same space, *[ch 1, 3 dc] into each ch 1 sp along side of square, ch 1, [3 dc, ch 3, 3 dc] into next ch 3 corner space; rep from * twice, [ch 1, 3 dc] into each ch 1 sp along side of square, ch 1, join with sl st into 3rd ch of ch 3. Sl st into next 2 dc to the next 3 ch sp.

Rnd 5: Join Yarn A to next 3 ch sp, holding Rnd 4 yarn in back. Ch 3, [2 dc, ch 3, 3 dc] into same space, *[ch 1, 3 dc] into each ch 1 sp along side of square, ch 1, [3 dc, ch 3, 3 dc] into next ch 3 corner space; rep from * twice, [ch 1, 3 dc] into each ch 1 sp along side of square, ch 1, join with sl st into 3rd ch of ch 3. Sl st into next 2 dc to the next 3 ch sp.

Break yarn and fasten off.

Pattern Notes

You can use this pattern to create a top that ends at the hip or a knee-length dress. Follow the directions for either within the pattern.

No two squares in this dress are identical and no two squares use the same three colors in the first three rounds. Use your imagination and play with the colors, or pick your favorites and make the dress/top in just those colors. The white and medium blue give the dress a more cohesive look.

Directions

Back

For the Dress

Make 32 (32, 40, 40) squares. For Rnds 1–3, use any combination of Yarns C through M. Use Yarn B for Rnd 4. Use Yarn A for Rnd 5.

Join squares together by holding the right sides of each square together and whipstitching in Yarn A through the back loops. For the back of the dress, make a rectangle 4 (4, 5, 5) squares across and 8 squares long.

For Size M and 1X dress only: With RS facing, join Yarn A to one long side of Back, ch 1 then sc in each stitch along the edge of the first 6 granny squares, turn. Rep this row 5 times for a total of 6 rows. Break yarn. Rep on other long side, starting at the third granny square and crocheting to the end of the piece.

For the Top

Make 20 (20, 25, 25) squares. For Rnds 1–3, use any combination of Yarns C through M. Use Yarn B for Rnd 4. Use Yarn A for Rnd 5.

Join squares together by holding the right sides of each square together and whipstitching in Yarn A through the back loops. Back of top is 4 (4, 5, 5) squares across and 5 squares long.

For Size M and 1X top only: With RS facing, join Yarn A to the long side of the piece (size 1X is square, so choose one side), ch 1 then sc into each stitch along the edge of the first 3 granny squares, turn. Rep this row 5 times for a total of 6 rows. Break yarn. Rep on other long side, starting at the third granny square from the top and crocheting to the end of the piece.

Front
For the Dress

Make 30 (30, 37, 37) squares. For Rnds 1–3, use any combination of Yarns C through M. Use Yarn B for Rnd 4. Use Yarn A for Rnd 5.

Squares are joined the same way as for the back. Neckline is formed by sewing a square at the top right-hand side and the top left-hand side only.

For Size M and 1X dress only: With RS facing, join Yarn A to the long side of the piece, ch 1 then sc along the edge of the first 6 granny squares, turn. Rep this row for a total of 6 rows. Break yarn. Rep on other long side, starting at the third granny square and crocheting to the end of the piece.

For the Top

Make 18 (18, 22, 22) squares. For Rnds 1–3, use any combination of Yarns C through M. Use Yarn B for Rnd 4. Use Yarn A for Rnd 5.

Squares are joined the same way as for the back. Neckline is formed by sewing a square at the top right-hand side and the top left-hand side only.

For Size M and 1X top only: With RS facing, join Yarn A to the long side of the piece, ch 1 then sc along the edge of the first 3 granny squares, turn. Rep this row for a total of 6 rows. Break yarn. Rep on other long side, starting at the third granny square from the top and crocheting to the end of the piece.

Sleeves

For each sleeve: Make 16 squares. For Rnds 1–3, use any combination of Yarns C through M. Use Yarn B for Rnd 4. Use Yarn A for Rnd 5.

Join squares together by holding the right sides of each square together and whipstitching in Yarn A through the back loops. Each sleeve is 4 squares across and 4 squares long.

Finishing

With RS facing, join the front and the back together at the shoulders by whipstitching through the back loops with Yarn A. Center the sleeves at the shoulder, making sure that the squares line up properly, then whipstitch to join.

Turn dress/top inside out and starting at the end of the sleeve, whipstitch through the back loops from the end of the sleeve to the underarm, then from the underarm to the hem. Rep on the other side. Turn right side out.

Make the trim: At one of the side seams at the bottom hem, in Yarn A, ch 1, then sc into the back loop of each granny square stitch all the way around. Sl st into first ch 1 st. Join Yarn B, ch 1, then sc all the way around to beginning chain, sl st into first ch 1 st. Rep this row.

Next row: Join Yarn A, ch 1 then sc around to beginning chain, sl st into first ch 1 st. Break yarn. Weave in end.

Rep at each sleeve hem.

For the neckline, join Yarn A at the back of neck. Work trim as you did for hem and sleeves.

Weave in and trim ends.

Rudies

by Caro Sheridan

Take one step beyond with Rude Boy and Rude Girl, our nod to ska music, style, and dance. These rock-steady sweaters feature a slim fit and checkerboard details that'll have you skanking in no time. Both sweaters have the checkerboard bands on the sleeves as well as cuff and waist hems. Peek inside the turned hems for even more detail. It's the little things that make us happy. An innovative, two-color applied I-cord finished the collars on both sweaters. The ladies' version has a scooped neck, three-quarter-length sleeves, and assertive waist shaping for a great fit.

Rude Boy

Sizes

S (M, L, XL, XL)

Note: This sweater is designed with 2" of ease.

Finished Measurements

Chest: 40 (42, 44½, 46, 48, 50)"

Materials

Valley Yarns Northampton (100% wool; 247 yd./100g per skein)

MC: #18 Burgundy; 5 (5, 6, 6, 7) skeins

CC1: #07 Black; 1 skein for all sizes

CC2: #02 Natural; 1 skein for all sizes

U.S. 8 (5mm) circular needles, 24" or 36" length, *or size needed to match gauge*

U.S. 7 (4.5mm) circular needles, 24" or 36" length

U.S. 8 (5mm) double-pointed needles or small circular needle for sleeves

U.S. 7 (4.5mm) double-pointed needles or small circular needle for sleeve cuffs

U.S. 6 (4mm) double-pointed needles for edging

Stitch markers

Darning needle

Gauge

18 sts × 25 rows = 4" in St st

Pattern Notes

This sweater is knit seamlessly in the round from the bottom up. Hems are knit and sewn down afterwards.

Directions

Right Sleeve

With larger dpns and MC yarn, CO 40 (40, 44, 48, 52, 56) sts. Place marker and join in the round, being careful not to twist. Knit 1 round.

Change to U.S. 7 dpns and work through the 4 rows of the chart below twice.

Switch back to MC, and knit 2 rows.

Change to larger dpn, purl 1 row to create a turning ridge, knit 1 row.

Work the 4 rows of the chart once.

In MC, knit 10 rows even.

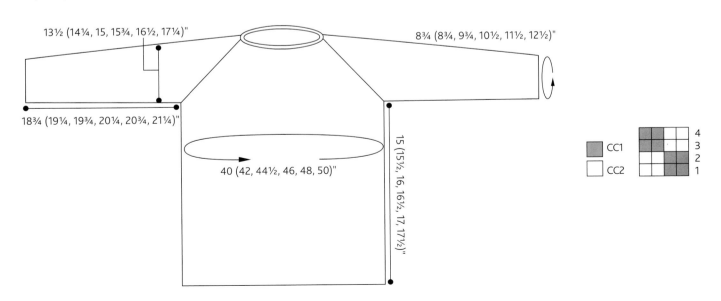

13½ (14¼, 15, 15¾, 16½, 17¼)"

8¾ (8¾, 9¾, 10½, 11½, 12½)"

18¾ (19¼, 19¾, 20¼, 20¾, 21¼)"

15 (15½, 16, 16½, 17, 17½)"

40 (42, 44½, 46, 48, 50)"

CC1
CC2

4
3
2
1

Begin Increases

Next row: Kfb, knit to 2 sts before marker, kfb, k1.

Knit 4 rows.

Rep those 5 rows 9 (11, 11, 11, 11, 11) times—60 (64, 68, 72, 76, 80) sts.

Work even until sleeve measures 17 (17½, 18, 18½, 19, 19½)" from purl turning ridge.

Knit the 4 rows of the chart twice. Place 16 sts on scrap yarn or holder (8 sts before and after marker) for underarm. Leave the rest of the sts live and set aside sleeve.

Left Sleeve

Knit the same as right sleeve, but do not knit the patt on the upper arm. Instead continue with MC until the left sleeve measures the same as the right sleeve. Place 16 sts on scrap yarn or holder (8 sts before and after marker) for underarm. Leave the rest of the sts live and set aside sleeve.

Body

With larger needle and MC yarn, CO 180 (188, 200, 208, 216, 224) sts. Place marker and join in the round, being careful not to twist.

Knit 1 round.

Change to smaller needles and knit 4 rows of the chart twice.

Change to MC and knit 2 rows.

Change to larger needle and purl 1 row for turning ridge. Knit 1 row.

Knit 4 rows of chart once.

Continue in MC until body measures 15 (15½, 16, 16½, 17, 17½)" (or desired length to underarm) from purl turning edge.

K98 (102, 108, 112, 116, 120) sts; place the last 16 sts knit on a holder or scrap yarn, knit to 8 sts before marker and place the next 16 sts on a holder or scrap yarn without knitting them. These sts will later be grafted to the corresponding sts on the sleeve for the underarm. Do not break yarn.

Joining Sleeves to Body

Place marker for beginning of the round and, with working yarn from the body, k44 (48, 52, 56, 60, 64) right sleeve sts, pm, k74 (78, 84, 88, 92, 96) body sts for the back, pm, k44 (48, 52, 56, 60, 64) left sleeve sts, pm, knit rem body sts for front. 236 (252, 272, 288, 304, 320) sts total.

Begin Raglan Shaping

Rnd 1: Knit.

Rnd 2: *K1, ssk, knit to 2 sts before marker, k2tog, sm. Rep from * to end of round.

Rep these 2 rows until 12 shoulder sts rem between markers at the top of each sleeve.

Shape Neck

You will work back and forth on the back and shoulder sts to shape the neck.

Next rnd: Knit to last 6 sts, pm to indicate beg of neck shaping.

Next row: *K4, k2tog, sm, k1, ssk, knit to 6 sts before next marker. Rep from * 3 times more, k4. Turn.

Next row and following WS rows: Purl across to neck shaping marker.

Next row: *K3, k2tog, sm, k1, ssk, knit to 5 sts before next marker, rep from * 3 times more, k3.

Next row (RS): *K2, k2tog, sm, k1, ssk, knit to 4 sts before next marker, rep from * 3 times more, k2.

Continue shaping neck as set until 4 sts remain between markers on each shoulder.

On the RS, loosely bind off all sts. In the gaps between the shoulders and front neck, pick up and bind off 3 sts to ease the step transition and continue binding off all stitches.

Neck Finishing: Two-Color Attached I-Cord

The I-cord is knit directly onto the neck edge. One row of the I-cord is worked for each neck stitch.

On size 6 dpns, CO 4 sts with CC1. Do not turn. Slide the sts down to the right end of the needle and bring the yarn behind the sts to knit the next row.

Row 1: K3, slip the last st pwise, bring the yarn to the front (yo), and pick up and knit a stitch from the back neck near the right shoulder. Pass the yo and slipped stitch over the picked-up stitch. Slide the work down to the right-hand side of the needle.

Row 2: Rep Row 1.

Rows 3 and 4: Change to CC2 and rep Rows 1 and 2.

Continue in this method all the way around the neck, changing color every 2 rows until you meet up with the beginning row. Bind off all stitches and graft the beginning and ends of the I-cord together.

Finishing

Graft underarm stitches. Fold cuff and hems under and sew down. Weave in all ends.

Rude Girl

Sizes
S (M, L, 1X, 2X)

Finished Measurements
Chest: 36 (40, 44, 48, 52)"

Materials
Valley Yarns Northampton (100% wool; 247 yd./100g per skein)

MC: #10 Apple Green; 5 (5, 6, 6, 7) skeins

CC1: #07 Black; 1 skein for all sizes

CC2: #02 Natural; 1 skein for all sizes

U.S. 8 (5mm) 24" to 36" length circular needle, *or size needed to match gauge*

U.S. 7 (4.5mm) 24" to 36" length circular needle

U.S. 8 (5mm) double-pointed needles or small circular for sleeves

U.S. 7 (4.5mm) double-pointed needles or small circular for sleeves

U.S. 6 (4mm) double-pointed needles for I-cord

Stitch markers

Darning needle

Gauge
18 sts × 25 rows = 4" in St st

Pattern Notes
Sweater is knit seamlessly in the round from the top down. Hems are knit and sewn down afterward to prevent them from flipping up while wearing.

Directions

Body
With larger circular needle, CO 38 (38, 40, 40, 46) sts; do not join in the round.

Row 1 and following WS rows: Purl.

Row 2 (RS): Kfb, k1, pm, Kfb, k4 (4, 4, 4, 6) sts, Kfb, k1, pm, Kfb, k18 (18, 20, 20, 22) sts, Kfb, k1, pm, Kfb, k4 (4, 4, 4, 6) sts, Kfb, k1, pm, Kfb.

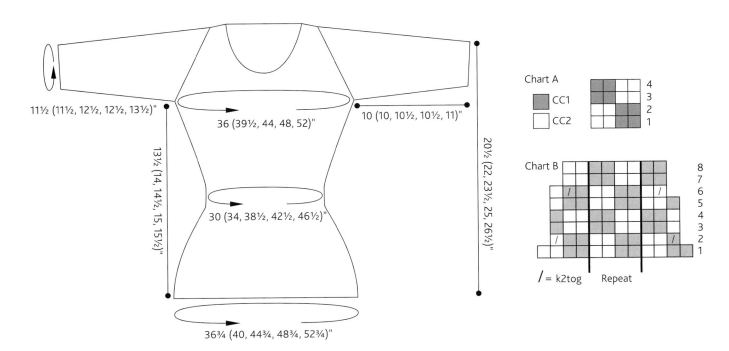

Row 4 (RS): K1, Kfb, k1, sm, Kfb, *k to 2 sts before next marker, Kfb, k1, sm, Kfb, rep from * to last st, k1.

Row 6 (RS): K2, Kfb, k1, sm, Kfb, *k to 2 sts before next marker, Kfb, k1, sm, Kfb, rep from * to last 2 sts, k2.

Row 8 (RS): K3, Kfb, k1, sm, Kfb, *k to 2 sts before next marker, Kfb, k1, sm, Kfb, rep from * to last 3 sts, k3.

Continue increasing in this manner 10 (10, 11, 11, 11) more times until there are 150 (150, 160, 160, 166) sts on the needle, ending with a WS row.

Begin Neck Edge Increases

Next row (RS): K1, Kfb, knit to 2 sts before next marker, Kfb, k1, sm, Kfb, rep from * 3 times, knit to last 2 sts, Kfb, k1.

Next row (WS): Purl.

Rep these 2 rows twice more, then rep the RS row once more.

Turn work and use the cable cast-on to add 10 (10, 12, 12, 14) sts. Turn work to RS, pm, and join in the round. This marker will denote the beginning of all subsequent rounds until the body is joined together. Knit 1 round plain.

Continue knitting in the round, increasing at each raglan marker as set every other round until you have 81 (88, 99, 108, 117) sts between markers for the front of the body. Finish with a non-increase round.

Separate the Sleeves and Join the Body

Knit to first raglan marker. Put first set of sleeve sts (between markers) on scrap yarn or a spare needle. Place a marker to denote the side seam and beginning of body rounds. Knit across the back sts, place second set of sleeve sts on scrap yarn or spare needle, place another side seam marker, and knit across the front body sts.

Next rnd: Sm, k2tog, knit to second side seam marker, sm, k2tog, knit to end.

Work even in St st for 3 (2, 1, 1, 1)".

Waist Shaping

Next rnd (Decrease Round): *K2, ssk, knit to 4 sts before marker, k2tog, k2, sm, rep from *.

Rep this decrease every 4th row 5 (5, 5, 5, 4) more times.

Work even for 1½ (1½, 1½, ½, ½)".

Next rnd (Increase Round): *K3, M1, knit to 3 sts before marker, M1, k3, sm, rep from *.

Rep this increase every 4th row 6 (6, 6, 6, 5) more times.

Work even until body measures 13½ (14, 14½, 15, 15½)" from underarm, or 1" shorter than desired length.

Hem

Work the 4 rows of Chart A once.

Knit 2 rows.

Purl 1 row to create turning ridge.

Change to smaller needles and knit 1 row.

Work Chart A twice.

Change back to MC and knit 2 rows plain.

Bind off all sts with the larger needle and leave a long enough tail to sew down the hem.

Sleeve 1

Return live sts to needle. Place marker at underarm to denote beginning of round, and with MC knit all sts, pick up one st at underarm. 68 (76, 84, 92, 100) sts.

Knit Chart B.

With MC, knit 1 round plain.

Decrease Round: K1, k2tog, knit to last 3 sts, ssk, k1.

Rep this Decrease Round every 3rd round to 52 (52, 56, 56, 60) sts.

Work until sleeve measures 9 (9, 9½, 9½, 10)" from underarm.

Knit Chart A once.

Knit 2 rows even.

Purl 1 row to create turning ridge.

Change to smaller needles and knit 1 row.

Work Chart A twice.

Change back to MC and knit 2 rows even.

Bind off all stitches with the larger needle and leave a long enough tail to sew down the hem.

Sleeve 2

Return live sts to needle. Place marker at underarm to denote beginning of round, and with MC knit all sts, pick up one st at underarm. 68 (76, 84, 92, 100) sts.

With MC, knit 1 round plain.

Decrease Round: K1, k2tog, knit to last 3 sts, ssk, k1.

Rep this Decrease Round every 3rd round to 52 (52, 56, 56, 60) sts.

Work until sleeve measures 9 (9, 9½, 9½, 10)" from underarm.

Knit Chart A once.

Knit 2 rows even.

Purl 1 row to create turning ridge.

Change to smaller needles and knit 1 row.

Work Chart A twice.

Change back to MC and knit 2 rows even.

Bind off all stitches with the larger needle and leave a long enough tail to sew down the hem.

Neck Finishing: Two-Color Attached I-Cord

The I-cord is knit directly onto the neck edge. One row of the I-cord is worked for each neck stitch on the back neck and bottom of the scoop. The sides of the scoop should be worked by picking up 3 sts for every 4 rows.

On size 6 dpns, CO 4 sts using CC1. Do not turn. Slide the sts down to the right side of the needle and bring the yarn behind the sts to knit the next row.

Row 1: K3, slip the last st pwise, bring the yarn to the front (yo) and pick up and knit a stitch from the back neck near the right shoulder. Pass the yo and slipped stitch over the picked-up stitch. Slide the work down to the right-hand side of the needle.

Row 2: Rep Row 1.

Rows 3 and 4: Change to CC2, rep Rows 1 and 2.

Continue in this method all the way around the neck, changing color every 2 rows until you meet up with the beginning row. Bind off and graft the beginning and ends of the I-cord together.

Finishing

Fold cuffs and bottom hem under and sew down. Weave in all ends.

Swanky Wristlet

Sometimes you just don't need a big, huge purse. When you do, by all means, you should use our Toasty Tote pattern to make one for yourself. But for those simpler days when all you need is a cell phone, keys, license, credit card, and maybe some lipstick—oh, and your sunglasses (you can't forget your sunglasses), and maybe your checkbook because you never know. And a hairbrush, that goes without saying . . . Wait. Back it up, Sister! We said simple—bare necessities for your day. Leave everything after the sunglasses at home. All that other stuff? Put it into our Swanky Wristlet and you're good to go. This is the perfect project for beginners and experienced sewists alike because they're easy to make, and you can never have too many. With so many fabrics to choose from, you can make them for every mood and occasion. And because of their compact size, you don't need a whole lot of material, so vintage fabric scraps and linens are just the thing to make your bag sing. Choose simple, embroidered tea towels for an afternoon jaunt. How could you not enjoy a wild and crazy night out without having a wristlet made with the bright colors and patterns of a repurposed 1970s skirt. For a more classic style, use vintage barkcloth or fancy it up with that bridesmaid's dress you were promised you'd wear time and time again. It'll feel good to take the scissors to that monstrosity, won't it?

Heavier-weight fabrics are best for this bag, but you can also use fusible interfacing on lighter-weight fabrics to give it enough body to stand up to whatever you put inside. Get creative and look for ways to reuse fabric from clothes you never wear. There's an entire fabric store waiting for you in the dark recesses of your closet. Then embellish away with buttons, trims, and costume jewelry to add some glamour.

What You'll Need

- 9" zipper
- 2 main pieces of fabric, 10½" × 5"
- 1 piece of fabric for the strap, 10½" × 1¼"
- Matching thread
- Sewing machine
- Zipper foot (optional, but worth the investment)
- 1" bias tape maker (optional)
- Pinking shears (optional)

Finished Measurement: 9¼" × 4¼"

Note: You can vary the size easily if you have a different length of zipper. Simply measure the full length of the zipper tape to determine the length to cut your fabric. (For instance, a 7" zipper usually has 8" of bias tape.)

What to Do

1. Center the closed zipper along the top of one the larger pieces of fabric with the right sides together, aligning the raw edge of the fabric with the edge of the zipper tape. (The right or "public" side of the fabric will face up and the public side of the zipper will face down.) Pin it in place. With the zipper foot on your sewing machine, stitch along the length with a ¼" seam allowance. Repeat with the other piece of fabric and the other side of the zipper.

2. Open the piece out flat and press the fabric away from the zipper.

3. With the zipper foot still on the machine, topstitch the fabric down about ⅛" from the fold along the length of the zipper. Do this on either side of the zipper.

4. Next up is the wrist strap. Run the long, skinny strip through your bias tape maker and press the whole thing lengthwise again. If you don't have a bias tape maker, you can simply press the edges in toward the middle, then fold the piece in half and press. Topstitch along the length of the strap to close it (using about ⅛" seam allowance).

5. Open the zipper at least two-thirds of the way and pin the bag pieces together with right sides of the fabric facing. Fold the wrist strap in half and, aligning all the raw edges, slip it into one

of the short sides parallel to the zipper about ½" down from the top. Sew the three sides closed, including the zipper ends, using ¼" seam allowance.

6. Clip your corners, zigzag stitch or pink along the raw edges and turn right side out.

7. Stand back and admire your handiwork! You just made a wristlet.

Step 1

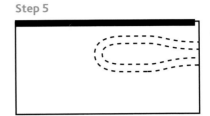

Zipper

Step 5

The strap is between the bag layers.

The right sides of the bag are facing each other (wrong side out).

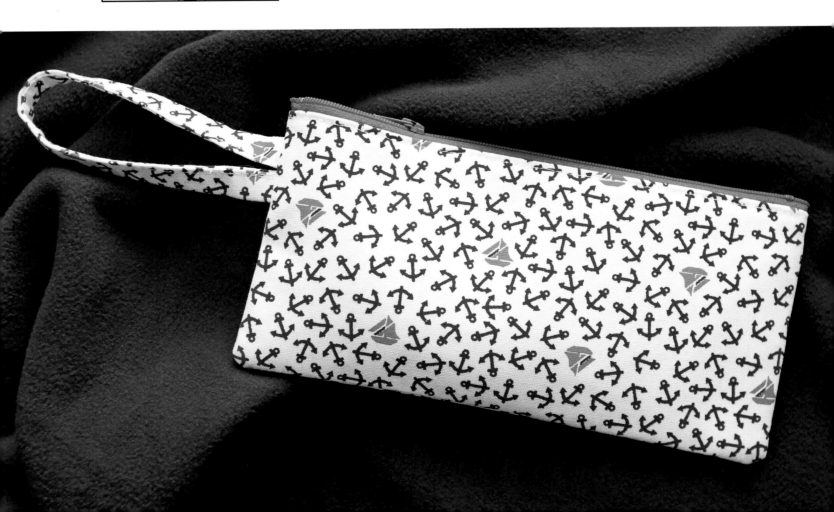

chapter 5

Sci-Fiber

I f we could write this intro in a monotone robot voice, we would. If you could read it that way, we would appreciate it. The future of the past was envisioned with personal supercomputers that took up an entire room and lumbering robots synthesized protein MREs in convenient pill form so there was no need to think about food sources. It's one of two ways—utopian or dystopian—and it's rarely something more middle of the road. Apparently the future is anything but ordinary.

Another thing we couldn't help but notice was that when it comes right down to it, the future also inevitably involves entire societies wearing the same clothing or at least just the one theme with minor variations. There's something almost comforting in knowing what you'll be wearing from one day to the next. And discerning a person's level of importance is easy as pie! Well, a pie pill. Just look at what color they're wearing. Every crew has a color chart that ranks people from experienced to expendable, so you always know where you stand. If you happen to be wearing red, chances are good you're standing inches from your doom and no one actually knows your name. On the plus side, it's more soylent green for everyone else!

Atomic Bowling Bag

by Regina Rioux

For the busy futurista on the go: take along your ray gun and a WIP or two. Don't forget your lip balm for those harsh solar winds. The roomy Atomic Bowling Bag will carry what-ever you need, whether you're off to your intergalactic knit night, battling Daleks, or trying to reason with Vogons. A sturdy zipper keeps everything secure, and two outer pockets warn of a looming hazard while keeping your keys or cell phone handy.

Finished Measurements

Bottom: 6½"

Top: 12" at widest point

Depth: 5½"

Materials

Lamb's Pride worsted (85% wool, 15% mohair; 190 yd./113g per skein)

MC: #M120 Limeade; 2 skeins

CC1: #M82 Blue Flannel; 2 skeins

CC2: #M78 Aztec Turquoise; 1 skein

U.S. G-6 (4mm) crochet hook, *or size needed to match gauge*

Tapestry needle

22" sport zipper

Sewing needle and coordinating heavy-duty thread

Pins

Stitch markers

Gauge

17 sts × 22 rows = 4" in sc

Directions

Main Panel

The main panel is worked from bottom to top in MC.

Foundation row: Chain 29.

Row 1 (RS): 1 sc in second ch from hook; 1 sc in each of the remaining ch sts; turn—2 sts added.

Rows 2, 4, and 6: Ch 1; 2 sc in first st; sc in each st to last st; 2 sc in last st; turn—34 sts.

Rows 3, 5, 7, and 8: Ch 1; sc in each st across, turn.

Row 9: Ch 1; 2 sc in first st; sc in the next 32 sts; 2 sc in last st; turn—36 sts.

Rows 10 and 11: Ch 1; sc in each st across, turn.

Row 12: Ch 1; 2 sc in first st; sc in the next 34 sts; 2 sc in last st; turn—38 sts.

Rows 13 and 14: Ch 1; sc in each st across, turn.

Row 15: Ch 1; 2 sc in first st; sc in the next 36 sts; 2 sc in last st; turn—40 sts.

Rows 16–18: Ch 1; sc in each st across, turn.

Row 19: Ch 1; 2 sc in first st; sc in the next 38 sts; 2 sc in last st; turn—42 sts.

Rows 20–22: Ch 1; sc in each st across, turn.

Row 23: Ch 1; 2 sc in first st; sc in the next 40 sts; 2 sc in last st; turn—44 sts.

Rows 24–26: Ch 1; sc in each st across, turn.

Row 27: Ch 1; 2 sc in first st; sc in the next 42 sts; 2 sc in last st; turn—46 sts.

Rows 28–30: Ch 1; sc in each st across, turn.

Row 31: Ch 1; 2 sc in first st; sc in the next 44 sts; 2 sc in last st; turn—48 sts.

Rows 32–34: Ch 1; sc in each st across, turn.

Row 35: Ch 1; 2 sc in first st; sc in the next 46 sts; 2 sc in last st; turn—50 sts.

Rows 36–38: Ch 1; sc in each st across, turn.

Row 39: Ch 1; 2 sc in first st; sc in the next 48 sts; 2 sc in last st; turn—52 sts.

Rows 40–42: Ch 1; sc in each st across, turn.

Row 43: Ch 1; 2 sc in first st; sc in the next 50 sts; 2 sc in last st; turn—54 sts.

Rows 44–49: Ch 1; sc in each st across, turn.

Row 50: Ch 1; sc first 2 sts tog; sc in the next 50 sts; sc last 2 sts tog; turn—52 sts.

Row 51: Ch 1; sc in each st across, turn.

Row 52: Ch 1; sc first 2 sts tog; sc in the next 48 sts; sc last 2 sts tog; turn—50 sts.

Row 53: Ch 1; sc in each st across, turn.

Rows 54–57: Ch 1; sc first 2 sts tog; sc in each st to the last 2 sts; sc last 2 sts tog; turn—42 sts.

Rows 58–60: Ch 1; sl st in next 2 sts, sc in each st to end of row; turn.

Fasten off.

Main Panel Border

With RS facing, hold the panel so that the foundation chain is at the top. This will be the bottom of the bag. Attach MC to the right-hand side of the foundation chain. Sc 28 along this edge, continue around, working 62 sc along side, 30 sc along top of panel, and 62 sc along remaining side, sl st to beg sc to join, fasten off.

Make a second panel the same as the first.

Sides, Bottom, and Top of Bag

With RS facing, attach CC1 at right corner of foundation chain. Working in back loops only, 182 sc around, pm in first st to denote beg of round—182 sts.

Begin working short rows, working through both loops.

Row 1: Sc in next 100 sc, turn.

Row 2: Sc in next 172 sc, turn.

Row 3: Sc in next 167 sc, turn.

Row 4: Sc in next 162 sc, turn.

Row 5: Sc in next 157 sc, turn.

Row 6: Sc in next 152 sc, turn.

Row 7: Sc in next 147 sc, turn.

Row 8: Sc in next 142 sc, turn.

Row 9: Sc in next 132 sc, turn.

Row 10: Sc in next 122 sc, turn.

Row 11: Sc in next 112 sc, turn.

Row 12: Sc in next 102 sc, turn.

Row 13: Sc in next 102 sc, ch 11, turn.

Row 14: Beg in 2nd ch from hook, sc in next 112 sc, ch 11, turn.

Row 15: Beg in 2nd ch from hook, sc in next 122 sc, ch 11, turn.

Row 16: Beg in 2nd ch from hook, sc in next 132 sc, ch 11, turn.

Row 17: Beg in 2nd ch from hook, sc in next 142 sc, ch 6, turn.

Row 18: Beg in 2nd ch from hook, sc in next 147 sc, ch 6, turn.

Row 19: Beg in 2nd ch from hook, sc in next 152 sc, ch 6, turn.

Row 20: Beg in 2nd ch from hook, sc in next 157 sc, ch 6, turn.

Row 21: Beg in 2nd ch from hook, sc in next 162 sc, ch 6, turn.

Row 22: Beg in 2nd ch from hook, sc in next 167 sc, ch 6, turn.

Row 23: Beg in 2nd ch from hook, sc in next 100 sc, do not turn.

Row 24: Sc in next 71 sc, ch 10, connect to opposite side, sc in next 101 sc. 182 sts.

Place rem panel with RS facing out atop finished piece. Make sure that main panels are aligned. Pin in place if needed. Secure panel to bag by making 1 rnd of sc through back loops of panel and front loops of sides, top, and bottom. Fasten off.

Panel Piping

*Attach CC2 in front post of main panel directly in front of seam. Make 1 rnd of FPsc all the way around main panel, making sure that you are as close to seam as possible, sl st to beg FPsc to join rnd. Fasten off.

Make a second piping round on the opposite side of the seam.

Attach CC2 in first piping round in back loop. Working in back loops piping round closest to you and front loops of the second piping round directly behind the first, sl st around to secure.

Rep from * on opposite side of bag. Weave in any rem ends.

Surface Crochet Stay Stitching

With CC2, make 1 row of surface sc on either side of bottom of bag and across sides of bag just below the bag top opening. Surface sc rows will add structure to sides and bottom of bag.

Atomic Pockets (Make 2)

When switching between two colors for the pockets, crochet over the unused color by laying it across the sts from the row below. For clean color changes, make the last yarn over on the last stitch of the old color with the new color.

Rnd 1: With CC1, ch 2, 6 sc in second ch from hook. Pm in beg st and begin to work in the round. Marker will move up as work progresses.

Rnd 2: 3 sc in every st. Drop CC1 and attach MC.

Rnd 3: With MC, sc in every st—18 sts.

Rnd 4: *With MC, 1 sc in next st, 3 sc in next st, 1 sc in next st, with CC1, 1 sc in next st, 3 sc in next st, 1 sc in next st, rep from * twice more—30 sts.

Work MC in MC sections and CC1 in CC1 sections for remainder of pattern.

Rnd 5 and following odd rnds: Work even.

Rnd 6: In each color section, 1 sc in next 2 sts, 3 sc in next st, 1 sc in next 2 sts—42 sts.

Rnd 8: In each color section, 1 sc in next 3 sts, 3 sc in next st, 1 sc in next 3 sts—54 sts.

Rnd 10: In each color section, 1 sc in next 4 sts 3 sc in next st, 1 sc in next 4 sts—66 sts.

Rnd 12: In each color section, 1 sc in next 5 sts, 3 sc in next st, 1 sc in next 5 sts—78 sts.

Rnd 14: In each color section, 1 sc in next 6 sts, 3 sc in next st, 1 sc in next 6 sts; fasten off CC1—90 sts.

Rnd 15: Sc in each st, make 1 more sc, fasten off.

Rnd 16: Attach CC2 and work 1 more rnd of sc, sl st to first sc to join, fasten off.

Weave in any remaining ends and sew to front of bags, leaving the top open so that atomic symbols function as pockets.

Straps (Make 2)
With CC1, ch 75.

Row 1: Beg in second ch from hook, sc in 74 sts across, turn.

Row 2: Ch 1, 1 sc in each st across, turn.

Row 3: Ch 1, sc in next 74 sts, do not turn. Work 5 dc in short end of strap, work 74 sc along bottom of foundation ch, work 5 dc in short end of strap, sl st to beg sc to join, fasten off.

Sew straps to top of bag.

Finishing
Make 1 rnd of evenly spaced sc around top opening of bag with CC1. Make 1 rnd of sc with CC2. Finish off with another rnd of CC2. Fasten off and pin zipper into top opening. Hand sew zipper into top of bag using needle and heavy-duty sewing thread.

Post-Apocalyptic

by Kellee Middlebrooks and Amy Herzog

Survived a robot war? Searching for a new world that's ripe for repopulation? Don't let the post apocalypse keep you from looking your best. Wear your survival on your sleeve with this set of matching sweaters we call Apocalyptus (for him) and Apocalypta (for her). Both sweaters were designed to look as though they've been through a barrage of laser blasts and are all the better for it. The men's version features reverse stitching at the seams, dropped stitches, and rolled hems. The ladies' version is knit with a gorgeous, drapey yarn that fits like a dream. Dropped stitches add shaping at the neck and at the end of the softly belled sleeves.

Apocalyptus

Sizes
XS (S, M, L, 1X, 2X)

Finished Measurements
Chest: 38 (40, 44, 48, 52, 56)"

Materials
Elsebeth Lavold Silky Wool (45% wool, 35% silk, 20% nylon; 191 yd./50g per skein); #61 Dark Brown; 9 (10, 12, 13, 14, 16) skeins

U.S. 6 (4mm) straight or circular needles, *or size needed to obtain gauge*

Stitch markers

Yarn needle

Opening stitch markers

Small, sharp scissors

Darning needle

Gauge
24 sts × 32 rows = 4" in St st

Pattern Notes

This is a simple, casual, modified drop-sleeve pullover. It is designed to be roomy in the shoulder and upper-arm area for ease of movement, yet with a modern, slim fit through the chest and torso. Exposed seams at the shoulders and neck provide structure, juxtaposing the worn-in, well-used feel with the dropped stitches.

Directions

Back
CO 116 (122, 134, 146, 158, 170) sts.

Work even in St st for 16 (16, 17, 17, 18, 18)", or until piece reaches desired length to armhole.

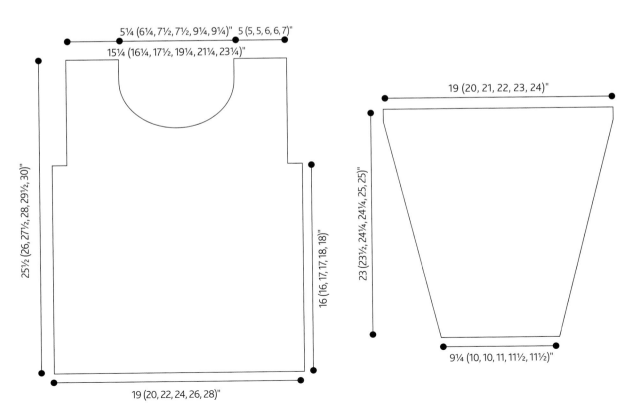

5¼ (6¼, 7½, 7½, 9¼, 9¼)"   5 (5, 5, 6, 6, 7)"

15¼ (16¼, 17½, 19¼, 21¼, 23¼)"

25½ (26, 27½, 28, 29½, 30)"

16 (16, 17, 17, 18, 18)"

19 (20, 22, 24, 26, 28)"

19 (20, 21, 22, 23, 24)"

23 (23½, 24¼, 24¼, 25, 25)"

9¼ (10, 10, 11, 11½, 11½)"

Armhole Shaping

Bind off 12 (12, 14, 14, 15, 15) sts at the beg of the next 2 rows. 92 (98, 106, 118, 128, 140) sts.

Work even in St st until armhole measures 9½ (10, 10½, 11, 11½, 12)". Bind off all sts.

Front

Work as for back through beg of armhole shaping. 92 (98, 106, 118, 128, 140) sts rem.

Work even in St st until armhole measures 5½ (6, 6½, 7, 7½, 8)", ending with a WS row.

Begin Neck Shaping

Next row (RS): K39 (42, 45, 51, 54, 60) sts, then slip these sts to a holder for left neck and shoulder.

Bind off 14 (14, 17, 17, 20, 20) sts, k39 (42, 44, 50, 54, 60) sts.

You will now work the right neck and shoulder only.

Next row (WS): Purl.

Next row (RS): Bind off 3 (3, 4, 4, 5, 5) sts at neck edge, knit to end of row.

Rep these 2 rows once more. 33 (36, 36, 42, 44, 50) sts.

Next row (WS): Purl.

Next row (RS): K1, ssk, knit to end of row.

Rep these 2 rows 4 (4, 6, 6, 8, 8) times more. 28 (31, 29, 35, 35, 41) sts.

Work even in St st until right armhole measures 9½ (10, 10½, 11, 11½, 12)".

Bind off rem sts.

Left Neck and Shoulder

Transfer the 39 (42, 44, 50, 54, 60) sts held for the left neck and shoulder to the working needles. Join the yarn at the neck edge.

Next row (WS): Bind off 3 (3, 4, 4, 5, 5) sts at neck edge, purl to end of row.

Next row (RS): Knit.

Rep these 2 rows once more. 33 (36, 36, 42, 44, 50) sts.

Purl 1 WS row.

Next row (RS): Knit to last 3 sts, k2tog, k1.

Next row (WS): Purl.

Rep these 2 rows 4 (4, 6, 6, 8, 8) times more. 28 (31, 29, 35, 35, 41) sts.

Work even in St st until left armhole measures 9½ (10, 10½, 11, 11½, 12)".

Bind off rem sts.

Sleeves (Make 2)

CO 56 (60, 60, 66, 68, 68) sts.

Work even in St st for 2", ending with a WS row.

Next row (Increase Row; RS): K1, M1, knit to last st, M1, k1.

Rep the Increase Row every sixth row 6 (7, 9, 9, 10, 11) more times. 70 (76, 80, 86, 90, 92) sts.

Then rep the Increase Row every 4th row 22 (22, 23, 23, 24, 26) times. 114 (120, 126, 132, 138, 144) sts.

Work even until piece is desired length to armhole or approximately 21 (21½, 22, 22, 22½, 22½)".

Mark each end for armhole placement and continue to knit even for 2 (2, 2.3, 2.3, 2½, 2½)".

Total sleeve length should be 23 (23½, 24.3, 24.3, 25, 25)".

Finishing

Block the pieces to the measurements given. Because the shoulder and armhole seams are exposed, the pieces should be held with RS facing and seamed with mattress stitch. The underarm and side seams are made with the WS facing, as usual for mattress-stitched seams.

Collar

Turn the garment inside out, and, using the circular needle, pick up and knit approximately 148 (156, 172, 172, 188, 188) sts around neck. The exact number of stitches isn't important, but a multiple of 4 is needed for the 2 × 2 ribbing. Picking the stitches up from the wrong side of the garment exposes the seam, just as seaming the pieces with the wrong sides facing does. It pays to take a little extra time here and pick these stitches up as neatly as possible, since this line will be exposed during wear.

Join in the round and work in k2, p2 rib for 2", then bind off all sts kwise.

Steam-block the collar.

Dropping Stitches

Using openable stitch markers, on the seamed, blocked, and completed garment, mark the desired beginning and ending points of all the runs you wish to add, keeping in mind typical areas of wear and potential damage points in a well-used sweater. I focused on the neckline, elbows, and the back shoulder areas.

Once you determine these points, cut 6" lengths of the same yarn used for the sweater to use as anchors. Very carefully, snip one stitch loop at *the top* of the dropped stitch, that is, where you want the runner to begin. Coax the dropped stitches all the way down to the desired ending point, and then, using the darning needle, thread one end of the anchor yarn through the loose stitch. Bring both tails of the anchor yarn to the back of the garment and simply weave in the ends as normal. This locks the loose stitch down and keeps it from running any further. Take the two loose ends from where you snipped to the wrong side, knot them firmly together, and weave in ends to secure the top of the run.

Apocalypta

Sizes

S (M, L, 1X, 2X)

Finished Measurements

Chest: 32 (36, 40, 44, 48)"

Materials

Berroco Seduce (100 yd./40g per skein); #4436 Rye; 7 (7, 9, 9, 11) skeins

U.S. 8 (5mm) circular needle, 24" or 32" length, *or size needed to obtain gauge*

U.S. 8 (5mm) circular needle or set of double-pointed needles for sleeves

Locking stitch markers or safety pins

Darning needle

Gauge

17 sts × 25 rows = 4" in St st

Pattern Notes

This pattern uses dropped stitches as styling accents in four places: Where side and sleeve seams would normally be, around the neckline, and for thumbholes in the sleeves. It is important to cast on (in the case of the side seams) and bind off (for the remainder) *very* loosely to accommodate the extra width of the dropped stitch.

This sweater is worked in the round from the bottom up; the front and back are divided at the armholes and worked separately. The sleeves are worked from the top down.

Directions

Body

CO 136 (154, 170, 188, 206) sts.

Join for working in the round, place side seam markers, and increase 2 sts as follows: K68 (77, 85, 94, 103) sts, pm, M1, pm, k68 (77, 85, 94, 103) sts, pm, M1, place end of round marker. 138 (156, 172, 190, 208) sts.

Work in St st for 2 (2, 2½, 2½, 3)".

Waist shaping set-up rnd: *K22 (25, 28, 31, 34) sts, place shaping marker, k24 (27, 29, 32, 35) sts, place shaping marker, k22 (25, 28, 31, 34) sts, knit marked side stitch, rep from *.

Decrease Round: *K to 2 sts before marker, ssk, knit to next marker and slip it, k2tog, knit to marked side stitch and knit it, rep from *. 4 sts decreased, 134 (152, 168, 186, 204) sts rem.

Work 3 rounds even.

Rep the last 4 rounds 6 times more; then rep the Decrease Round 1 additional time—32 sts decreased over 29 rounds. 106 (124, 140, 158, 174) sts rem.

Work 1½ (1½, 2, 2, 2)" even.

Increase Round: *Work to shaping marker, M1R, sm, k24 (27, 29, 32, 35) sts between markers, sm, M1L, knit to marked side stitch and knit it, rep from *. 4 sts increased, 110 (128, 144, 162, 178) sts.

Work 3 rounds even.

Rep these 4 rounds 6 times more, then rep the Increase Round once more: 32 sts increased over 29 rounds. 138 (156, 172, 190, 208) sts on the needle. Remove shaping markers, but keep side seam sts marked.

Work 1½" even—piece will measure approximately 14 (14, 15, 15, 15½)" in length.

The front and back will now be worked separately.

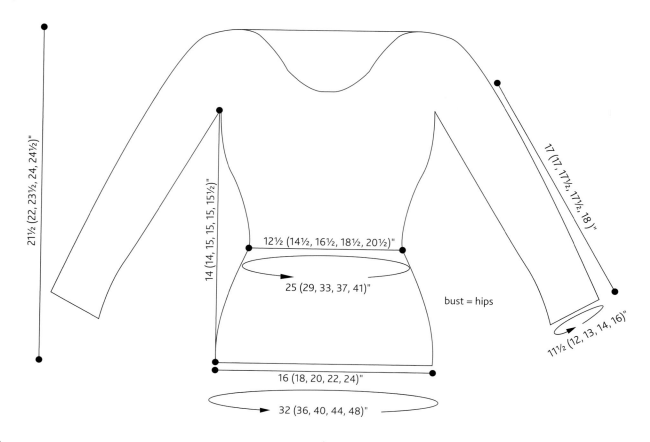

21½ (22, 23½, 24, 24½)"

14 (14, 15, 15, 15½)"

12½ (14½, 16½, 18½, 20½)"

25 (29, 33, 37, 41)"

17 (17, 17½, 17½, 18)"

bust = hips

11½ (12, 13, 14, 16)"

16 (18, 20, 22, 24)"

32 (36, 40, 44, 48)"

Back

Drop sts to form faux side seams as follows: Knit to marked side st and drop it from the needle, allowing the sts to run down to the cast-on edge; knit to second marked st and drop it from the needle.

Now divide the front and back. Bind off 4 (4, 4, 4, 5) sts, k64 (73, 81, 90, 98) sts to side seam.

Slip next 68 (77, 85, 94, 103) sts to holder for front and continue in St st on sts for back only.

Turn and begin working back and forth. Bind off 4 (4, 4, 4, 5) sts, purl to end of row. 60 (69, 77, 86, 93) sts rem for back.

Bind off 3 at the beginning of the following 2 rows. 54 (63, 71, 80, 87) sts rem.

Work 1 row even.

Next row (RS): K1, ssk, knit to last 2 sts, k2tog, k1.

Next row: Purl.

Rep these 2 rows 2 (2, 3, 3, 4) times more. 48 (57, 63, 72, 77) sts rem.

Continue working even until the back measures 7½ (8, 8½, 9, 9½)" from the beginning of armhole shaping.

Shape Shoulders

Bind off 6 (7, 8, 9, 10) sts at the beginning of the next 2 rows. 36 (43, 47, 54, 57) sts.

Bind off 5 (6, 7, 8, 9) sts at the beginning of the following 2 rows.

Bind off rem 26 (31, 33, 38, 39) sts.

Front

Return sts held for front to working needles and rejoin yarn with RS facing.

Bind off 4 (4, 4, 4, 5) sts at the beginning of the next 2 rows.

Bind off 3 at the beginning of the following 2 rows. 54 (63, 71, 80, 87) sts rem.

Work 1 row even.

Next row (RS): K1, ssk, knit to last 2 sts, k2tog, k1.

Next row: Purl.

Rep these 2 rows 2 (2, 3, 3, 4) times more. 48 (57, 63, 72, 77) sts rem.

Continue working even until the front measures 2½ (3, 3½, 4, 4½)" from the beginning of armhole shaping, ending with a WS row.

Over the next 10 rows, you will make and mark 4 sts that will be dropped before binding off to create the neck detailing.

The process of creating the sts is identical for each: Work until the proper placement, pm, M1, pm, work to end of row. If the sts to be dropped are lettered A, B, C, D from left to right, you will make them in the following order: C, A, D, B.

Next row (RS): K16 (19, 20, 25, 27) sts, pm, M1, pm, work to end of row.

Work 1 row even.

Next row (RS): K35 (41, 42, 48, 52) sts, pm, M1, pm, work to end of row.

Work 3 rows even.

Next row (RS): K14 (16, 18, 21, 23) sts, pm, M1, pm, work to end of row.

Work 1 row even.

Next row: K21 (26, 26, 33, 34) sts, pm, M1, pm, work to end of row.

Work even until the front measures 4½ (5, 5½, 6, 6½)" from the beginning of armhole shaping, ending with a WS row.

Shape Neck and Right Shoulder

Note: The marked sts (for dropping) should be ignored for the following counts. Bind off or decrease over the sts as appropriate, dropping them before you do so.

Next row (RS): K20 (23, 26, 29, 32) sts and place them on a holder for left shoulder, bind off 8 (11, 11, 14, 13) sts, and knit to end of row. Continue with RS of neck only.

Next and following WS rows: Purl.

Next row (RS): Bind off 2 (3, 3, 3, 4) sts at the beginning (neck edge) of the row, knit to end.

Next row (RS): Bind off 2 (2, 2, 3, 3) sts, knit to end of row.

Bind off 1 st at beginning of next and following 4 (4, 5, 5, 5) RS rows. 11 (13, 15, 17, 19) sts rem.

Work even until piece measures the same as back to the shoulder, ending with a RS row.

Next row (WS): Bind off 6 (7, 8, 9, 10) sts.

Next row (RS): Bind off rem 5 (6, 7, 8, 9) sts.

Left Shoulder

Return 20 (23, 26, 29, 32) sts held for left side of neck to needles and join yarn at neck edge with WS facing.

Next row (WS): Bind off 2 (3, 3, 3, 4) sts, purl to end of row.

Next and following RS rows: Knit.

Next row (WS): Bind off 2 (2, 2, 3, 3) sts, purl to end of row.

Bind off 1 st at neck edge of next and following 4 (4, 5, 5, 5) WS rows: 11 (13, 15, 17, 19) shoulder sts rem.

Work even until the piece measures the same as back to the shoulder, ending with a WS row.

Next row (RS): Bind off 6 (7, 8, 9, 10) sts.

Next row (WS): Bind off rem 5 (6, 7, 8, 9) sts.

Sleeves

Sleeves are worked from the shoulder down to the wrist, joining to be worked in the round after the sleeve cap is shaped. Both sleeves are alike to the thumbhole.

CO 10 (10, 10, 10, 12) sts.

Beginning with a knit row, work in St st and CO 3 sts at end of next 2 rows, then 2 sts at end of following 2 rows. 20 (20, 20, 20, 22) sts.

Increase 1 st at each end of the needle every row 0 (1, 0, 3, 4) times, then every third row 1 (2, 2, 1, 3) times, then every sixth row 3 (2, 3, 3, 3) times, then every third row 2 (2, 2, 2, 1) times, then every row 4 (4, 4, 6, 7, 7) times.

CO 4 (4, 4, 4, 5) sts at end of following 2 rows. The sleeve cap is completed, and there are 48 (50, 54, 60, 68) sts.

Join for working in the round and knit 2 rnds.

Next rnd: K48 (50, 54, 60, 68) sts, pm, M1, place round marker. The marked st should be opposite the middle of the top of the sleeve cap. This st will be dropped when the sleeve is completed, making a "seam" of dropped sts as on the sides of the sweater.

Work even until the sleeve measures 15½ (15½, 16, 16, 16½)" from join.

Right Sleeve

K12 (13, 14, 15, 17) sts, pm, M1, pm, work to end of round. 50 (52, 56, 62, 70) sts total, including 2 marked sts.

Work straight until the sleeve measures 17 (17, 17½, 17½, 18)" or desired length. Bind off loosely, dropping marked sts as you bind off, and binding off extremely loosely over the dropped sts.

Left Sleeve

K36 (38, 41, 45, 51) sts, pm, M1, pm, work to end of round. 50 (52, 56, 62, 70) sts total, including 2 marked sts.

Work even until the sleeve measures 17 (17, 17½, 17½, 18)" or desired length. Bind off loosely, dropping marked sts as you bind off, and binding off extremely loosely over the dropped sts.

Finishing

Sew shoulder seams.

Sew in sleeves, pinning center of top of sleeve cap to shoulder seam, and dropped stitch to dropped stitch to assist in easing the sleeve in.

Wet-block to finished measurements, and get yourself a pair of ultra-cool sunglasses.

Galileo

by Christy Varner

It's a fact, the guy in charge of
the crew always gets the most
handsome uniform. Galileo is
our version of a fleet com-
mander's sweater from classic
sci-fi movies of the 1950s.
Colors always signify rank, so
we chose a simple putty color
for the main body and paired it
with blue so everyone would
know who to salute. A manly
shawl collar adds an air of cozy
confidence that will have the
Martians retreating in no time.

Sizes

S (M, L, XL, XXL)

Finished Measurements

Chest: 38 (42, 46, 50, 54)"

Materials

Berocco Pure Merino (100% merino wool; 92 yd./50g per skein)

MC: #8503 Barley; 13 (13, 15, 17, 19) skeins

CC: #8565 New Navy; 5 (5, 6, 6, 7) skeins

U.S. 8 (5mm) circular needle, 32" length, *or size needed to match gauge*

U.S. 6 (4mm) circular needle, 24" length

U.S. 7 (4.5mm) circular needle, 24" length

U.S. 8 (5mm) circular needle, 24" length

Stitch markers

Darning needle

Gauge

18 sts × 24 rows = 4" in St st

Special Stitches and Terms

Jogless join: When you switch from CC to MC on the body, you will want to do a jogless join. To do this, join MC and knit 1 row. Begin the next row by lifting the back of the stitch below the first stitch on the left needle up onto the left needle without twisting it. Knit this stitch together with the first stitch on the needle.

Pattern Notes

This sweater is knit in the round up to the armscye. Then the front and back are knit separately.

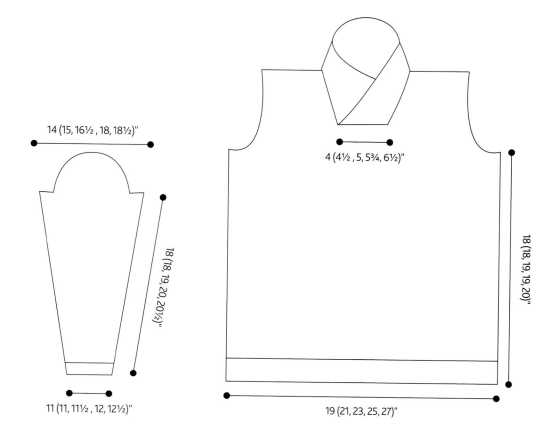

14 (15, 16½ , 18, 18½)"

4 (4½ , 5, 5¾, 6½)"

18 (18, 19, 20, 20½)"

18 (18, 19, 20)"

11 (11, 11½ , 12, 12½)"

19 (21, 23, 25, 27)"

Directions

Body

Using CC and longer size 8 needles, CO 154 (170, 186, 202, 218) sts.

Place marker and join in the round.

Knit 7 rows.

Next rnd (Increase Round): 16 (18, 20, 22, 24) sts evenly spaced around. 170 (188, 206, 224, 242) sts. This round creates the hem turn.

K85 (94, 103, 112, 121) sts, place second marker to indicate left side seam.

Knit 10 rows.

Join MC using jogless join and cut CC.

Work even until sweater measures 19½ (19½, 20½, 20½, 21½)" from cast-on edge and 18 (18, 19, 19, 20)" from hem turn.

Front

Bind off 3 (4, 4, 6, 6) sts, knit to marker. Turn. You will work back and forth on the sts for the front only. Place 85 (94, 103, 112, 121) back sts on holder or scrap yarn.

Next row (WS): Bind off 3 (4, 4, 6, 6) sts, purl to end of row. 79 (86, 95, 100, 109) sts.

Bind off 2 (2, 3, 2, 2) sts at beg of next 2 rows. 75 (82, 89, 96, 105) sts.

Next row (RS): K1, ssk, knit to last 3 sts, k2tog, k1.

Next row (WS): Purl across.

Rep these 2 rows 1 (2, 2, 2, 3) more times.

For size S only: Work 2 rows even. 71 (76, 83, 90, 97) sts.

Begin Neck Shaping

Next row (RS): K27 (28, 30, 32, 34) sts and place these sts on holder for left shoulder, bind off 17 (20, 23, 26, 29) sts, k27 (28, 30, 32, 34) sts.

Right Neck and Shoulder

Beginning with a WS row, work 5 (5, 7, 7, 7) rows in St st.

Next row (RS): K1, ssk, knit to end.

Work 9 (9, 11, 11, 13) rows even.

Rep these 10 (10, 12, 12, 14) rows 3 more times. 23 (24, 26, 28, 30) sts.

Continue in St st until 8½ (8, 8½, 9, 9)" from beginning of neck shaping.

Place sts on holder or scrap yarn and cut yarn, leaving a 12" tail.

Left Neck and Shoulder

Transfer held sts for left neck to working needles. Reattach yarn at neck edge and purl across.

Work 4 (4, 6, 6, 6) rows in St st.

Next row (RS): Knit to last 3 sts, k2tog, k1.

Work 9 (9, 11, 11, 13) rows even.

Rep these 10 (10, 12, 12, 14) rows 3 more times. 23 (24, 26, 28, 30) sts rem.

Continue in St st until 8½ (8, 8½, 9, 9)" from beginning of neck shaping.

Place sts on holder or scrap yarn and cut yarn, leaving a 12" tail.

Back

Transfer sts held for back to working needles.

Begin Armhole Shaping

With RS facing, attach yarn.

Bind off 3 (4, 4, 6, 6) sts at beg of next 2 rows.

Bind off 2 (2, 3, 2, 2) sts at beg of next 2 rows. 75 (82, 89, 96, 105) sts.

Next row (RS): K1, ssk, knit to last 3 sts, k2tog, k1.

Next row (WS): Purl across.

Rep these 2 rows 1 (2, 2, 2, 3) more times. 71 (76, 83, 90, 97) sts. Mark this row with a safety pin or detachable marker.

Work even until back measures 8 (7½, 8, 8½, 8½)" from this marked row.

Begin Neck Shaping

K26 (27, 29, 31, 33) sts, place the rem 45 (49, 54, 59, 64) sts on holder or scrap yarn.

Right Neck and Shoulder

Continue working the 26 (27, 29, 31, 33) sts on needles as follows:

Next row (WS): Bind off 2 sts, purl across.

Next row (RS): Knit.

Next row: Bind off 1 st, purl across.

Place remaining 23 (24, 26, 28, 30) sts on holder or scrap yarn, and cut yarn.

Left Neck and Shoulder

Transfer 26 (27, 29, 31, 33) sts from left side to needles. You will leave the middle 19 (22, 25, 28, 31) sts on holder for neck.

With WS facing, attach yarn and purl across.

Next row (RS): Bind off 2 sts, knit across.

Next row (WS): Purl.

Next row: Bind off 1 st, knit across.

Next row: Purl. 23 (24, 26, 28, 30) sts.

Use three-needle bind-off to attach front and back shoulders.

Sleeves (Make 2)

Using size needles and CC, CO 45 (45, 47, 48, 50) sts.

Work 7 rows in St st (starting with a WS row).

Next row (Increase Row; RS): 5 (5, 5, 6, 6) sts evenly spaced around. 50 (50, 52, 54, 56) sts.

Work 9 rows even in St st.

Join MC and cut CC.

Work 4 rows in St st.

Next row (RS): K2, M1, knit to last 2 sts, M1, k2.

Work 11 (9, 9, 7, 7) rows even.

Rep these 12 (10, 10, 8, 8) rows 6 (8, 10, 12, 13) more times. 64 (68, 74, 80, 84) sts.

Work even until the sleeve measures 19½ (19½, 20½, 21½, 22)" from cast-on edge and 18 (18, 19, 20, 20½)" from hem turn, ending with a WS row.

Shape Sleeve Cap

Bind off 5 (6, 7, 8, 8) sts at beg of next 2 rows. 54 (56, 60, 64, 68) sts.

Next row (RS): K1, ssk, knit to last 3 sts, k2tog, k1.

Next row: Purl.

Rep these 2 rows 14 (15, 16, 17, 18) more times. 24 (24, 26, 28, 30) sts.

Bind off 2 sts at beg of next 6 rows.

Bind off rem 12 (12, 14, 16, 18) sts.

Rep for second sleeve.

Collar

With the RS facing, using U.S. 6 needles and CC, beg at the bottom of the right side of the front neck, pick up and knit 38 (39, 41, 43, 44) sts to the sts held for the back neck, knit across the 19 (22, 25, 29, 31) neck sts on holder, pick up and knit 38 (39, 41, 43, 44) sts on left side of neck. 95 (100, 107, 115, 119) sts. You will not pick up sts along the bottom of the neck. Do not join.

Work back and forth in k1, p1 rib for 1 (1½, 1½, 1½, 1½)".

Switch to size 7 needles, continue in patt for 1½ (1½, 1½, 2¼, 2½)".

Switch to size 8 needles, continue in patt until collar measures a total of 4 (4½, 5, 5¾, 6½)" from the picked-up edge.

Bind off using a tubular bind-off.

Finishing

Sew sleeve seams. Ease sleeves into armscyes and sew into place.

Sew bottom of collar to neck opening, overlapping the ends as shown.

Turn up hems on sleeves and body, and attach using whipstitch.

Not An Extra

by Julia Vesper

Just got a sweet gig on an exploratory spaceship? Let's hope you're not the new guy and gal on the away mission. Let them know that you're Not An Extra with these matching his and hers crew sweaters. Both sweaters have a coordinated two-tone color combination for that clean fleet-uniform look without looking like you're straight out of the Academy. Stand-up V-shaped collars and an easy fit make these sweaters a comfortable, fun choice for everyday wear. The men's version has long sleeves, and the ladies' version has three-quarter-length sleeves.

He's Not An Extra

Sizes

S (M, L, XL, XXL)

Finished Measurements

Chest: 36 (40, 44, 48, 52)"

Materials

Plymouth Yarns Galway (100% wool; 210 yd./100g per skein)

MC: #116 Bright Blue; 4 (5, 5, 6, 6) skeins

CC: #66 Dark Brown; 3 (3, 3, 4, 4) skeins

U.S. 7 (4.5mm) circular needle, 32" length, *or size needed to match gauge*

U.S. 7 (4.5mm) double-pointed needles, or 16" circular needle

U.S. 5 (3.75mm) circular needle

U.S. 5 (3.75mm) double-pointed needles, or 16" circular needle

Stitch marker

Darning needle

Length of scrap yarn or stitch holders

Gauge

20 sts × 26 rows = 4" in St st on larger needles

Special Stitches and Terms

Wrap and turn (w&t): see page 47.

Pattern Notes

The body of this sweater is worked in the round from the bottom up, then divided for the top front and back, and the top of each piece is worked flat. Stitches are picked up around the armholes, and the sleeve cap is worked back and forth using short rows to create a set-in-sleeve cap. The sleeve is then worked in the round to the cuff.

The only seams sewn are the shoulder seams.

To finish, stitches are picked up along each side of the neck edge, and an attached I-cord is worked.

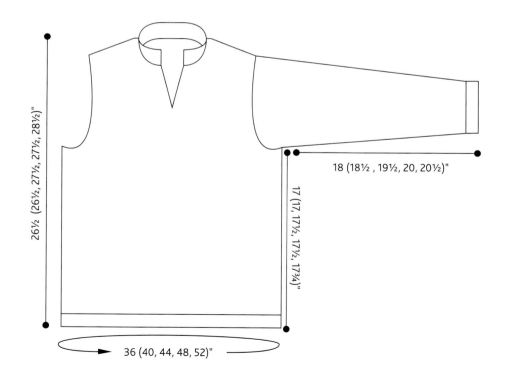

26½ (26½, 27½, 27½, 28½)"

18 (18½ , 19½, 20, 20½)"

17 (17, 17½, 17½, 17¾)"

36 (40, 44, 48, 52)"

Directions

Body

With smaller 32" circular needle and CC, CO 180 (202, 222, 240, 258) sts.

Work in k3, p3 rib for 2".

Switch to larger 32" circular needle and MC.

Next rnd: *P1, k89 (100, 110, 119, 128) sts, pm, rep from * once more.

Rep this round for 3½"; the column of purl sts up each side creates a "seam" along each side.

Discontinue the purl "seam" and work in St st until the sweater measures 17 (17, 17½, 17½, 17¾)" from cast-on edge, or desired length to underarm.

Divide Front and Back for Armholes

Next rnd: K88 (99, 109, 118, 127) sts, bind off 3 sts for underarm, k86 (97, 107, 116, 125) sts and place these sts on a holder for the front, bind off 3 sts for underarm.

Back

Next row (Decrease Row; RS): K2, ssk, knit to last 2 sts, k2tog, k2.

Rep this Decrease Row every RS row 3 times more. 80 (91, 101, 110, 119) sts.

Continue in St st until piece measures 4½" from beg of armhole. Cut MC, and join in CC. Continue in St st for a further 4 (4, 4½, 4½, 5)", ending with a WS row.

Begin Short Row Shoulder Shaping

Set-up row: Knit across 27 (31, 34, 37, 40) sts, pm, k26 (29, 33, 36, 39) sts, pm, k27 (31, 34, 37, 40) sts.

Next row: P20 (25, 28, 31, 34) sts, w&t; knit back to end.

Next row: P15 (20, 23, 26, 29) sts, w&t; knit back to end.

Next row: P10 (15, 18, 21, 24) sts, w&t; knit back to end.

Next row: P5 (10, 13, 16, 19) sts, w&t; knit back to end.

Next row: P0 (5, 8, 11, 14) sts, w&t; knit back to end.

Next row: P0 (0, 3, 6, 9) sts, w&t; knit back to end.

Next row: P0 (0, 0, 0, 9) sts, w&t; knit back to end.

Next row: Purl across all sts, picking up and purling the wraps together with the sts they wrap.

Next row: Bind off these 27 (31, 34, 37, 40) sts.

Place center 26 (29, 33, 36, 39) sts on holder.

Rejoin yarn to rem sts at armhole edge, ready to begin a RS row.

Next row: K20 (25, 28, 31, 34) sts, w&t; purl back to end.

Next row: K15 (20, 23, 26, 29) sts, w&t; purl back to end.

Next row: K10 (15, 18, 21, 24) sts, w&t; purl back to end.

Next row: K5 (10, 13, 16, 19) sts, w&t; purl back to end.

Next row: K0 (5, 8, 11, 14) sts, w&t; purl back to end.

Next row: K0 (0, 3, 6, 9) sts, w&t, purl back to end.

Next row: K0 (0, 0, 0, 9) sts, w&t, purl back to end.

Next row: Knit across all sts, picking up and knitting the wrap together with the sts they wrap.

Next row: Bind off these 27 (31, 34, 37, 40) sts.

Front

Transfer the 86 (97, 107, 116, 125) sts held for front onto needles.

Join the yarn at the right edge with RS facing.

Next row (Decrease Row; RS): K2, ssk, knit to last 2 sts, k2tog, k2.

Rep this Decrease Row every RS row 2 times more. 80 (91, 101, 110, 119) sts.

When piece measures 4½" from beg of armhole, break MC, join CC, and continue in St st.

When piece measure 5" from beg of armhole, ending with a WS row, divide for neck shaping as follows:

Next row: K39 (44, 49, 53, 57) sts, transfer these sts to a holder, bind off 2 (3, 3, 4, 5) sts, knit to end of row.

Right Front

Next row: Purl to last 3 sts, p2tog tbl, p1.

Work 2 rows even.

Next row: K1, ssk, knit to end of row.

Work 2 rows even.

Next row: Purl to last 3 sts, p2tog tbl, p1. 36 (41, 46, 50, 54) sts.

Continue in St st until the neck opening measures 2" ending with a WS row.

Next row (RS): Bind off 5 (5, 6, 7, 7) sts, knit to end of row.

Next row (WS): Purl.

Next row (RS): K1, ssk, knit to end of row.

Rep the last row every RS row 3 (4, 5, 6, 7) times. 27 (31, 34, 37, 40) sts.

Work even until piece measures 8½ (8½, 9, 9, 9½)" from beg of armhole, ending with a WS row.

Shape Shoulder

Next row: K20 (25, 28, 31, 34) sts, w&t, purl back to end.

Next row: K15 (20, 23, 26, 29) sts, w&t, purl back to end.

Next row: K10 (15, 18, 21, 24) sts, w&t, purl back to end.

Next row: K5 (10, 13, 16, 19) sts, w&t, purl back to end.

Next row: K0 (5, 8, 11, 14) sts, w&t, purl back to end.

Next row: K0 (0, 3, 6, 9) sts, w&t, purl back to end.

Next row: K0 (0, 0, 0, 9) sts, w&t, purl back to end.

Next row: Knit across all sts, picking up and knitting wraps as you go.

Next row: Bind off these 27 (31, 34, 37, 40) sts.

Left Front

Transfer the 39 (44, 49, 53, 57) sts held for left front onto needles. With WS facing, attach yarn at neck edge.

Next row: P1, p2tog, purl to end of row.

Work 2 rows even.

Next row: Knit to last 3 sts, k2tog, k1.

Work 2 rows even.

Next row: P1, p2tog, purl to end of row. 36 (41, 46, 50, 54) sts.

Continue in St st until neck opening measures 2", ending with a RS row.

Next row (WS): Bind off 5 (5, 6, 7, 7) sts, purl to end of row.

Next row (RS): Knit to last 3 sts, k2tog, k1.

Rep the last row every RS row 3 (4, 5, 6, 7) times. 27 (31, 34, 37, 40) sts.

Work even until piece measures 8½ (8½, 9, 9, 9½)" from beg of armhole, ending with a RS row.

Shape Shoulder

Next row: P20 (25, 28, 31, 34) sts, w&t, knit to end of row.

Next row: P15 (20, 23, 26, 29) sts, w&t, knit to end of row.

Next row: P10 (15, 18, 21, 24) sts, w&t, knit to end of row.

Next row: P5 (10, 13, 16, 19) sts, w&t, knit to end of row.

Next row: P0 (5, 8, 11, 14) sts, w&t, knit to end of row.

Next row: P0 (0, 3, 6, 9) sts, w&t, knit to end of row.

Next row: P0 (0, 0, 0, 9) sts, w&t, knit to end of row.

Next row: Purl across all sts, picking up and purling wraps as you go.

Next row: Bind off these 27 (31, 34, 37, 40) sts.

Sleeves

Sew shoulder seams.

Pick up sts for sleeve cap as follows:

With MC and larger 16" needles, begin at center of underarm. Pick up 4 sts over underarm shaping; pick up and knit 15 sts in MC, switch to CC as it is reached, using a short length of CC yarn, pick up and knit 13 (13, 15, 15, 16) sts. Place marker at shoulder seam. Pick up and knit 13 (13, 15, 15, 16) sts more in CC, switch to MC as it is reached, using a short length of MC, pick up and knit 15 sts, then 4 sts more over underarm shaping. 64 (64, 68, 68, 70) sts.

At center of underarm, pm, and using the same short length of MC, knit to CC join.

With CC, k11 sts past center shoulder marker. Remove shoulder marker. Turn work.

Next row: P22 sts. Turn.

Next row: K23 sts. Turn.

Continue in this way, working 1 more st than previous row, until 5 sts rem on either side of center underarm marker, switching from CC to MC as it is reached.

On the next RS row, knit all sts and begin working in the round.

Work for 2" in St st.

Then decrease as follows:

Next rnd: K1, k2tog, knit to 3 sts before underarm marker, ssk, k1.

Rep this round every ninth round 4 (4, 4, 5, 5) times, and then every seventh round 6 times. 42 (42, 48, 48, 48) sts.

Knit 12 rounds more.

Switch to smaller needles and CC. Knit 1 round.

Work in k3, p3 rib for 16 rounds.

Bind off.

Rep for second sleeve.

Finishing
Collar

With smaller needle and CC, begin at second bind off on the right front neck and pick up and knit 5 (5, 6, 7, 7) sts from the bound-off edge and 8 (9, 11, 13, 15) sts up right side of neck, knit the 26 (29, 33, 36, 39) sts held from back neck, then pick up and knit 8 (9, 11, 13, 15) sts from left side of neck and 5 (5, 6, 7, 7) sts from bound-off left front neck sts. 52 (57, 67, 76, 83) sts.

Next row (WS): Purl.

Continue working in St st for 2", ending with a WS row.

Next row (RS): Purl across to create turning ridge.

Next row (WS): Purl.

Continue in St st until collar measures 4" from where you picked up sts. Bind off loosely.

Sew bound-off edge to picked-up edge.

Neck Edging

The sides of the neck slit are finished with attached I-cord.

With larger needles and CC, begin at bottom of neck slit and pick up and k3 sts for every 4 rows of knitting up right side of neck edge. Continue to the top of the collar. Break yarn.

Begin I-Cord

With larger dpn and CC, cast on 3 sts. *Do not turn. Slide sts to opposite end of needle, bring working yarn snugly across the back, k2, ssk using last st from dpn and 1 st from the picked-up sts of edging. Rep from * until all the picked-up sts have been worked. Bind off.

Rep for left side.

Sew center neck edges of I-cords to center of neck.

Weave in all ends. Block if desired.

She's Not An Extra

Sizes

S (M, L, 1X, 2X)

Finished Measurements

Chest: 34 (38, 42, 46, 48)"

Materials

Plymouth Yarns Galway (100% wool; 210 yd./100g per skein)

MC: #107 Salmon; 4 (4, 5, 5, 6) skeins

CC: #152 Light Brown; 2 (2, 2, 3, 3) skeins

U.S. 7 (4.5mm) circular needle, 32" length, *or size needed to* match gauge

U.S. 7 (4.5mm) double-pointed needles, or 16" circular needle

U.S. 5 (3.75mm) circular needle, 32" length

U.S. 5 (3.75mm) double-pointed needles, or 16" circular needle

Stitch marker

Darning needle

Length of scrap yarn or stitch holders

Gauge

20 sts × 26 rows = 4" in St st on larger needles

Special Stitches and Terms

Wrap and turn (w&t): see page 47.

Pattern Notes

The body of this sweater is worked in the round from the bottom up, and then divided for the front and back, which are worked flat. Stitches are picked up around the armholes, and the sleeve cap is worked back and forth using short rows to create a set-in-sleeve cap. The sleeve is then worked in the round to the cuff.

The only seams sewn are the shoulder seams.

Stitches are picked up along each side of the neck edge, and an attached I-cord is worked.

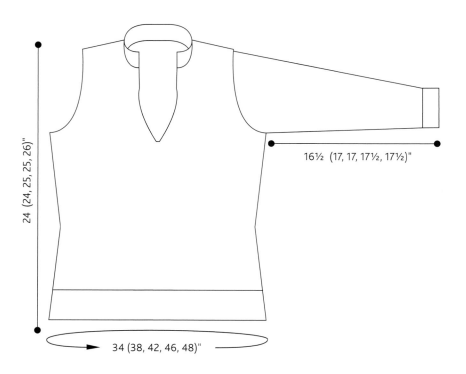

24 (24, 25, 25, 26)"

16½ (17, 17, 17½, 17½)"

34 (38, 42, 46, 48)"

Directions

Body

With smaller 32" circular needle and CC, cast on 162 (186, 204, 222, 242) sts.

Work in k3, p3 rib until piece measures 2" from beg.

Switch to larger 32" circular needle and MC.

Dec 0 (4, 2, 0, 0) sts around. 162 (182, 202, 222, 242) sts.

Row 1: *P1, k80 (90, 100, 110, 120) sts, pm, rep from * once more.

Rep this round until the piece measures 4" from the cast-on edge. The purl st creates a "seam" along each side of the body piece.

Begin Waist Shaping

Next rnd (Decrease Round): *Sm, p1, k1, k2tog, knit to 3 sts before marker, ssk, k1, rep from * once more.

Rep Decrease Round every eighth round twice more. 150 (170, 190, 210, 230) sts.

Work 12 rows even.

Next rnd (Increase Round): *Sm, p1, k1, M1, knit to 2 sts before marker, M1, k1. Rep from * once more.

Rep Increase Round every tenth round 4 more times. 170 (190, 210, 230, 250) sts.

Work even until piece measures 14½ (14½, 15, 15, 15½)" from cast-on edge.

Divide for Front Neckline

Next rnd: Sm, p1, k41 (46, 51, 56, 61) sts, bind off 3 sts, k41 (46, 51, 56, 61) sts, sm, p1, knit to end of round. 83 (93, 103, 113, 123) sts for front, 84 (94, 104, 114, 124) sts for back, 167 (187, 207, 227, 247) sts total.

Next row: Turn. Work sts as they appear to bound-off sts for neck.

Next row: K2, ssk, knit to side "seam" and purl that st, knit across to second seam and purl that st, knit to last 4 sts, k2tog, k2.

Work 1 row even.

Rep the last 2 rows once more. 78 (90, 98, 108, 118) sts total across front.

Divide Front and Back

Next row (RS): K38 (44, 48, 53, 58) sts and place these sts on a holder, bind off 3 sts for underarm, k82 (92, 102, 112, 122) sts, bind off 3 sts for underarm, knit across rem front sts and place them on a holder for later.

With RS facing, attach yarn to back and shape armholes as follows:

Next row (RS): K2, ssk, knit to last 4 sts, k2tog, k2.

Rep this row every RS row twice more. 76 (86, 96, 106, 116) sts.

Continue even in St st until piece measures 4" from beg of armhole. Cut MC, and join CC. Continue in St st until piece measures 7 (7, 7½, 7½, 8)" from beg of armhole, ending with a WS row.

Begin Short Row Shoulder Shaping

Set-up row: K26 (29, 32, 36, 39) sts, pm, k24 (28, 32, 34, 38) sts, pm, k26 (29, 32, 36, 39) sts.

Next row: P21 (24, 27, 31, 34) sts, w&t, knit to end.

Next row: P16 (19, 22, 26, 29) sts, w&t, knit to end.

Next row: P11 (14, 17, 21, 24) sts, w&t, knit to end.

Next row: P6 (9, 12, 16, 19) sts, w&t, knit to end.

Next row: P0 (4, 7, 11, 14) sts, w&t, knit to end.

Next row: P0 (0, 0, 6, 9) sts, w&t, knit to end.

Next row: P0 (0, 0, 0, 9) sts, w&t, knit to end.

Next row: Purl across all sts, picking up wraps and purling them together with the sts they wrap as you go.

Next row: Bind off these 26 (29, 32, 36, 39) sts.

Put center 24 (28, 32, 34, 38) sts on holder.

Rejoin yarn to rem 26 (29, 32, 36, 39) sts at armhole edge.

Next row: K21 (24, 27, 31, 34) sts, w&t, purl to end.

Next row: K16 (19, 22, 26, 29) sts, w&t, purl to end.

Next row: K11 (14, 17, 21, 24) sts, w&t, purl to end.

Next row: K6 (9, 12, 16, 19) sts, w&t, purl to end.

Next row: K0 (4, 7, 11, 14) sts, w&t, purl to end.

Next row: K0 (0, 0, 6, 9) sts, w&t, purl to end.

Next row: K0 (0, 0, 0, 9) sts, w&t, purl to end.

Next row: Knit across all sts, picking up and knitting wraps together with the sts they wrap as you go.

Next row: Bind off these 26 (29, 32, 36, 39) sts.

Right Front

When the front measures 4" from beg of armhole shaping, switch to CC. *At the same time*, shape the neckline as follows:

Transfer 38 (44, 48, 53, 58) sts for right front from holder back onto needles. Join yarn at neck edge.

Armhole Decrease Row (RS): Knit to last 4 sts, k2tog, k2.

Work 1 row even.

Rep these 2 rows twice more. 35 (41, 45, 50, 55) sts.

Work 4 rows even.

Neck Decrease Row (RS): K1, ssk, knit to end of row.

Work 9 rows even.

Rep these 10 rows once more, and then rep the neck decrease row once.

Work 1 row even.

Next row (RS): Bind off 5 (5, 6, 6, 7) sts for neck, knit to end of row.

Work 1 row even.

Next row (RS): K1, ssk, knit to end of row.

Rep this row every RS row 0 (4, 4, 5, 6) times. 26 (29, 32, 36, 39) sts.

Work even until piece measures 7 (7, 7½, 7½, 8)" from beg of armhole, ending with a RS row.

Shape Shoulder

Next row: P21 (24, 27, 31, 34) sts, w&t, knit to end.

Next row: P16 (19, 22, 26, 29) sts, w&t, knit to end.

Next row: P11 (14, 17, 21, 24) sts, w&t, knit to end.

Next row: P6 (9, 12, 16, 19) sts, w&t, knit to end.

Next row: P0 (4, 7, 11, 14) sts, w&t, knit to end.

Next row: P0 (0, 0, 6, 9) sts, w&t, knit to end.

Next row: P0 (0, 0, 0, 9) sts, w&t, knit to end.

Next row: Purl across all sts, picking up and purling wraps as you go.

Next row: Bind off these 26 (29, 32, 36, 39) sts.

Left Front

When the front measures 4" from beg of armhole shaping, switch to CC. *At the same time,* shape the armhole and neckline as follows:

Transfer 38 (44, 48, 53, 58) sts for left front from holder back onto needles. Join yarn at the armhole edge.

Armhole Decrease Row (RS): K2, ssk, knit to end of row.

Work 1 row even.

Rep these 2 rows twice more. 35 (41, 45, 50, 55) sts.

Work 4 rows even.

Neck Decrease Row (RS): Knit to last 3 sts, k2tog, k1.

Work 9 rows even.

Rep these 10 rows once more, then rep the Neck Decrease Row once. Work 2 rows even.

Next row (WS): Bind off 5 (5, 6, 6, 7) sts for neck, purl to end of row.

Next row (RS): Knit to last 3 sts, k2tog, k1.

Rep this row every RS row 0 (4, 4, 5, 6) times. 26 (29, 32, 36, 39) sts.

Work even until piece measures 7 (7, 7½, 7½, 8)" from beg of armhole, ending with a WS row.

Shape Shoulder

Next row: K21 (24, 27, 31, 34) sts, w&t, purl to end.

Next row: K16 (19, 22, 26, 29) sts, w&t, purl to end.

Next row: K11 (14, 17, 21, 24) sts, w&t, purl to end.

Next row: K6 (9, 12, 16, 19) sts, w&t, purl to end.

Next row: K0 (4, 7, 11, 14) sts, w&t, purl to end.

Next row: K0 (0, 0, 6, 9) sts, w&t, purl to end.

Next row: K0 (0, 0, 0, 9) sts, w&t, purl to end.

Next row: Knit across all sts, picking up and knitting wraps as you go.

Next row: Bind off these 26 (29, 32, 36, 39) sts.

Sleeves

Sew shoulder seams.

Pick up sts for sleeve cap as follows:

With MC and larger 16" needles, begin at center of underarm. Pick up and k4 sts from underarm shaping. Pick up and knit 14 sts in MC, switch to a small length of CC and pick up and knit 11 (11, 12, 12, 13) sts. Place a marker at the shoulder seam. Pick up and knit 11 (11, 12, 12, 13) sts more with CC, switch to a short length of MC and pick up and knit 14 sts and 4 sts more at underarm shaping. 58 (58, 60, 60, 62) sts.

Place marker at center of underarm, and, using the same short length of MC, k18.

Join CC, and knit to 9 sts past center shoulder marker. Remove shoulder marker. Turn work.

Next row: P18; turn work.

Next row: K19; turn work.

Continue in this way, working 1 more st than previous row, until 4 sts rem on either side of center underarm marker, switching from CC to MC as it is reached. End with a WS row.

Next row (RS): Knit all sts and begin knitting in the round.

Work for 2" in St st.

Next rnd (Decrease Round): K1, k2tog, knit to 3 sts before marker, ssk, k1.

Work Decrease Round every 14 (15, 15, 16, 16) rnds 7 (7, 8, 8, 9) times more. 42 sts rem.

Knit 3 rnds more.

Switch to smaller needles and CC. Knit 1 round.

Work in k3, p3 rib for 13 rnds.

Bind off.

Rep for second sleeve.

Finishing
Collar

With smaller needle and CC, begin at the right front of the neck and pick up and knit 5 (5, 6, 6, 7) sts from the bound-off edge, 15 sts up right side of neck, k24 (28, 32, 34, 38) sts from holder for back neck, pick up and knit 15 sts down left side of neck, and k5 (5, 6, 6, 7) sts from left neck cast-off. 60 (64, 74, 76, 86) sts.

Next row (WS): Purl.

Continue working in St st for 2", ending with a WS row.

Next row (RS): Purl across to create turning ridge.

Next row (WS): Purl.

Continue in St st until collar measures 4" from where you picked up sts.

Bind off loosely.

Sew bound-off edge to picked-up edge.

Neck Edging

The sides of the neck slit are finished with attached I-cord.

With larger needles and MC, begin at the bottom of the neck slit and pick up and knit 3 sts for every 4 rows of knitting up right side of neck edge, switching to CC as it is reached. Continue to the top of the collar. Break yarn.

Begin I-Cord

With larger dpn and MC, cast on 3 sts. *Do not turn. Slide sts to opposite end of needle, bring working yarn snugly across the back, k2, ssk using last st from the dpn and 1 st from the picked-up sts of edging. Rep from * until all the picked-up sts have been worked. Bind off.

Rep for left side.

Sew center neck edges of I-cords to center of neck.

Weave in all ends. Block if desired.

Hello World

by Christy Varner

Are spy rays penetrating your brain and reading your thoughts? No worries. Deflect those rays in style and comfort with our Hello World hat, complete with coded message for those in the know.

Size

One size fits most adults

Finished Measurements

Circumference: 20"

Height: 7½"

Materials

Pigeonroof Studios Siren Two Sport (80% superwash merino wool, 10% cashmere, 10% nylon)

MC: Indigo Ink; 1 skein

CC1: Green Ochre; 1 skein

CC2: Smoulder; 1 skein

U.S. 4 (3.5mm) circular needle, 16" length

U.S. E-4 (3.5mm) crochet hook for provisional cast-on

Stitch markers

Darning needle

Gauge

22 sts × 32 rows = 4" in St st

24 sts × 30 rows = 4" in colorwork

Special Stitch and Terms

Provisional cast-on: see page 172.

Pattern Notes

This hat uses small amounts of the two contrasting colors. You will need approximately 30 yards of CC1 and 10 yards of CC2.

On Rnd 4 of the chart on page 157, knit the round plain with MC. The stitches in CC1 should be worked later in duplicate stitch.

This hat is meant to fit 22–23" heads snugly. If you would like to make a looser-fitting hat, work 1 × 1 rib (without decreasing) instead of 3 × 1 rib over the last 2 rounds of the brim, and finish with a tubular bind-off.

Directions

Brim

With MC and your favorite provisional cast-on, CO 120 sts.

Place marker and join in the round.

Begin working from chart, beginning with Rnd 1.

Work through all 14 rows of the chart (see Pattern Note about Rnd 4).

Knit 1 round with MC.

Next rnd: [(k3, p1) twice, k3, p2tog] 7 times, (k3, p1) 4 times—112 sts.

Next rnd: Work in k3, p1 rib.

Bind off in pattern.

Hat

Turn the brim WS out, so that the color work floats are facing the outside.

Transfer the sts from your provisional cast-on to the working needle—120 sts.

Attach MC and knit 1 round.

Next rnd: [K8, k2tog] around. 108 sts.

Next rnd: [K3, p1] around.

Continue in k3, p1 rib until the hat measures 5½" from the brim fold.

Next rnd: *K3, p1, k3, p1, k1, k2tog, p1, rep from * to end of round—99 sts.

Work sts as they appear for 5 rounds.

Next rnd: *K3, p1, ssk, k1, p1, k2, p1, rep from * to end of round—90 sts.

Work sts as they appear for 2 rounds.

Next rnd: *K1, k2tog, p1, k2, p1, k2, p1, rep from * to end of round—81 sts.

Work sts as they appear for 1 round.

Next rnd: *K2, p1, ssk, p1, k2tog, p1, rep from * to end of round—63 sts.

Work sts as they appear for 1 round.

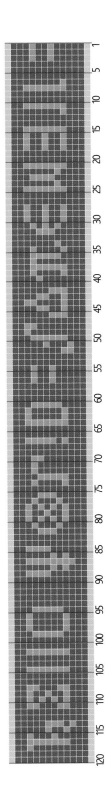

Next rnd: *K2tog, p1, s2kp, p1, rep from * to last st, ending round with s2kp. This is the new end of round. Move marker to this position—36 sts.

Next rnd: K2tog, p1, k1, rep from * to last st, ending round with p1. This is the new end of round. Move marker to this position—27 sts.

Next rnd: Sk2p around—9 sts.

Cut tail and draw through rem sts; pull gently to tighten and secure end.

Finishing
Using tapestry needle and CC2, duplicate st Rnd 4 of chart.

Fold brim up at cast-on edge and tack in place if desired.

Intergalactic Pals

by Paola Navarro

Looking for some intergalactic pals? Look no further; Mitma and his furry friend, Kusku, will be your friends to the end of the universe. These adorable crocheted creatures have uniquely detailed eyes with a shiny look that will melt your heart. Mitma's eye stalks, floppy ears, pudgy sucker fingers, and irresistible belly button make him the cutest alien visitor a planet could hope for. His loyal pet, Kusku, is a must-have companion that will bring a smile to the face of everyone who meets him. I, for one, welcome our new crochet overlords.

Mitma the Alien

Finished Measurement
Height: 15"

Materials
Any Aran weight yarn (100% acrylic)

MC: Purple; 1 skein

Small amounts of orange, brown, white, and black DK or sport-weight yarn

U.S. C-2 (2.75 mm) crochet hook

Tapestry needle

Polyester stuffing

Gauge
Approximately 22 sc = 4"

Special Stitches and Terms
Double adjustable ring: To avoid a hole at the beginning of each piece, make a double adjustable ring by looping the yarn twice around your finger and then beginning to crochet into the ring. After the first round, pull the tail snug to close.

Directions
You will start with your alien eyes, head, and facial features. When those are complete, you'll make the legs, the body, and finally the extremities.

Eye (Make 2)
Make a double adjustable ring with white yarn.

Rnd 1: Make 6 sc in ring; pull tail to close ring.

Rnd 2: 2 sc in each st—12 sts.

Rnd 3: *1 sc in next st, 2 sc in next st, rep from * around—18 sts.

Rnd 4: *1 sc in next 2 sts, 2 sc in next st, rep from * around—24 sts.

Rnd 5: *1 sc in next 3 sts, 2 sc in next st, rep from * around—30 sts.

Rnds 6 and 7: Sc in each st.

Rnd 8: Switch to MC and sc in each st.

Rnd 9: *1 sc in next 3 sts, sc next 2 sts tog, rep from * around—24 sts.

Rnd 10: Sc in each st.

Rnd 11: *1 sc in next 2 sts, sc next 2 sts tog, rep from * around—18 sts.

Rnd 12: Sc in each st.

Rnd 13: *1 sc in next st, sc next 2 sts tog, rep from * around—12 sts.

Rnds 14–33: Sc in each st.

Cut yarn and secure end. Once you've finished Rnd 33 of the second eye, do not cut the yarn. Join both eyes together at the base with slip sts over 3 sts. Then, continue crocheting the head around both eyes.

Head
Rnd 1: 18 sc around.

Rnd 2: *1 sc in next 2 sts, 2 sc in next st, rep from * around—24 sts.

Rnd 3: *1 sc in next 3 sts, 2 sc in next st, rep from * around—30 sts.

Rnd 4: *1 sc in next 4 sc, 2 sc in next st, rep from * around—36 sts.

Rnds 5 and 6: Sc in each st.

Rnd 7: *1 sc in next 5 sc, 2 sc in next st, rep from * around—42 sts.

Rnds 8–12: Sc in each st.

Rnd 13: *1 sc in next 6 sc, 2 sc in next st, rep from * around—48 sts.

Rnd 14: *1 sc in next 7 sc, 2 sc in next st, rep from * around—54 sts.

Rnd 15: *1 sc in next 8 sc, 2 sc in next st, rep from * around—60 sts.

Rnd 16: *1 sc in next 9 sc, 2 sc in next st, rep from * around—66 sts.

Rnd 17: *1 sc in next 10 sc, 2 sc in next st, rep from * around—72 sts.

Rnds 18–25: Sc in each st.

Rnd 26: *1 sc in next 10 sc, sc next 2 sts tog, rep from * around—66 sts.

Rnd 27: *1 sc in next 9 sc, sc next 2 sts tog, rep from * around—60 sts.

Rnd 28: *1 sc in next 8 sc, sc next 2 sts tog, rep from * around—54 sts.

Rnd 29: *1 sc in next 7 sc, sc next 2 sts tog, rep from * around—48 sts.

Rnd 30: *1 sc in next 6 sc, sc next 2 sts tog, rep from * around—42 sts.

Rnd 31: *1 sc in next 5 sc, sc next 2 sts tog, rep from * around—36 sts.

Rnd 32: *1 sc in next 4 sc, sc next 2 sts tog, rep from * around—30 sts.

Rnd 33: *1 sc in next 3 sc, sc next 2 sts tog, rep from * around—24 sts.

Rnd 34: *1 sc in next 2 sc, sc next 2 sts tog, rep from * around—18 sts.

Cut yarn and secure end. Stuff the head.

Eyelids

The eyelids are crocheted directly onto the eyeballs over Rnd 8 (the first MC round).

Rnd 1: Work 30 sc over Rnd 8.

Rnds 2–5: Sc in each st.

Cut yarn and secure end.

Iris

Make a double adjustable ring with orange yarn.

Rnd 1: Work 6 sc into ring; pull tail to close.

Rnd 2: Work 2 sc in each st from last round—12 sts.

Rnd 3: *1 sc in next sc, 2 sc in next st, rep from * around—18 sts.

Rnd 4: *1 sc in next 2 sc, 2 sc in next st, rep from * around—24 sts.

Cut yarn and secure end.

Brown Circle

With brown, make a double adjustable ring.

Rnd 1: Work 6 sc into ring; pull tail to close.

Rnd 2: Work 2 sc in each st from last round—12 sts.

Rnd 3: *1 sc in next sc, 2 sc in next st, rep from * around—18 sts.

Cut yarn and secure end.

Pupil

With black, make a double adjustable ring.

Rnd 1: Work 6 sc into ring; pull tail to close.

Rnd 2: *2 sc in next 2 sts, 2 hdc in next 2 sts, 2 sc in next 2 sts—12 sts.

Cut yarn and secure end.

Assemble Eyes

Over the white zone of the eyeballs, first sew the orange circle, then the brown circle, and finally the pupil. The inner border of all these pieces should be touching the round where you've exchanged colors between purple and white. With white yarn, embroider 2 points of light of different sizes on each pupil.

You can insert wire or pipe cleaners into the eyes in order to make them bend, if desired; the sample shown has no wire.

Ears (Make 2)

Make a double adjustable ring with MC.

Rnd 1: Work 6 sc into ring; pull tail to close.

Rnd 2: Sc in each st.

Rnd 3: 2 sc in first st, 1 sc in each rem st—7 sts.

Rnds 4–6: Rep Rnd 3—10 sts.

Rnd 7: *1 sc in next 4 sc, 2 sc in next st, rep from * (12 sts).

Rnd 8: *1 sc in next 5 sc, 2 sc in next st, rep from * (14 sts).

Rnd 9: *1 sc in next 6 sc, 2 sc in next st, rep from * (16 sts).

Rnd 10: *1 sc in next 7 sc, 2 sc in next st, rep from * (18 sts).

Rnd 11: *1 sc in next 2 sc, 2 sc in next st, rep from * (24 sts.)

Rnd 12: Sc in each st.

Rnd 13: *1 sc in next 3 sc, 2 sc in next st, rep from * (30 sts).

Rnds 14–18: Sc in each st.

Rnd 19: *1 sc in next 3 sc, sc next 2 sts tog, rep from * around—24 sts.

Rnds 20 and 21: Sc in each st.

Rnd 22: *1 sc in next 2 sc, sc next 2 sts tog, rep from * around—18 sts.

Rnds 23 and 24: Sc in each st.

Join the ear's borders with a sc row (9 sts). Cut yarn and secure end.

Fold the ears in half vertically and sew the base of the ears with a few sts. Sew the ears to both sides of the head, over the union between the eyes and head.

Lips (Make 2)

With orange, make a double adjustable ring:

Rnd 1: Work 5 sc into ring; pull tail to close.

Rnd 2: 2 sc in first st, 1 sc in each st to end of round—6 sts.

Rnd 3: 2 sc in first st, 1 sc in each st to end of round—7 sts.

Rnd 4: 2 sc in first st, 1 sc in each st to end of round—8 sts.

Rnd 5: 2 sc in first st, 1 sc in each st to end of round—9 sts.

Rnd 6: 2 sc in first st, 1 sc in each st to end of round—10 sts.

Rnds 7–14: Sc in each st.

Rnd 15: Sc next 2 sts tog, 1 sc in each st to end of round—9 sts.

Rnds 16–19: Rep Rnd 15—5 sts. Add a bit of stuffing to lip.

Cut yarn and secure end. With the tapestry needle, draw yarn through each st of last round and pull tightly to close.

Sew the lips to the face, under Rnd 21 on the head and centered under the eyes. Sew the lips together where they meet.

Legs (Make 2)

With MC, make a double adjustable ring:

Rnd 1: Work 6 sc into ring; pull tail to close ring.

Rnd 2: Work 2 sc in each st—12 sts.

Rnd 3: *1 sc in next st, 2 sc in next st, rep from * around—18 sts.

Rnds 4 and 5: Sc in each st.

Rnd 6: *1 sc in next 2 sc, 2 sc in next st, rep from * around—24 sts.

Rnds 7 and 8: Sc in each st.

Rnd 9: *1 sc in next 3 sc, 2 sc in next st, rep from * around—30 sts.

Rnds 10 and 11: Sc in each st.

Rnd 12: *1 sc in next 4 sc, 2 sc in next st, rep from * around—36 sts.

Rnds 13 and 14: Sc in each st.

Cut yarn and secure end. Once you've finished Rnd 14 of the second leg, without cutting the yarn, join both legs with 6 sc (this is the alien's crotch) and continue crocheting the body around the legs:

Body

Rnd 1: Work 64 sc around both legs to begin the body.

Rnds 2–15: Sc in each st.

Rnd 16: *1 sc in next 14 sc, sc next 2 sts tog, rep from * around—60 sts.

Rnds 17 and 18: Sc in each st.

Rnd 19: *1 sc in next 8 sc, sc next 2 sts tog, rep from * around—54 sts.

Rnds 20 and 21: Sc in each st.

Rnd 22: *1 sc in next 7 sc, sc next 2 sts tog, rep from * around—48 sts.

Rnds 23 and 24: Sc in each st.

Rnd 25: *1 sc in next 6 sc, sc next 2 sts tog, rep from * around—42 sts.

Rnds 26 and 27: Sc in each st.

Rnd 28: *1 sc in next 5 sc, sc next 2 sts tog, rep from * around—36 sts.

Rnds 29 and 30: Sc in each st.

Rnd 31: *1 sc in next 4 sc, sc next 2 sts tog, rep from * around—30 sts.

Rnds 32 and 33: Sc in each st.

Rnd 34: *1 sc in next 3 sc, sc next 2 sts tog, rep from * around—24 sts.

Rnds 35 and 36: Sc in each st.

Rnd 37: *1 sc in next 2 sc, sc next 2 sts tog, rep from * around—18 sts.

Rnds 38 and 39: Sc in each st.

Cut yarn and secure end. Fill the body with stuffing. Join the body and head by sewing together their openings, adding more stuffing in the neck area if necessary in order to get the head standing in the right position.

Belly

With orange yarn, make a double adjustable ring:

Rnd 1: Work 6 sc in ring; pull tail to close.

Rnd 2: 2 sc in each st from last round—12 sts.

Rnd 3: *1 sc in next st, 2 sc in next st, rep from * around—18 sts.

Rnd 4: 1 sc in next st, 2 sc in next st, *1 sc in next 2 sc, 2 sc in next st rep from * to last st, 1 sc in last st—24 sts.

Rnd 5: *1 sc in next 3 sc, 2 sc in next st, rep from * around—30 sts.

Rnd 6: 1 sc in next 2 sc, 2 sc in next st, *1 sc in next 4 sc, 2 sc in next st, rep from * to last 2 sts, 1 sc in next 2 sts—36 sts.

Rnd 7: 1 sc in next st, 2 sc in next st, *1 sc in next 5 sts, 2 sc in next st rep from * to last 4 sts, 1 sc in next 4 sts—42 sts.

Rnd 8: 1 sc in next 3 sts, 2 sc in next st, *1 sc in next 6 sts, 2 sc in next st, rep from * to last 3 sts, 1 sc in next 3 sts—48 sts.

Rnd 9: *2 sc in next st, 1 sc in next 7 sc, rep from * to end—54 sts.

Rnd 10: 1 sc in next 5 sts, 2 sc in next st, *1 sc in next 8 sts, 2 sc in next st, rep from * to last 3 sts, 1 sc in next 3 sts—60 sts.

Rnd 11: *1 sc in next 9 sc, 2 sc in next st, rep from * around—66 sts.

Rnd 12: 1 sc in next 6 sc, 2 sc in next st, *1 sc in next 10 sc, 2 sc in next st, rep from * to last 4 sts, 1 sc in next 4 sts—72 sts.

Cut yarn and secure end. Sew the belly to the front side of the body. With orange yarn, embroider a round of chain sts over the belly's border. Finally, at the belly's center, embroider the alien's navel.

Feet (Make 2)

The feet are crocheted from toe to heel and have to be filled with stuffing while crocheting.

Big Toe (Make 1 per Foot)

With orange, make a double adjustable ring.

Rnd 1: Work 6 sc into ring; pull tail to close.

Rnd 2: Work 2 sc in each st from last round—12 sts.

Rnd 3: *1 sc in next st, 2 sc in next st, rep from * around—18 sts.

Rnd 4: *1 sc in next 2 sc, 2 sc in next st, rep from * around—24 sts.

Rnds 5 and 6: Sc in each st.

Rnd 7: *1 sc in next 2 sc, sc next 2 sts tog, rep from * around—18 sts.

Rnd 8: *1 sc in next st, sc next 2 sts tog, rep from * around—12 sts.

Rnds 9–16: Sc in each st.

Cut yarn and secure end. Stuff the toe.

Small Toe (Make 2 per Foot)

With orange, make a double adjustable ring:

Rnd 1: 6 sc sts.

Rnd 2: 2 sc in each st from last round—12 sts.

Rnd 3: *1 sc in next st, 2 sc in next st, rep from * around—18 sts.

Rnds 4 and 5: Sc in each st.

Rnd 6: *1 sc, sc next 2 sts tog, rep from * around—12 sts.

Rnds 7–10: Sc in each st.

Cut yarn and secure end. Once you've finished crocheting the second small toe, do not cut the yarn. Place the three toes next to each other (with the big one on one side) and connect them together. Then continue crocheting the foot around the toes.

Cut yarn and secure end. Use tapestry needle to bring yarn through each stitch of previous round; pull to close up hole. Sew the feet underneath the legs, placing the big toes next to each other.

Hands and Arms (Make 2)

Each arm is crocheted in as a single piece, from bottom to top, starting on the hands, and has to be filled with stuffing while crocheted. Each hand consists of three fingers: one big finger and two small fingers.

Big Finger

With orange yarn, make a double adjustable ring.

Rnd 1: Work 6 sc into ring; pull tail to close.

Rnd 2: Work 2 sc in each st from last round—12 sts.

Rnd 3: *1 sc in next st, 2 sc in next st, rep from * around—18 sts.

Rnds 4 and 5: Sc in each st.

Rnd 6: *1 sc in next st, sc next 2 sts tog, rep from * around—12 sts.

Rnd 7: *Rep Rnd 6—8 sts.

Rnds 8–15: Sc in each st.

Cut yarn and secure end. Stuff.

Small Finger (Crochet 2 per Hand)

With orange, make a double adjustable ring.

Rnd 1: Work 5 sc into ring; pull tail to close.

Rnd 2: Work 2 sc in each st from last round—10 sts.

Rnd 3: *1 sc in next st, 2 sc in next st, rep from * around—15 sts.

Rnds 4 and 5: Sc in each st.

Rnd 6: *1 sc, sc next 2 sts tog, rep from * around—10 sts.

Rnd 7: *1 sc in next 3 sc, sc next 2 sts tog, rep from * (8 sts).

Rnds 8–10: Sc in each st.

Cut yarn and secure end. Once you've finished crocheting the second small finger, do not cut the yarn. Place the fingers next to each other and connect them together with 2 sts. Then, with orange yarn, continue crocheting the hand around the fingers:

Rnd 1: Work 24 sc around hand.

Rnds 2–6: Sc in each st.

Rnd 7: *1 sc in next 4 sc, sc next 2 sts tog, rep from * around—20 sts.

Rnd 8: Sc in each st.

Switch to purple yarn to start crocheting the arm:

Rnds 9–14: Sc in each st.

Rnd 15: *1 sc in next 8 sc, sc next 2 sts tog, rep from *. (18 sts.)

Rnds 16–21: Sc in each st.

Rnd 22: *1 sc in next 7 sc, sc next 2 sts tog, rep from *. (16 sts.)

Rnds 23–28: Sc in each st.

Rnd 29: *1 sc in next 6 sc, sc next 2 sts tog, rep from *. (14 sts.)

Rnds 30–35: Sc in each st.

Rnd 36: *1 sc in next 5 sc, sc next 2 sts tog, rep from *. (12 sts.)

Rnds 37–42: Sc in each st.

Rnd 43: *Sc 2 sts tog, rep from * around—6 sts.

Stuff the arm. Cut yarn and secure end. With the tapestry needle, draw yarn through all sts from last round and pull tightly to close.

With a tapestry needle and purple yarn, embroider a chain stitch round over the color exchange between orange and purple. Sew the arms to the body, placing the big finger forward.

Kusku the Alien Sidekick

Finished Measurements

Height: 6"

Materials

Any Aran weight yarn (100% acrylic)

MC: Spring Green; 1 skein

Small amounts of black, white, and turquoise DK or sportweight yarn

U.S. C-2 (2.75mm) crochet hook

Tapestry needle

Polyester stuffing

Gauge

Approximately 22 sc = 4"

Special Stitches and Terms

Double adjustable ring: see page 159.

Loop stitch: Start with a row (or round) of single crochet stitches.

Step 1: Insert the hook in the first stitch. Form a loop, wrapping the yarn clockwise around your left index finger. Rotate your hook in the opposite direction from the way you usually would. It goes over the yarn first and then behind both sides of the loop.

Step 2: Catch both sides of the loop and pass them through the stitch where you inserted the hook in Step 1. Now you'll have the hook in the front side of the work with 3 loops on it and 1 loop in the back side of the work. Yarn over the hook (you'll have 4 loops on the hook) and pass the strand through the other 3 loops on your hook to finish the stitch.

Step 3: Repeat Steps 1 and 2 till the end of the row.

Directions

Body

The body is crocheted from top to bottom, starting on the eyeball, and has to be filled with stuffing while crocheting.

Make a double adjustable ring.

Rnd 1: With black, work 6 sc into ring. Pull tail to close ring.

Rnd 2: Work 2 sc in each sc—12 sts.

Rnd 3: Switch to white and *1 sc in next st, 2 sc in next st, rep from * around—18 sts.

Rnd 4: *Sc in next 2 sts, 2 sc in next st, rep from * around—24 sts.

Rnds 5 and 6: Sc in each st.

Rnds 7 and 8: Switch to MC and sc in each st.

Rnd 9: *Sc in next 2 sts, sc next 2 sts tog (decrease), rep from * around—18 sts.

Rnd 10: *Sc in next st, sc next 2 sts tog, rep from * around—12 sts. Stuff the eyeball.

Rnd 11: *Sc in next st, sc next 2 sts tog, rep from * around—8 sts.

Rnds 12–25: Sc in each st.

Beginning with the next round, you'll start crocheting the body in loop stitch. In order to get the loops on the front side of your work, turn the work and then continue crocheting:

Rnd 26: Work 2 loop sts in each st—16 sts.

Rnd 27: *Work 1 loop st in next st, 2 loop sts in next st, rep from * around—24 sts.

Rnd 28: *Work 1 loop st in next 3 sts, 2 loop sts in next st, rep from * around—30 sts.

Rnd 29: *Work 1 loop st in next 4 sts, 2 loop sts in next st, rep from * around—36 sts.

Rnds 30–35: Loop st in each st around.

Rnd 36: *Work 1 loop st in next 4 sts, work 1 loop st in next 2 sts tog (decrease), rep from * around—30 sts.

Rnd 37: *Work 1 loop st in next 3 sts, work 1 loop st in next 2 sts tog, rep from * around—24 sts.

Rnd 38: *Work 1 loop st in next 2 sts, work 1 loop st in next 2 sts tog, rep from * around—18 sts.

Rnd 39: *Work 1 loop st in next st, work 1 loop st in next 2 sts tog, rep from * around—12 sts. Stuff the body.

Rnd 40: *Work 1 loop st in next 2 sts tog, rep from * around—6 sts.

Secure the end and cut the yarn. With tapestry needle, thread yarn through sts from last round and pull tightly to close.

Eyelid

The eyelid is crocheted directly over the eyeball on Rnd 7 (first MC round).

Rnd 1: Join MC at beg of round and sc in each st—24 sts.

Rnds 2 and 3: Sc in each st.

Rnd 4: 12 sc with MC; cut yarn. Join black yarn and crochet the picot eyelashes as follows: *ch 3, sc in next st, rep from * 6 times. Cut yarn and secure the end.

Muzzle

Make a double adjustable ring with MC to begin.

Rnd 1: Work 6 sc into ring; pull tail tight to close.

Rnd 2: Work 2 sc in each st—12 sts.

Rnd 3: *1 sc in next st, 2 sc in next st, rep from * around—18 sts.

Rnd 4: *1 sc in next 2 sts, 2 sc in next st, rep from * around—24 sts.

Rnds 5–12: Sc in each st around.

Cut yarn, secure end, and fill the muzzle with stuffing.

Nose

With black, make a double adjustable ring:

Rnd 1: Work 6 sc in ring; pull tail tight to close.

Rnd 2: Work 2 sc in each st—12 sts.

Rnds 3 and 4: Sc in each st around.

Cut yarn and secure end. With the tapestry needle, draw yarn through each stitch from last round, put some stuffing in the center of the nose, and then pull the yarn tightly to close.

Ears (Make 2)

Make a double adjustable ring with black:

Rnd 1: Work 6 sc in ring, pull tail tight to close.

Rnd 2: Work 2 sc in each st—12 sts.

Rnd 3: *Work 1 sc in next 5 sts, 2 sc in next st, rep from * (14 sts).

Rnd 4: *Work 1 sc in next 6 sts, 2 sc in next st, rep from * (16 sts).

Rnds 5–8: Sc in each st.

Rnd 9: *Work 1 sc in next 6 sts, sc 2 sts tog, rep from * (14 sts).

Rnd 10: Sc around.

Rnd 11: *Work 1 sc in next 5 sts, sc 2 sts tog, rep from * (12 sts).

Rnd 12: Sc around.

Rnd 13: *Work 1 sc in next 4 sts, sc 2 sts tog, rep from * (10 sts).

Rnds 14–16: Sc around.

Cut yarn and secure end.

Feet (Make 2)

The feet are crocheted from front to back and have to be filled with stuffing while crocheted.

With MC, make a double adjustable ring.

Rnd 1: Work 6 sc in ring; pull tail to tighten.

Rnd 2: Work 2 sc in each st—12 sts.

Rnd 3: *Sc in next st, work 2 sc in next st, rep from * around—18 sts.

Rnd 4: *Sc in next 2 sts, 2 sc in next st, rep from * around—24 sts.

Rnds 5–8: Sc in each st around.

Rnd 9: *Sc in next 10 sts, sc next 2 sts tog, rep from * (22 sts).

Rnd 10: Sc in each st around.

Rnd 11: *Sc in next 9 sts, sc next 2 sts tog, rep from * (20 sts).

Rnd 12: Sc in each st around.

Rnd 13: *Sc in next 8 sts, sc next 2 sts tog, rep from * (18 sts).

Rnd 14: Sc in each st around.

Rnd 15: *Sc in next 7 sts, sc next 2 sts tog, rep from * (16 sts).

Rnd 16: Sc in each st around.

Rnd 17: *Sc in next 6 sts, sc next 2 sts tog, rep from * (14 sts).

Rnd 18: Sc in each st around.

Rnd 19: *Sc in next 5 sts, sc next 2 sts tog, rep from * (12 sts).

Rnd 20: *Sc next 2 sts tog, rep from * around—6 sts.

Cut yarn. With the tapestry needle, draw yarn through each st of last round and pull tightly to close.

Tail

With MC, make a double adjustable ring.

Rnd 1: Work 6 sc in ring; pull tail to close up ring.

Rnd 2: Work 2 loop sts in each st—12 sts.

Rnd 3: *Work 1 loop st in next st, work 2 loop sts in next st, rep from * around—18 sts.

Rnd 4: Loop st in each st.

Turn work so that loops are on the outside, and continue in the round.

Rnd 5: *1 sc in next st, sc next 2 sts tog, rep from * (12 sts).

Rnd 6: *Sc next 2 sts tog, rep from * (6 sts).

Rnds 7–15: Sc in each st around.

Cut yarn and secure the end.

Finishing

To finish the eye, with turquoise yarn and chain sts, embroider all around at the transition from black to white. Then, with white yarn, embroider 2 points of light of different sizes, one on the outside of the pupil and the other inside the pupil.

Sew the muzzle to the body, 2 rounds under the eye stalk and with the eyelashes on the top side of the eye. Then sew the nose on the tip of the muzzle. With black yarn and chain stitches, embroider the mouth as shown in the photo on page 158.

Sew the ears to both sides of the body 2 sts away from the eye stalk.

Sew the feet underneath the body. Thread a tapestry needle with black yarn and make 3 long stitches from bottom to top on each foot, pulling firmly and knotting in place to create toes.

Sew the tail to the back side of the body.

Enjoy!

Toasty Tote

Sometimes a sweater isn't just a sweater. Sometimes it's an awful mess. We've all been there. Most of us still have the first sweater we ever made, whether out of pride or as a warning to avoid future mishaps. For better or worse, they're part of our handmade history. What about that vest crocheted by a mysterious relative that has never met you, but by the looks of the bouclé fringe across the chest, clearly doesn't like you. Maybe you have spied a stunning 1980s sweater at the thrift store—the one with the bat-wing sleeves, giant intarsia tiger head with rhinestone eyes, and metallic pleather stripes. You know you want it, but you're not sure why.

Why let these twisted treasures sit idly by when you could be sporting them around town in convenient non-sweater form! Of course, you wouldn't wear a non-ironic fuzzy kitten sweater or a cardigan that has been enthusiastically over-bobbled, but who doesn't want a tote bag made of one? It's like a trophy that proves you found the best worst sweater ever without having to actually wear it. Plus recycling and all that. Frankly, it's your duty to the planet.

What You'll Need

- 1 sweater that is as wide as you'd like your bag and that you don't mind chopping up
- ½ yard of fabric for lining (or enough fabric to cut two pieces of lining that are the same size as your finished bag)
- Coordinating twill tape measuring at least 1" wide, and the length of the bag handle you want plus 4"
- Matching thread
- Sewing machine

What to Do

1. Find a sweater that you love, but would never in a million years actually wear. Turn the sweater inside out.

2. Determine how long you want your new bag to be. Anything below the armpits of the sweater is fair game. (If you can, keep the finished edge of the sweater uncut so you have less unraveling to worry about.)

3. Before you cut the sweater, sew across at your measurement line to keep it from unraveling. This will become the bottom seam of your bag. For extra security, sew this line twice.

4. Cut across the sweater ½" away from the seam you just made. Now, through the magic of scissors, it is no longer a sweater. It is now the exterior of a bag. Voila!

5. Press your lining fabric and cut two pieces the exact same size as your freshly cut bag-in-progress.

6. Pin the fabric pieces with right sides together, and sew along the two sides and bottom using a ¼" seam allowance. Do not sew the top edge. Leave a 5" section along the bottom open, backstitching at either end of this opening to keep the stitches from ripping out. You're going to be pulling the bag-formerly-known-as-a-sweater (heretofore known as *BFKAAS*) through this hole shortly.

7. Okay. Take a deep, cleansing breath and maybe a sip of a small cocktail. We're going to attach the lining now and frankly, if spatial thinking isn't your thing, it may take a couple of tries. Don't worry, it's natural and happens to everyone. It's not you, it's physics, our dimensional universe, and possibly the time-space continuum, and there's nothing we can do about that, is there?

8. Here we go. Make sure the BFKAAS is inside-out so the right sides are facing each other. Easy, right?

9. Turn the lining out so the right sides are facing out. Don't over-think this part, and forget about the concept of "inside-out" as it relates to the lining. Trust us. Just turn it so the right sides are facing out in the most Zen way possible. Do not fall down the

rabbit hole that we did—I mean, that some people might. The confused stares are amusing, but they're also confusing. Just remember, there is no spoon.

10. Now, insert the lining into the bag. This bit can get fiddly because the fabric kind of clings to the sweater fabric, but just work it in there and line up the edges of the bag and lining as best as you can. Are the right sides of the lining facing the right sides of the bag? Awesome! Pin it in place all the way around.

11. Breathe. You did it! It's all cake from here. Sew all the way around about ½" from the edge.

12. This part is like a magic trick, so work in some jazz hands and a mysterious stare for some extra credibility. Pull out the lining, reach into the hole, and pull out the BFKAAS. Now you'll see the right sides of both the bag and the lining.

13. Press the edge of the lining where you left the opening so the edges are turned in, and then sew the opening closed. You can seam along the entire bottom to make it all even. Sew about ⅛" away from the edge either way.

14. Push the lining into the bag and—*hot dog*—you've got a lined bag. Made from that old sweater. Huh!

15. Take your measured twill tape, turn each end under ½", press, and sew down to finish ends.

16. Sew 1½" at each end of the twill tape to the inside of the bag along the side seam in the lining. We recommend using the classic box-style stitching for extra stability.

17. Put all your knitting into your new bag, head off to your weekly knit night, and prepare to be complimented (or yelled at because, "Hey, isn't that the sweater I lent you last year?!").

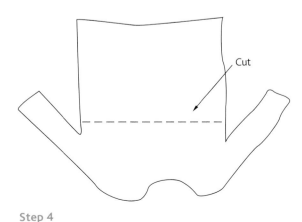

Step 4

Step 6

Step 7

About the Designers

Snowden Becker (St. Moritz)   If you see a woman knitting near the campus of the University of Texas, Austin, it's probably Snowden Becker, who is a doctoral student in the School of Information there. Her blog is filed under the appropriate LC heading at tt820classy knitting.blogspot.com, and her designs have been featured by Knitty and Knit Picks, among others. If you see her, tell her to put down her needles and get back to work on that dissertation she's supposed to be writing.

Adrian Bizilia (Peppermint Lounge hat and mitten set)   Adrian lives in Shelburne Falls, MA. She knits a lot and sometimes writes down the patterns she comes up with. In her spare time, she cooks for people, takes photos of her dog, watches lots of movies, and eats cheese. You can find her online at helloyarn.com.

Kelly Bridges (Apres Ski Skirts)   Kelly lives in sweet little Gilmanton Ironworks, NH and is the manager at the Elegant Ewe Yarn and Fiber Shop in Concord, NH where she also teaches and enjoys knitting vicariously through her customers. You can find more of her designs and thoughts in general at www.elegantewe.com.

Cheryl Burke (Staghorn pullover and hat)   Cheryl loves using yarn to explore color, texture, and all sorts of patterns. She teaches knitting classes and has a small collection of knitwear designs available through WEBs. She loves spreading the contagious joy of knitting to friends, family, really anyone who shows the remotest interest. A graphic designer by day, Cheryl has a master's degree in design from the Rhode Island School of Design. Cheryl can be found at www.yarnbee.blogspot.com.

Robyn Chachula (Wiley Wahine)   Robyn's winding path to a crochet career began as a structural engineer with a specialty in historic preservation and renovation. Her designs have been published in Interweave Crochet, Crochet Today!, and CrochetMe.com; as well as in books, including Crochet, Son of Stitch & Bitch, and Sensual Crochet. You can see all of her architecturally inspired pieces at www.crochetbyfaye.com.

Tammy George (Snowmates For Her)   Tammy (a.k.a. PuNk rAwK pUrL) shares a Technicolor Victorian Flat with her opinionated cat, Rosco in Oakland, CA. She is known for her KNIT & PURL tattooed knuckles (yeah, for reals!). She's been called the Andy Warhol of Wool, but prefers to be the Punky Brewster of Textiles. You can spy on, shop from, and contact her at www.punkrawkpurl.com.

Jodi Green (Pump Jockey)   Jodi is an artist, art educator, and independent knit designer living and working in Windsor, Ontario. You can view her portfolio at www.jodigreen.ca. Jodi's already well on her way to becoming the weird old lady down the street, and on warm days can be found on her front porch rallying the neighbor kids to collect bugs for her or trying to get them interested in yarn.

Amy Herzog (Apocalypta, Lady Speedway)   Amy lives near Boston, MA and blogs at www.stashknitrepeat.com. Her years of knitting have gradually led to an obsession for well-fitting sweaters, fueled by a seemingly never-ending supply of yarn. Amy's other designs can be found at www.stashknitrepeat.com/designs/.

Stephen Houghton (Snowmates For Him)   Stephen lives in the never-snowy San Francisco, having survived a chilly East Coast childhood. Since 2004, he's been a needle junkie online at www.hizknits. com. When he's not slinging pixels at his day job, he trains to be a circus freak, travels the globe with his photographer husband Christopher Hall, and snuggles Janie Sparkles, their French Bulldog.

Kirsten Kapur (Swing Time)   Kirsten has been knitting for as long as she can remember and began designing knitting patterns about 4 years ago. She lives in New Jersey (a much maligned, yet beautiful state) with her husband and three teenaged children. You will find her blogging about her knitting on Through the Loops at www. throughtheloops.typepad.com.

Melissa LaBarre (Watusi Topper)   Melissa lives in Massachusetts and likes making hats and sweaters out of scratchy wool and wearing them next to her bare skin. She's just tough like that. Melissa is co-author of the book New England Knits (Interweave 2010) and blogs at knittingschooldropout.com.

Caryn Lantz (Fast Lane)   Caryn knits and spins so the Minnesota winters don't kill her. She blogs at www.fuzzynoodleknits.com, and schleps her handspun at www.fuzzynoodleknits.etsy.com.

Diana Loren (Ahoy, Sailor)   Diana spends her days looking at old things and her nights knitting new things, which are sometimes inspired by old things. She posts occasionally at bestitched.typepad.com.

Marnie MacLean (Saucy Convertible, Cheeky Hot Pants) Marnie has been designing since 2003 and offers an assortment of patterns and tutorials on her site, marniemaclean.com. She also has two exceptionally adorable dogs whose pictures make their way onto her blog on a regular basis.

Kellee Middlebrooks (Apocalyptus)   Kellee loves making things, and she's really good at it. From handspun yarn to cheese, she quilts to a small redheaded child and is a force to be reckoned with. She lives in and perpetually remodels a 100-year-old house in Somerville, MA with her husband, Rick and her son and greatest craft project ever, Beckett. You can find her online at www.obsessiondujour.typepad.com/.

Annie Modesitt (Sunday Drive)   Annie lives in St Paul, MN with her husband, kids, and assorted pets and can be found online at www.anniemodesitt.com. Her work has appeared in magazines like *Interweave Knits, Vogue Knitting, Knitters Magazine* and *McCalls Needlework*. She is also the author of *Confessions of a Knitting Heretic* and *Knitting Millinery*. Annie has also contributed to many knitting books including *Stitch N' Bitch, Scarf Style, Weekend Knitting* and *Men Who Knit And The Dogs Who Love Them*.

Claire Moore (Clara)   Claire Moore lives and knits under the radar in the heat of Austin, TX. She can usually be found making beer, playing pinball, fixing up her Citroen or hanging with her husband, dog, cats, and miscellaneous chickens and ducks.

Paola Navarro (Intergalactic Pals)   Paola is from Tucuman, Argentina and she really loves crocheting. She started with this wonderful craft as a kid but became a real crochet junkie 12 years ago or so. She works as a web-designer with her husband Ricardo, and together they built www.deliciouscrochet.com. Also you can find her patterns on Etsy at www.etsy.com/shop/DeliciousCrochet.

Staci Perry (Watusi dress)   Staci has been knitting practically since birth, and is now a knitwear designer and knitting teacher in sunny Austin, TX. When she puts the needles down, she spends her time volunteering for Basenji Rescue and keeping up with her own three Basenjis. Staci blogs at www.verypink.com, where she has several knitting tutorial videos. She also sells handknit, heirloom baby knits at www.etsy.com/shop/staciiii.

Regina Rioux (Hala Kahiki, Atomic Bag)   Regina is many things, including but not limited to artist, mother, crocheting-knitting-spinning-weaving-sewing fool, wanderer, creator, and knower of adhesive tools. She is also known for turning yarn into unexpected objects that yarn never dreamed it could be. You can find Regina designing and blogging at www.monstercrochet.com.

Cirilia Rose (Double Decker cardigan and hat)   Cirilia Rose knits and designs in the Northeast and is inspired by all things cinematic. When she isn't knitting in darkened theaters, she enjoys visiting friends who are scattered around the US and making messes in the kitchen.

Maryse Roudier (Go-Go Granny, Sunshine Day)   Maryse lives in the Boston metro area with her husband and two cats and blogs erratically at www.monster-yarn.com. When not at her day job, she takes pictures, crochets, knits, spins, reads trashy novels, obsesses about color and cruises around in her chili red Mini. She has never met a granny square she didn't like.

Erin Slonaker (Sock Hop)   All of Erin's claims over the year to being stashless are proving untrue, as she finds yarn in the corner of every room and hidden in all the closets of her Brooklyn apartment. Years of blogging mean she now happily answers to "Mintyfresh." Her crafty pursuits can be seen at pepperknit.com/blog.

Tamie Snow (Bottle Buddy)   Tamie Snow lives in Northern California with her husband William and son, Jackson. She spends her days chasing her little boy and her nights crocheting her guts out! She blogs all about being in Snow biz at http://tamiesnow.typepad.com/snow_business/. Look for her book *Tiny Yarn Animals: Amigurumi Friends to Make and Enjoy* in bookstores and check out her patterns at www.roxycraft.com/.

Christy Varner (Galileo, Hello World)   Christy started life cranky due to her lack of handknits to wear. She makes up for this now by knitting obsessively and occasionally attempting to be a blogger at www.neitherhipnorfunky.com. After five years of knitting, a day that she is not wearing a handknit is rare.

Julia Vesper (He's Not an Extra, She's Not an Extra)   Julia is a full-time fiber artist and a once in awhile designer. She and her new husband have recently relocated from Pittsburgh to Michigan, to trade city life for family. Read more about it at www.knitterlythings.com.

Pamela Wynne (Rally)   Pamela is a child of the 80s who has dabbled in countless now-retro crafts, including macrame, decoupage, and Extreme Puffy Painting. These days, she lives and knits in Flint, MI. Find her online at www.flintknits.com.

Resources

Crochet

Abbreviation	Meaning	Abbreviation	Meaning
beg	beginning	RS	right side
Bl	work into the back loop of the stitch	sc	single crochet
ch	chain	sk	skip
dc	double crochet	sl st	slip stitch
Fl	work into the front loop of the stitch	st(s)	stitch(es)
FPsc	front post single crochet	sp	space
hdc	half double crochet	t-ch	top of chain stitches when working in the round or top of turning chain when working in rows
pm	place marker	tog	together
rep	repeat	tr	treble crochet
rnd(s)	round(s)	WS	wrong side

Knitting

Abbreviation	Meaning	Abbreviation	Meaning
(·)	repeat the instructions in the parentheses the specified number of times	p2tog	purl 2 stitches together
*	repeat the instructions after the * as instructed	patt	pattern
beg	beginning	pfb	purl into front and back of next stitch (1 stitch increase)
CA	color A	pm	place marker
CB	color B	psso	pass slipped stitch over
CC	contrasting color	pwise	purlwise
CO	cast on	rem	remaining
dec	decrease; decreasing	rep	repeat
dpn(s)	double-pointed needle(s)	rnd(s)	round(s)

Abbreviation	Meaning	Abbreviation	Meaning
est	establish(ed)	s2kp	Slip 2 stitches as if to k2tog, k1, pass the 2 slipped stitches over the stitch just to knit.
g	gram	sl	slip
inc	increase	sm	slip marker
k	knit	ssk	slip, slip, knit
k2tog	knit 2 stitches together	st(s)	stitch(es)
kfb	knit into front and back of same stitch (increase)	St st	stockinette stitch
kwise	knitwise	tbl	through back loop
M1	make 1 stitch by picking up the bar between the last stitch worked and the next st and knitting through the back loop (1 stitch increase).	w&t	wrap and turn (see also page 47)
M1R	make 1 right—pick up the bar between the stitches from back to front, and place it on the left needle. Knit through the front loop.	WS	wrong side
M1L	make 1 left—pick up the bar between the stitches from front to back and place it on the left needle. Knit through the back loop.	wyib	with (working) yarn in back
MC	main color	wyif	with (working) yarn in front
mm	millimeter(s)	yd.	yard(s)
p	purl	yo	yarn over
RS	right side	yo2	Between 2 knit stitches, bring the yarn to the front below the needles, wrap it up over the right needle, and return it to the front below the needle before knitting the next stitch.

Cast-On Methods

Judy's Magic Cast-On Variation

This technique is an invisible stockinette provisional cast-on over two needles, resulting in a row of live stitches on both needles: one ready to be worked, the other to lie in wait as if a provisional cast-on. This is Cat Bordhi's alternate to Judy Becker's original, resulting in all stitches properly mounted (not twisted). Cat's video of this technique can be found on YouTube (www.youtube.com/watch?v=lhBIS0AhhQY). The original variation appeared on Knitty.com (knitty.com/ISSUEspring06/FEATmagiccaston.html) and on Judy's Blog (www.persistentillusion.com/blogblog/techniques/magic-cast-on/magic-cast-on-2).

1. Hold two needles (double-pointed needles or circular) together horizontally in your right hand with the tips pointing to the left to a 9 o'clock position. The top one is Needle #1, the lower one is Needle #2.

2. Place the yarn on Needle #1, with the working yarn (attached to the ball going behind the needles) behind and the tail end between the needles (hanging down and behind Needle #2). This loop will become your first stitch.

3. Holding the stitch in place, move the tail end around to the right and behind the working/ball yarn. Cinch the loop on Needle #1 tight by separating the yarn, creating the triangle as if to long-tail cast-on, with the tail end over your left index finger and the working/ball yarn going over the outside of your left thumb. Keep tension on the yarn on the needles and over fingers by holding both tail end and working/ball yarn taut against your palm with the left ring and/or pinky finger. This is your starting position.

4. Cast 1 stitch on Needle #2: Rotate the points of the needles clockwise up/away from you toward the tail end over your left index finger to an 11 o'clock position. Wrap a loop of tail end yarn around Needle #2 (the bottom one) with your index finger moving the yarn from below, over Needle #2 and between the needles. Return to starting position by rotating the points of the needles counterclockwise back to 9 o'clock.

5. Cast 1 stitch on Needle #1: Rotate the points of the needles down/toward you near the working/ball yarn over your left thumb, pointing to a 7 o'clock position. Wrap a loop of working yarn around Needle #1 with your thumb, bringing the yarn from behind through to between the needles up and over Needle #1. Return to starting position by rotating the points of the needles counterclockwise back to 9 o'clock.

6. Cast 1 stitch on Needle #2: Rotate the points of the needles clockwise up/away from you toward the tail end over your left index finger to an 11 o'clock position. Wrap a loop of tail end yarn around Needle #2 (the bottom one) with your index finger moving the yarn from below, over Needle #2 and between the needles. Return to starting position by rotating the points of the needles counterclockwise back to 9 o'clock.

7. Repeat Steps 5 and 6, casting on pairs of stitches (one each to Needle #1 and Needle #2) until desired number of stitches are cast on each needle.

8. After your last stitch is cast on Needle #2, rotate the needles 180-degrees to point to 3 o'clock, securing the last cast-on stitch by wrapping the tail end of yarn in front of the working/ball end and cinching to tighten. Needle #2 is now on the top, Needle #1 on the bottom.

9. If using circulars, slide Needle #1 (the bottom one) to the middle of the cable, to wait until it is their turn to be knit and/or joined as a hem. Begin knitting the stitches from Needle #2 across the entire row. If specified, follow instructions to join in the round (for neck collar), joining the last stitch to the first stitch on Needle #2. Otherwise, attach to body by knitting across Needle #2 and continue around body of garment. To complete the round, join garment to first JMCO stitch (for armpits).

Knitted Cast-On

Add stitches at the beginning of a row by inserting the right needle knitwise into the end stitch, and make a new stitch. But instead of passing the new stitch onto the right needle, slip it onto the left needle to be worked as a new stitch. Work as many additional stitches as needed in the same fashion.

Provisional Cast-On

Make a slip knot with waste yarn, and put it on the crochet hook. Holding the circular needle below the crochet hook in the same hand, *wrap yarn around the needle and the hook and pull a loop through with the hook as you would to chain. One new stitch is on the needle. Repeat from * until you have cast on as many stitches as required. Chain a couple more stitches on the hook only. Break yarn and pull through last stitch to secure. Mark this end of the yarn with a knot so you will remember which end to unravel.

Index